Leaving Legacies

Reflections from the Prickly Path to Leadership

K. CANDIS BEST

BookSurge Publishing

ISBN-13: 978-1-4196-7738-1 - Paperback
ISBN-13: 978-1-4196-8032-3 - Hardcover
Library of Congress Control Number: 2007908250
Publisher: BookSurge Publishing
North Charleston, South Carolina

Acknowledgements

I owe a debt of thanks to more people than I could possibly list. But I must pay special thanks to Dawn Best, Claudine Brown and Christy Hicks for braving through the first (very rough) draft of this book. Their comments provided me with timely and much needed course corrections. Similar thanks goes to Erica Simone Turnipseed for sharing her time and expertise in the early stages of this project and to Ruth Coughlin for her attention to detail in polishing my little gem.

I also need to acknowledge Rev. Anthony L. Trufant for being a friend as well as a pastor. Similarly, I want to acknowledge the many mentors whose support and guidance shaped my development as a leader and as a person. They include Huey Cotton, Theodis Thompson, Lynda Curtis and Marc Bard. Heartfelt appreciation goes to the host of family and friends whose support and encouragement made this project possible. But finally and perhaps most importantly, I wish to acknowledge all of the dedicated employees of the New York City Health & Hospitals Corporation with particular fondness for the staff of the North Brooklyn Health Network, who not only provided me with stories to tell, but with memories that will stay with me for a lifetime.

To Mom, Dad and Dawn,

my enduring sources of inspiration and the
ultimate proof that God truly loves me.

Author's Note

This is a memoir about leadership. I did not approach this project like a journalist nor did I intend to present it as a historical account. It reflects my independent recollections of interactions I had with my supervisors, staff and colleagues as those events unfolded over an eleven-year period. No interviews were conducted to verify the extent to which my memories matched those of others who were participants in the same events. As such, I'm sure there will be some who may remember the same events differently.

In a few isolated instances, conversations that took place over the course of different meetings were condensed into a single event for editorial purposes. But in none of these instances was the content of the conversations altered. The stories included here were selected in large part because of how significant those experiences were to me, both then and now. So other than the provisos stated, the accounts that follow accurately reflect the exchanges that took place at the time to the best of my recollection and I stand by every word that has been written on these pages.

With the exception of my name and that of the Mayor of the City of New York (because what would be the point?) the names of individuals have been changed as a courtesy to those involved. The names of locations have not been changed except where indicated.

INTRODUCTION

I KNEW IMMEDIATELY UPON leaving the New York City Health & Hospitals Corporation that I wanted to write a book about leadership. My first-hand experiences as both a purveyor and a consumer of leadership made the subject almost a preoccupation for me, especially during my final months and weeks there. I came to understand among other things that to accept the mantle of leadership means not having the option of ethical ambiguity. The stakes are too high. Too many people are impacted by the decisions that leaders make. How you shade your beliefs is your choice but you need to believe in something. In truth, we all believe in something, even if it's nothing more than the quest for the almighty dollar. The leaders who make the greatest impact are the ones who are willing to wear their beliefs across their chest so that the people who follow them know what they're getting into.

During my eleven years as a healthcare executive, watched person after person violate the rules of sound managerial judgment and move right up the corporate ladder anyway. So much so that it no longer surprised me. What I found amazing, however, were the ubiquitous displays of shock and bewilderment that occurred when the areas these people led began to founder. The character of the leader is a mirror image of the character of the individual. Hire a weak person and you hire a weak leader; shallow person, shallow leader; inspired person, inspired leader. You get the picture.

1

This book became a *leadership memoir* when I realized that, ultimately, so much had already been written about the mechanics of how to lead effectively that there was little new academic insight for me to share on the subject. So instead, I chose to share my experiences and reflections in the hope that they might benefit others, just as the experiences and reflections of the people who influenced me most benefited me.

It took a long time for me to speak my passions out loud. I was sailing along on a professional trajectory that seemed to be lifted from a case study on career advancement. There is no doubt in my mind that any number of my colleagues, familiar and estranged, would have traded places with me in a heartbeat. But in the deepest recesses of my heart I knew that while others may have been pining away for the positions I was being offered, I was not. I was grateful for the opportunities but there were moments, fleeting moments but moments nonetheless, when I knew that I was living out the dreams of others, not my own.

I also knew something else, however. Something that became one of several personal creeds I learned to live by early in my life. I came to trust that while my life did not always proceed along the path where I wanted it to go, it always went where it was supposed to go. It always took me to places that kept me safe or taught me lessons I would need later when I returned to the stretch of road that I was actually looking for. This book covers an eleven year detour that was so rich and engaging that for a time I thought the detour was my destination. Of course it wasn't. But along the way it gave me a story to tell.

In the end, we are drawn inexorably back to the deepest desires of our heart. For me that desire was to write a book that offered a story worth sharing. In the one that I am about to share with you, I hope I have succeeded.

Chapter One

"See, you young people don't know shit!"
I knew it was going to be a long afternoon when Charles started a conversation by casting me among the young people. And yes, his lectures could be peppered with well-placed profanity from time to time if he thought that's what it took to get his point across. Sometimes I would just listen and other times, like now, when I thought he was full of it himself, I would push back. "Yeah, well whatever we don't know, you all didn't teach us. So it's as much your fault as it is ours."

I knew from the moment I met Dr. Charles Montgomery that we were going to be fast friends. I've always liked people who are direct and candid even when candor flies in the face of political correctness; someone who doesn't waste time with superficial conversation but has enough levity to make what little conversation they do grant you enjoyable. I also appreciated the way he wore his sense of self. You knew you were in the presence of a self-assured man within minutes of meeting him. But the air of arrogance he hinged to that presence stopped short of the pretentiousness one often encounters with a person when he or she is the only Ph.D. in the room. Charles was all of these things and one more…he was now my new boss.

"I grew up on a farm in the backwoods of Alabama," he told me one day. "And I remember one of my grammar school teachers telling me, 'you're a poor little black-ass boy from nowhere. That means you're

3

starting out with three strikes against you. So you'd better get yourself an education. And always make sure that you present yourself well.' I never forgot that."

Dr. Montgomery grew up in the South at a time when circumstances denied the men who educated him access to the jobs for which they were actually qualified. Fired in the kiln of a segregated South, it made their surfaces hard and their colors glossy. That's how young Black boys from Alabama came to be influenced by articulate Black men who wore three-piece suits pressed to a razor's edge and wing-tips polished to a high shine. Their rebukes weren't insults. These men lived their warnings. Sometimes it takes one to make one.

The sharp lines and vivid luster of his particular brand of earthenware made working with Charles as rewarding as it was taxing. His mercurial temperament meant that you never knew which "Doc" would show up from one day to the next. One day he might call me into his office and we would talk from afternoon to dusk. The very next morning I'd hear him come into the administrative suite and approach him to say good morning. Only to have him walk past me and anyone else who was present, go into his office and close the door without saying a word. He'd run through several assistants that way and it explained why very few employees passed through the suite. Most chose to adopt the "I'll speak when spoken to" approach.

I'm sure that having a law degree had something to do with how an isolated consulting project that required me to rewrite an employee manual turned into a twice-weekly consulting engagement. When Charles asked me to develop and then manage the center's Human Resources department, I jumped at the chance. The arrangement provided me with the exit from practicing law that I was looking for.

The novelty of hanging up a shingle right after graduation wore off within the first eighteen months. It wasn't *L.A. Law*, not by a long shot. File a motion, get yelled at by a judge, chase your clients down for the balance of your fees – the thought of spending the next twenty years on that hamster wheel wasn't whetting any of my appetites. But I had student loans to pay and there wasn't a rich husband in sight. At the time, that was my sole motivation for considering full time employment at the Fort Greene Community Health Center[*]. But I would soon discover that Charles was also introducing me to a vocation that I would quickly grow to love.

"So you think you want to be a healthcare administrator?" Charles asked me one day.

"Maybe," I said. "I like it so far."

"Well, healthcare jobs are dirty and difficult," he went on to say. "Serving the communities we serve is easy to talk about but it gets real when someone is spitting at you or cursing you out because it's taking too long for them to be seen. You've got to know this is what you want to do and you'd better know why."

The center occupied a modest two-story brick building at the corner of a three-way intersection. Located just steps away from the hustle and bustle of downtown Brooklyn, I'd probably passed the building hundreds of times but never really noticed it before a chance encounter brought me to its front door. It was a federally qualified health center, which meant that it received funding from an arm of the Department of Health and Human Services that subsidizes healthcare services for the uninsured. In addition to that unfortunate group, the center also served the neighborhood's Medicaid and Medicare populations.

The patients who walked through the center's door were a lot like the clients I represented during my internship at a legal clinic in Chester, Pennsylvania, when I was a third-year law student. They were always on the

---

[*] *Fictitious name*

verge of one crisis or another. Their lives were not their own. They belonged to criminal court or family court, a welfare agency or a methadone clinic. Most of their daily deeds proceeded by instruction not by choice. These are the conditions that can make a person feel voiceless, and when people don't think they're being heard, they tend to scream.

Nonetheless, as I considered allowing two days a week to turn into five, I couldn't escape the feeling that I was being presented with a compelling opportunity. I had an entrepreneurial spirit that I can only assume I inherited from my parents. But I also knew that I wanted to do work that was meaningful. Now I could fulfill both these needs.

"There's plenty to do around here if you're interested," he said. "I'll teach you as much as you want to learn."

I didn't know it at the time but accepting his offer meant that I'd just stepped off a subway platform and onto the ride of my life.

Settling in was surprisingly easy. I enjoyed learning about Charles' many facets by seeing him through the eyes of others. "We would have closed years ago if it wasn't for Doc," said one of his many admirers. When only one man commands the nickname "Doc" in a place that is full of doctors, it says a lot about how those people feel about that man. Interestingly, he never expected anyone to call him Dr. Montgomery. He always introduced himself as Chuck. So of course I always called him Charles. Every staff person I met made sure I knew that Charles was the reason the center's doors were still open. It is that rare ability to inspire stories told with wide-eyed wonderment that turns myth to legend for the famous and the infamous alike.

"We were hundreds of thousands of dollars in debt when the Feds sent him in," said Edith, the Finance Director. "He had us in the black within six months."

Charles' version of events was lackluster by contrast. "They were living off grant money from the federal government," he said. "They hadn't even tried to bill for their services. I brought a company in to bill for the claims that hadn't expired. That's how we wiped out the deficit. It didn't take a genius to figure out what to do. They were just being lazy."

Perhaps it was that simple. Perhaps anybody could have done what he did, but it still didn't explain everything. One of the first things about the center that captured my attention was how unlike a typical clinic it was. In fact, "clinic" was a word that Charles never permitted anyone to associate with his center.

I surmised that he was sensitive about it because of the images that clinics usually invoke - dank and grimy walls, disaffected staff and foul-smelling corridors – places of last resort. It is the sort of indelible stereotype that brands the kinds of places that this place clearly was not. The fact that someone cared about what happened within its walls was readily apparent the moment you stepped through the center's doors. It was an atmosphere of high expectations that clearly extended from the top. Edith had a story to explain that too.

For years after the center took over the building that housed them, much of the first floor was left unoccupied. But that didn't mean it could be neglected as far as Charles was concerned.

"Doc happened to come downstairs while one of the janitors was mopping the floor," Edith told me one day. Like so many other stories I heard about Charles, she retold it with a mixture of pride, awe and trepidation. "I guess he wasn't putting enough effort into it," she continued. "Because Doc grabbed the handle and mopped that entire floor all by himself with the janitor right on his hip. And he was giving him an ear full of cleaning tips all the way across."

I was impressed. It was a big floor.

"But that's Doc for you," Edith said. "He's definitely not the stand and point type."

I learned quickly that in addition to a persnickety attention to detail, Charles also had never heard the word self-censorship. As more of the complexities of his personality began to emerge, they served to explain why a man who clearly bordered on brilliant was spending the twilight years of his career in a job for which he was grossly overqualified.

"Don't you ever want to get a husband?" he said to me one day.

No matter how hard I tried to steel myself to his unconventional style, he still managed to come up with comments that stunned me into slack-jawed silence.

"With all of the pharmaceutical reps we have coming in here," he continued, "you might get asked out on a date once in a while if you didn't come to work looking like an unmade bed sometimes."

The transition from self-employment to working a steady 9 to 5 job was not an easy one for me. But I was able to ease my way back into the unfamiliar territory of a structured schedule much like one would slip into a hot bath – one limb at a time. It wasn't just the work schedule. It took effort for me to adjust to something as simple as putting on work attire everyday. Clearly it was a struggle I didn't always win.

"If you wanted me to come to work in suits, all you had to do was say so," I said with the whine of the wounded. I wish I could have come up with a better emotional response than "ouch" but I couldn't. So I fumbled my way through that equally lame reply.

"I don't really care how you dress as long as you get my work done," he said over his shoulder. "I'm just trying to help you."

He was the quintessential enigma. Disciplined in some aspects of his life and thoroughly undisciplined in others. He had this uncanny ability to hold two contradictory concepts in his mind at the same time and make them make sense. I guess that's how a man whose desk was always clear, office spotless and who always came to work looking like new money could take on a protégé who came to work wearing flip-flops and sundresses, burned incense in her office and hadn't seen the top of her desk since the day it was delivered.

At the same time, he could be sensitive and exceedingly generous. He made sure that the board of directors compensated him handsomely for his contributions past and present. But unlike many others I've encountered in similar positions, he always shared the wealth. As he said to me once, "Every time I get a raise, everybody in here gets a raise. I'm not doing this by myself." As a result, for an organization its size, the employees at every level were well paid. I benefited as well and not just monetarily.

Enigma or not, Charles kept his promise to teach me everything I wanted to know about running a health center. As I came up with ideas for how to improve operations, he let me run with them. Taking the time to navigate his mood swings was worth the pressure and the heat because if you could hold on long enough, you were sure to find a diamond within the lump of coal.

But the true value in our working relationship came in ways I wasn't able to identify at the time. Working for a man like Charles forced me to grow up. At that point in my career, I suffered from the same delusion that many people bring to their jobs. I expected to be stroked with love and appreciation for each and every job well done. But his was a style that was generous with verbal criticism and sparse with praise. At least it felt that way to me. Over time it taught me to appreciate praise but to "expect" a paycheck - and nothing more. And by "over time" I mean it took a while.

I was taking on more and more responsibility and I decided that my title should be upgraded to Chief Operating Officer. Charles agreed in principle but for some reason he was taking his sweet time in making it official. During one of my attempts to nag him into compliance, he called me spoiled and it really set me off. So I held a conference call with my top two advisors — my mother and my only sister.

"I'm so sick of him!" I said. "He doesn't appreciate anything I do." It was one of the now near monthly venting sessions where I seriously contemplated quitting and I was on a roll. "And do you know what he had the nerve to say to me today? He called me spoiled. Spoiled! Can you believe that ... hello ... hello?"

It was only after an unusually long pause that my sister finally said something.

"Sorry. I was waiting for the part where he said something that wasn't true."

I am fortunate to have in my own family smart women who have had their own careers. Over the years, they often provided me with ready and much-needed access to caring yet professional advice. In addition to being smart, my sister is easily the most perceptive person I know. If you can only bring one person with you to a negotiation, she's the one you want. She has an almost supernatural ability to notice all of the little details that everyone else misses. So despite being loving and protective as every big sister should be, whenever I ask her to put on the hat of an impartial advisor, she does so without reservation and she's pretty damn good at it. In other words, she will tell me when I have my ass on backwards.

My mother is another story. Easily my best friend, she also gives excellent advice. This is probably why she's managed to maintain her own relationships with so many of the people I've worked with over the years, long after I've moved on. But unlike my sister, she'll never put any role ahead of the role of being my mother. So while I can count on her to give me valuable insight most of the time, if doing so could be construed as her not coming down on the side of her baby girl, she'll opt for the diplomat's way out. This explains her response when I accused my sister of treason for inferring that Charles may have been justified in calling me spoiled. "Mom! Did you hear what she just said?" I asked.

"Well, honey, he was probably a little harsh but . . . ."

As we entered the spring of 1996, we began preparing in earnest for a very important review. Every few years the center's federal funding source conducted something called a Primary Care Effectiveness Review (or "PCER") of its grant recipients. The ebb and flow of working with Charles had subsided a bit because he was spending more and more time away from the center consulting, attending conferences or spending time with his family out of town.

Whenever he was away he left me in charge. But with the PCER getting closer I expected him to cut down on the travel to give me more direction. He didn't and I was growing concerned. My career as a healthcare administrator was only a little more than a year old. There was so much that I still didn't know in general and I had never been through anything like a review before. The center was receiving a seven-figure grant allocation. So, failing the review would have had fatal consequences. But none of that seemed to raise enough concern with Charles to cause him to curtail his travel plans. He just handed me some material to read and left me to figure it out. As the review drew closer, my mood shifted from concern to frustration.

I was in my office late one night when he passed by on his way out. "You getting things ready for the survey?" he asked. He was so blasé when he asked the question that I could feel my blood start to boil.

"I guess," I said without looking up.

"Well you're the boss around here," he said with a smirk. I was in no mood for sarcasm.

"You'd think that as much as you're gone," I quipped. "But you seem to forget I've never done this before. A little help would be nice."

"I don't do survey prep anymore," he said. "That's why I hire smart, energetic people like you." It was now my turn for sarcasm. "That sounds like a Chief Operating Officer's job and last I checked, that's not my title," I responded.

I had stopped mentioning the promotion months ago. But he kept plucking my last good nerve. Bringing it up now the way I did was the kind of move that usually lit the wick with him. But instead of an angry diatribe he slipped me a precious trinket that I've kept with me ever since. He said, "When you're really ready for a promotion, the staff should be treating you like you already have it. The title is just a formality."

I sat with that one for a long while. And I never brought the promotion up again. Instead, I focused on the opportunity that he was giving me by being away so much. I took another look at the materials he left me with, discovered my instincts and began to figure it out. I went through each of the chapters of the review manual and started working with the departments they impacted. That meant the physicians, the finance department, the front desk, facilities, even the board of directors.

The board members were volunteers so there was a limit to how much of their attention I could expect. So I decided to prepare a primer for them with samples of the kinds of questions they might be asked and some examples of how they might want to answer.

They were thrilled. But preparing the staff required a different approach.

I needed input from them on how they performed their jobs so that I could figure out and then explain to them how their work might intersect with what the reviewers would want to know. For the most part, I encountered no resistance – that was except for the Finance Director.

"I don't need help," Edith said. "I've done this before."

That was her response whenever I tried to set up an appointment to go over the review manual. So after three unsuccessful attempts, I left her section with her with highlights on the areas she needed to work on. Beyond that I didn't push it.

It was during this same period that the board of directors approved Charles' plan for a lay off or "Reduction in Force" as he liked to call it. I can think of one reason the department directors at the center were happy to see me come on board as Director of Human Resources. My presence meant they no longer had to do their own dirty work when they wanted to fire someone.

It was a part of the job that I certainly didn't enjoy but I had a practical streak made of titanium. It was my job, it wasn't personal, and so I did it. Even with having to terminate so many people who I'd come to know personally, the lawyer in me was still able to distinguish between what I wanted to do and what was expected of me. That was until I arrived at one name on the list. Charles had put his own assistant on it – the woman who introduced me to him and was arguably the reason why I had my job.

I had taken on a part-time position teaching at a small Catholic college in Brooklyn. This was shortly after I returned to New York following my graduation from law school. I taught management and business law classes on nights and weekends to working adults who were going back to school to finish their undergraduate degrees. It was early one Saturday morning when Charles' executive assistant approached me.

"I want you to meet my boss," she said. "He's looking for a consultant to rewrite our Human Resources manual. I think you would be perfect for the job."

What we think we know about a person is strongly influenced by the positions they hold. As teacher and student, the interactions between me and Charles' executive assistant had been limited and highly structured. But once we became co-workers I suspect that our perceptions of each other changed dramatically.

The aura of the college professor who wore conservative dresses, glasses and her hair in a bun turned to mist during our daily contacts. Since I no longer held the kind of lofty position that once impressed her, she now felt free to behave in ways that showed me how impressed she was with herself. On an almost daily basis she would demonstrate an acutely accurate impersonation of someone suffering from delusions of grandeur. She exaggerated about everything, even silly insignificant things and it came back to haunt her.

Charles had been mulling over the possibility of conducting layoffs for weeks, and her close proximity to the information gave her another topic to pontificate about. She made statements like, "I hope they lay me off. I need a break." and "My husband works so I don't really need this job." She even went as far as to say, "I'd rather they laid me off so that someone else who really needs their job can stay. I really don't mind."

In the weeks before the layoffs were approved, she was so glib about her job that I really wasn't surprised when I saw her name on the list. But I also suspected that she wasn't really prepared for someone to call her bluff. Either way, I didn't want that person to be me. So I spoke with Charles about it. I knew it was my responsibility to handle the layoffs – all of them, not just the ones I wanted to do. But I was hoping he would let me off the hook when it came to her. Thankfully, he did. He offered to tell her himself. Unfortunately, it turned out that I would have to do it anyway.

Early on the morning after the board approved the final plan, she came into my office. We were alone and she looked pale and anxious.

"Are they doing layoffs today?"

The question caught me by surprise because I didn't think anyone knew that we were implementing them so soon. "Yes," I said. My stomach tightened. I knew what was coming next.

"Am I on the list?"

It was the only time in all of our interactions that I ever actually saw her look scared. I struggled to find a way to avoid telling her that she was indeed on the list. Apparently, "you'll have to discuss that with Dr. Montgomery" didn't do the trick. Just that quick, she snapped back to her old self and said, "I don't have to talk to him. It's fine. I'll pack."

Charles did speak to her when he came in but she was gone by noon. With that bit of unpleasantness behind me I turned to the equally disagreeable task of letting the rest of the people on the list know that they were being let go and explaining the terms of their severance packages. What I remember most about the experience is the thick cloud that the specter of layoffs cast over the center. Even our best employees were worried.

I decided that no matter how many layoffs there were, I was going to finish them in one day. That way the staff would know that if they still had a job at the end of the day, they still had a job. It may seem like an insignificant gesture but I feel strongly that anything you can do to put people at ease in such a difficult situation is worth the extra effort. If the people who eliminate thousands of jobs with the flick of a pen actually had to look each of their victims in the face when they did it, they would probably give a little more thought to those decisions.

Despite his frequent absences, Charles always made sure he knew what was going on at the center. As the week of our survey drew closer, he held an impromptu meeting with key members of the senior staff to get an update on our progress. I brought my binder to the meeting. In it I had all of my notes for every section of the PCER Review manual. Every section that is, except for finance.

"Alright, take me through the manual," he said.

He didn't hold many staff meetings but when he did his commanding presence had the same effect as when he walked through the hallways. All eyes were on him and everyone was quiet until he gave them an indication that he wanted them to speak.

We went through the governance section first. I showed him the primer I gave the board members. He nodded without expression. That was as much of an endorsement as I could expect. "Medical Staff," he said next. The Medical Director began to respond. He was new to the post and had a thick accent. That coupled with his visible anxiety made the first few minutes of his report a little tense. But I'd worked with him on his sections so I jumped in to amplify an answer if it looked like Charles was about to go on the attack. Before long we managed to make it through that section.

Next up was Nursing. Charles was always hard on the Nursing Director. He snapped at her when her answer was a little vague. I jumped in where I could with the notes I had and then he snapped at me. "Your word isn't good enough," he said. "They want examples." "We were going to give them a book with the minutes from our meetings," the Nursing Director said timidly.

"Don't make them look for it! The more time they spend with their nose in our minutes the more places they'll find to dig," he barked. "Make copies of the pages that give examples of what they're looking for and put them in a separate folder."

It was all so easy to him. That's why your behind needs to be here, I thought. I thought it; I didn't say it. I had enough sense to know that in this setting a sarcastic remark would have led to a public beheading. After a few more slaps on the wrist, he let Nursing off the hook.

"Okay. What about finance?" he said.

I'd been co-presenting up to that point. But I knew nothing about how the finance department had been preparing so I had nothing to add. The abrupt pause in the conversation caused Charles to turn his gaze toward me. I didn't want to make an issue of the fact that Edith and I had been at odds, so instead of commenting I forwarded his glance to her.

"I don't have anything," she said.

You could feel a frost move through the room as Charles tipped his head forward to peer over his horn-rimmed glasses.

"Why not?" he asked.

I could tell he was annoyed but he was surprisingly calm. Without blinking or looking in my direction for that matter, Edith said, "I thought Candis was handling this."

Words cannot do justice to how dramatically Edith's reply altered my blood pressure. I was so unprepared for her response that I couldn't come up with one of my own. It would have been inappropriate for me to try to explain what had really been going on, right there in the middle of the meeting. So under the circumstances, the only alternative available was for me to brace for impact and straighten it out after the meeting was over. But to everyone's surprise, Charles said nothing more about it. He just moved to the next topic.

I think the reason I'd been able to work around Charles' mood swings with reasonable dexterity was that in temperament he was very much like my father. He blew up about little things that any normal person would never get that upset about. Big things that really should cause him to detonate he would respond to without any emotion at all. I'd lived with this kind of unpredictable behavior all my life. It ceased to unnerve me around age nine. But I also knew from experience that sometimes it was just the calm before the storm.

Later that day when I cautiously went into his office to explain, he listened without reacting as I told him about my attempts to work with Edith. When I was finished all he said was, "Don't worry about it." I left his office not knowing what that meant. Did he believe me? Or did he just think this was proof I wasn't up to the task?

Ready or not, the PCER survey team arrived in July of 1996. I was filled with anxiety but Charles showed no signs of concern one way or another. The butterflies in my stomach started executing kamikaze dives as soon as the opening conference was over. I watched each surveyor pair up with the appropriate department director and leave the room. Then I paced back and forth, nervously tracing my index finger around the rim of my cup of tea. Our Director of Community Affairs approached me in the corner of the conference room.

"Don't be nervous," she said. "You did a great job getting us ready."

"Thanks, but I'd still feel better if Dr. Montgomery had been more involved," I said. "I don't know if I've missed something. I really expected him to be around more these last few weeks."

"He must think you can handle it," she said. I wasn't persuaded.

"Yeah right," I said. With just the two of us alone in an empty conference room, I didn't bother to hide my skepticism.

"Well," she said "he hired me a few months after he came here and in all these years I've never known him to be away from the center as much as he has been since you got here. Believe me, for him, that's a compliment."

I had the opportunity to sit in on some of the interviews during the survey. The staff did a terrific job. When the meeting with the board of directors was over, the Vice-Chairman of the board found me in my office.

"Candis, I had to stop by your office to thank you," he said grinning from ear to ear.

"You're welcome. But for what?" I asked.

"Every question they asked us you covered in that little handout you gave us," he said. "I can't remember ever being so well-prepared before. You are really an asset around here. Don't you even think about leaving us," he said with a smile as he darted out the door.

We gathered in the conference room on the last day of the survey. It was Charles, the Medical Director, the Nursing Director, Edith, the Community Affairs Director, the Chairman of the Board of Directors and me. Our program officer from the Bureau of Primary Health Care spoke first.

"I don't know what to say," he said.

My heart raced just a little. There was more than one way to take that statement.

"It's like I'm visiting this place for this first time. Dr. Montgomery, I don't know what new magic you're working here this time, but whatever you're doing keep it up."

When Charles looked directly at me and smiled it made up for all of the arguments we'd had over the previous year. And the accolades kept coming. Each of the three surveyors had nothing but glowing remarks.

"I feel like I haven't done my job if I don't write down something for the center to improve but I really couldn't find anything. So I'm telling you now that your areas for improvement from me will sound petty. They are," the next surveyor said.

Only the surveyor for the finance section of the review had concrete recommendations. But even those weren't significant enough to mar what turned out to be the best review the center had ever had.

When the summation was over, there were plenty of hugs and smiles to go around. The smile from Charles during the meeting was all the praise I would receive from him about how we'd performed. But by then he'd so sufficiently toughened me up that it was more than enough. I drifted away from the others and out into the administrative suite. Janice, the new executive assistant, was sitting at her desk smiling.

Janice had been working at the front desk for a few years but her new supervisor wanted her fired. She began having attendance problems and there was constant friction between them. But she had also once been voted employee of the month and the patients loved her. I suspected that her recently developed pattern of absenteeism had more to do with morale than ability. So I asked Charles if we could give her a chance to work with us back in the suite instead of firing her. He was skeptical but he went along with the idea.

I didn't know if she had any real secretarial skills and as it turned out she didn't. Both Charles and I typed faster than she did. But since his assistant was now our assistant, that flaw wasn't fatal. Those weren't the skills that we needed. Charles was one of the most independent bosses I'd ever seen. He typed his own memos and answered the phone, as did I. The only thing he couldn't seem to do for himself was arrange for his breakfast and lunch. He needed a caretaker and Janice was happy to oblige with those sorts of details.

Beyond that, what we really needed was someone with an easygoing demeanor who could be the crème filling between our hard-cookie surfaces. Those were skills she brought in abundance. In her own unassuming way she managed to douse more than a few small brush fires between Charles and me before they flared out of control.

"Congratulations," she said.

"Thanks, but the credit goes to the CEO. He's in charge," I replied. I meant it. Somehow Charles managed to know when to be present and when to stay out of the way. Even though I fussed about him leaving me on my own so much, I had to admit he was there when I needed him.

"Maybe," Janice said without looking up, "but he and just about everybody else in that room was here for the last survey. . . except for you."

She looked up just long enough to give me a wink. At least I thought she was winking at me. Charles passed by me on his way to his office at about the same time. There was no way he could have missed what she said. I was sure that we were both going to pay for her remark. That was until I saw his face. He winked back at both of us, smiled and closed the door.

The mood in the office was easy and light for weeks after the survey. "Candis, your mom's on the phone and when you're finished Dr. Montgomery wants to see you," Janice called out to me one afternoon. My voice conveyed my confusion when I picked up the phone.

"I heard the phone ring ten minutes ago," I said.

"Oh yeah, Janice and I were just chatting," my mother said through light-hearted laughter.

"Could you please stop co-opting my staff?"

"I can't help it if they l-u-u-v me."

I could hear her mischievous little grin through the phone. She'd called me to relay news from my cousin. Her son had gotten sick at a party and was taken to Woodhull Hospital.

"Woodhull??? Why would she take him to that dump?" I asked horrified.

"She didn't," my mother replied. "The ambulance did. You have to let her tell you how bad it was. You know she has a gift for storytelling. I can't do it justice."

"Well how is he now?"

"Better. She had him transferred to another hospital."

My thoughts drifted to all the horror stories I'd heard about Woodhull over the years. It had one of the worst reputations in Brooklyn if not the entire city.

"I need to go work a little of my magic over at that place," I said. I was only partially joking. Clearly I was still feeling the after effects of the ether from the center's success on its review. But of course my mother thought it was a thoroughly plausible idea.

"You should," she said. "They certainly could use some help. You're probably just what they need."

We were deep in conversation when I remembered that Charles wanted to see me. I cut the call short and hurried to his office. "Sorry it took me so long," I said. "Do you want me to close the door?" I knew I'd better enter humbly because I'd kept him waiting.

"Talking to Mommy?" he asked with a cutting edge that bordered on derision. Charles thought it absurd that my mother and I spoke everyday. Periodically, he let me know as much. But on that point there was nothing he could do or say to make me bend. I didn't bite the bait for another argument so he proceeded to the point of why he'd called me into his office.

"I let Edith go," he said.

I didn't know what to say. Edith had been with the center for almost two decades. Charles' penchant for venting meant that if he was thinking about doing something he couldn't hold it any better than a sieve holds soup. But he never gave me any indication that he was thinking about this.

"Why?" I asked.

"Because the Finance Director will have to report to the Chief Operating Officer just like everybody else and I knew she was never going to work with you."

That's how I found out I was being promoted to Chief Operating Officer. It was so typical of him. He wasn't even looking at me when he told me. He was rifling though papers on his desk, acting as if he'd just asked me to order his lunch. But it was just as he said it would be. My promotion was met with very little fanfare.

With the formality of my title finally settled, Charles gave me more autonomy than ever. One of the tasks he immediately turned over to me was responsibility for writing the annual grant application for our federal funding. Now there wasn't an aspect of the center's operations, including finance, that I wasn't intimately involved in. I applied for other grants on the center's behalf and we were awarded $400,000 to expand our HIV program. The new grant required more staff and that meant we had to find space for them. We hired contractors to renovate the unused space on the first floor. But we needed a project manager to make sure the renovations would be finished by the time the new staff started. Who got the job? Me, of course. I definitely loved my work.

By the middle of 1997, I felt like I'd been a healthcare administrator all of my life. So when I learned that another federally qualified health center in Far Rockaway was looking for an Executive Director, my insatiable hunger for the next big challenge prompted me to apply. But I was conflicted. I was happy where I was. And I was comfortable.

The ups and downs between Charles and me had settled into a predictable rhythm. He was still stingy with the compliments in my presence but I'd come to learn that when I wasn't around he bragged to everyone else about what a smart and talented deputy he had. I presented at health care conferences because of him. I co-authored my first article because of him. He may have been unconventional but he had been the definition of a mentor to me. I owed him a great deal. I decided to speak to him about the position to see what he thought.

"I saw an ad in the New York Times last Sunday," I said. "There's a center in Far Rockaway that's looking for an Executive Director."

"Yeah I know which one you're talking about," he said. "I heard their Director was leaving."

I took a deep breath.

"I was thinking about applying. What do you think?"

I watched his face carefully for any sign of how he might feel about my applying for another job. But it didn't seem to bother him at all.

"You could definitely do that job," he said. "It's a dinky little center. They could use somebody like you to turn it around. I know the Bureau would love to see you there."

"Really?"

"Sure. You're starting to make a name for yourself after how well the review went," he said. "I'll write you a recommendation if you want to apply. And I'll make some calls."

I was so relieved that he wasn't upset. I sent in my resume and they called me for an interview right away. In the meantime, everyone working in healthcare in New York State had a new target to focus on. The state was finally making serious preparations to move its Medicaid program into a managed care model and there were billions of dollars at stake.

President Clinton's attempt to revamp healthcare made its spiraling costs front-page news. Most people have a vague idea of what the Medicaid program is – health insurance for the poor. But far fewer know how complex the program's structure can be. The benefits participants receive vary from state to state and the differences can be dramatic. Some states cover prescription drugs, some states don't. Some states pay for transportation to and from the doctor, some states don't. Medicaid is a matching grant program. That means a state can offer as many of the federally approved benefits as it likes as long as the state pays half the cost.

New York's Medicaid program is one of the most generous in the country. So, naturally, that makes it one of the most expensive. The cost control features of managed care made it only a matter of time before New York would be forced to embrace it. That it had taken so long to reach a state that spends so much on healthcare is a credit to how many powerful constituencies exist here. Between the healthcare workers union and the public health advocates, New York's Medicaid program was a Goliath that no one wanted to tangle with.

By 1997, however, "David" had entered the ring. As a compromise to the warring factions, an impressive amount of money in the form of multi-year grants was being appropriated to help New York healthcare providers with the transition to managed care. Organizations that served the largest proportion of Medicaid patients stood to receive the largest proportion of the grant funds. And it was adding up to an obscene amount of money.

It was obvious early on that no matter how the pie was sliced New York City's public hospitals were positioned to take home the lion's share of the money.

That was due to the sheer volume of Medicaid patients they treated on an annual basis. Cries went out all over the city from the smaller agencies that stood to be left out. In response, early drafts of the legislation were being rumored to require the city's public hospital system to demonstrate alliances with small community-based healthcare providers that were not part of their system. I'm certain that's how the small constellation of federally qualified health centers in New York City came to be sucked into the gravitational pull of a planet called the New York City Health and Hospitals Corporation.

As public health institutions go, HHC is a behemoth. It has 11 hospitals, 6 large outpatient facilities (called Diagnostic & Treatment Centers or D&TCs in New York), well over 100 smaller clinics and school health programs. It operates nursing homes and rehabilitations centers; it has its own home health agency and its own insurance plan. Nearly one-and-half million of New York City's eight million residents receive some sort of treatment at an HHC facility on an annual basis. The Veterans Health Administration operates more facilities but as an integrated public health system, HHC is by far the largest in the country. In public health circles, it is the 800-pound gorilla.

I knew very little about "the Corporation" except for what my mother shared from her 30 years of city employment. "I know that whenever a social worker had the chance to leave our agency to work at HHC, they jumped at the chance. HHC always paid better," she'd say.

Every community health center in the city received personal invitations to a meeting hosted by HHC to discuss how we could work together. Charles took me to that meeting and it was the kind of droning gabfest you would expect when you bring the leaders of thirty or forty agencies of different sizes together in one room. Everyone wanted their turn at the mike even after there was nothing new left to say. After a few hours, it was decided that committees would be formed and broken up by borough. I knew I would be representing our center before Charles and I got back into the car. There was no way he had the patience for something like that.

It was at the first Brooklyn meeting that I was able to learn names and faces. The center of attention was Shaina Green, HHC's Sr. Vice-President for Planning and Government and so on and so forth. From the very first meeting, she impressed me as someone who was smart and articulate but with a dash of bullshit mixed in for good measure.

She came breezing into the meeting fifteen minutes late already in full conversation mode. The meeting was held at HHC's Cumberland Diagnostic & Treatment Center, which is located on the north side of Fort Greene Park just below the Brooklyn-Queens Expressway. Cumberland's proximity to our center should have made them a competitor but they were three times our size. Beyond that, in Brooklyn an eighth of a mile can span three zip codes. So we weren't really seeing the same patients.

Cumberland's Executive Director was Donna Wilson and unlike Shaina, I detected nothing but sincerity in her. Shaina and one of her Assistant Vice President's discussed a scope for the Brooklyn committee and then suggested that we form sub-committees. We all bounced around ideas about what each subcommittee should focus on. Then we settled on assignments that each of these teams would flesh out and then report on at a subsequent meeting. For some reason, I was hoping to be put on a team with Donna but I ended up working with the COO from another health center like ours. The HHC representative on our subcommittee was a woman named Lois and she, as it turned out, was the Executive Director at Woodhull Hospital.

The HHC collaboration project turned out to be an interesting and welcome diversion for me. We'd finished the renovations to the center's ground floor months earlier. Our newly expanded HIV program received high praise during its first review. Visits were up. Life was good. I was getting bored. Working on this committee gave me something new to do.

By that point I'd made my way to the final round for the job at the center in Far Rockaway but they selected someone else. I suspected that once again my age had something to do with it. Somewhere around the point in time when I skipped my senior year in high school to become a 15- year-old freshman at St. John's University, people started treating me like a wunderkind.

Sometimes that meant the people around me would marvel at the kinds of tricks I could perform. But just as often they acted as if they didn't know what to do with me. Now that the possibility of being the head of my own center was out, I was left with that all too familiar wanderlust. If I didn't find a path to redirect that energy to soon, it would eventually lead me to my "advisors" lamenting over what I should do with my life. I always seemed to need something new to do.

I was sitting in the small waiting area outside of Charles' office one day, talking with Janice when a phone call interrupted us. One of Janice's talents could be found in her delightful speaking voice and professional demeanor. I could tell from her end of the conversation that the call was for me. So I stood up to go into my office. But I found myself fixed in place by the bewildered look on Janice's face and the awkwardness of her conversation.

"Uh hold on . . hold. . . yes . . .okay she's here . . .um hmm."

Obviously the other person was still talking but Janice looked like she was listening to an alien on the other end. Finally she said, "Okay . . . would you hold on please?" When she put the person on hold I asked her what the problem was. "You'll see," she replied and then calmly went back to stuffing envelopes.

I went into my office, sat down and picked up the phone. "Hello, this is Candis Best."

"Candis . . . ?"

"Yes."

"Candis Best?"

"Yes."

"Ohhhhh . . . it is so nice to finally meet you . . . well we're not actually meeting are we, we'd have to be face to face but we are talking aren't we and it's s-o-o-o nice to be talking to you."

I took the receiver away from my ear and looked at it the same way Janice had moments earlier. I glanced up in time to see her peering at me from the doorway to my office. She didn't say anything. She just gave me a look that said, "See what I mean." Then she drifted back to her desk. When I put the receiver back to my ear the woman on the other end of the line was still talking in a steady stream of conversation all by herself. Her voice alternated between high pitches and soft whispers and a visual image flashed in my mind that wherever she was, there were little humming birds circling her head.

"Excuse me but who am I talking to?" I asked.

"My goodness! What a dingleberry I am! All this time I'm talking to you and I haven't even told you my name. What terrible manners. My name is Velma. I'm Ms. Wilson's assistant here at Cumberland," she said.

"Hello Velma. It's nice to . . ." That's as far as I got before she cut me off again.

"And I have heard so much about you - so many wonderful things. Ms. Wilson was talking about what a lovely young lady you are and I can just tell now by talking to you that she's right! Oh I could tell that right away. You know . . ."

This went on for five more minutes. She never paused to take a breath. I finally had to interrupt her abruptly just to get a word in. "Velma, what can I do for you?"

"Listen to me going on and on . . . of course yes, I called for a reason didn't I. Yes well Ms. Wilson would like to know if she and her Deputy could meet with you."

I was happy to comply. "Sure," I said. "I'll put you back on with my assistant."

I put her on hold before she could crank herself up again. I got up to tell Janice to pick up the phone just so I could enjoy the look on her face when she learned she'd have another chance to chat with Velma.

Donna and Vonetta, her Deputy Director, came to the center the following week to discuss the Women, Infants and Children or WIC Program that provides nutritional classes and food vouchers to low income women and children. Cumberland was a WIC site and many of our patients went there for their WIC subsidies.

"We were wondering if you would like for us to sponsor a WIC site for you here at your center," Donna offered.

"What would we need to do?" I asked.

"Just provide the space," Donna said.

"We need an office for the dietician, some space for classes and a secure location to dispense the WIC checks," Vonetta added.

"We can do that," I said. "What about staff?"

"We'll provide the staff," Donna replied. "It's easier for us to get approval to add you to our license than it would be for you to apply on your own. We see quite a few of your patients. So we thought this might work well for you."

It was a terrific idea and quite generous of them. Every WIC patient of ours that went to Cumberland presented them with the opportunity to entice our patient to become their patient. Having our own site would not only allow us to keep our patients in the building but we would have access to new WIC clients who might not have a healthcare provider of their own. I agreed immediately.

"Great," Donna said. "Vonetta will work out the details with you."

"Thank you," I said. "This is a very thoughtful gesture for you to make."

"Not at all," Donna replied. "There's enough business for both of us. Besides it's more convenient for the patients. That's why we're here, right?"

I knew there was a reason why I got a good feeling from her. And she was efficient as well. We had worked the entire deal out in less than 15 minutes.

"By the way, how's your committee working out?" she asked as she gathered her things to leave.

"Funny you should mention it," I said.

I offered to host our first sub-committee meeting. I ordered refreshments and my colleague from the other health center arrived on time. We waited and waited but Lois never showed up. I called her the next day and she said, "Was that last night? Oh I forgot. I had a retirement party to go to. We'll host the next meeting here at Woodhull."

When I finished relaying the story to Donna and Vonetta they exchanged knowing glances but said nothing.

"I'll call you once I've been in touch with the state," Vonetta said.

Our new WIC program was up and running in a matter of weeks. Velma would call to set up follow-up meetings and I would so enjoy watching Janice try in vain to bring her to the point of the call. The HHC -

31

Community Health Center collaborations did not proceed as swimmingly. We had one or two more meetings. I became the chair of my subcommittee and submitted detailed reports to the larger committee. For what little good it did, I enjoyed participating while it lasted. But by early in 1998, it was clear that HHC was going to get its money with or without the community health centers. As soon as the ink was dry on that deal, they quickly lost interest in collaborating.

Unfortunately, in the meantime my working relationship with Charles had once again become turbulent. He read one of my reports to the HHC Collaboration Committee and went ballistic.

"Why are you doing all this work!" he shouted at me one day. "You've got work to do here."

Things had been so placid between us in the preceding months that his outburst caught me off guard.

"My work is getting done here," I said.

"That's not for you to decide, it's for me to decide. You don't need to be drawing attention to yourself. The next thing you know they'll be offering you a job," he said.

I looked at him like he had lost his mind.

"What are you talking about? No one's offering me a job." It was as if I hadn't even spoken.

"I don't want you working on that committee anymore," he said. "The center is a mess!"

Every other week we were bickering about one thing or another. More often than not, the "bickering" was loud enough to be heard through the walls. Then he called me into his office and handed me my annual performance evaluation. It was awful and I had a holy fit.

"What the hell is this?" I screamed.

He was unusually calm, given my tirade. He actually seemed to enjoy seeing me lose my temper.

"You know what it is," he said wryly. "Now sit down. You're not going to stand over my desk and yell at me in *my* office. I know you think I work for you but I'm still the CEO here."

"I'll tell you what I think! I think you're out of your mind!" I said.

I was still standing and I was still yelling. He wasn't enjoying it anymore. A look of irascibility was inching up his face and I'd seen that look before. But there was also something devilish about the look in his eyes. It taunted me like a dangling steak just beyond the reach of a hungry pit bull. Then the chain broke.

"This is garbage and I'm not accepting it!" I said. I tore my evaluation into pieces and threw it on his desk. Then I turned on my heels, went back to my office and slammed the door.

I knew he was coming for me. Before I left his office I witnessed rage overtake shock as he looked at the pieces of my evaluation now strewn across his desk. I was long past the point of concern over losing my job. We were so furious at each other that I knew one of us was going to the hospital and the other one was going to jail before it was all over. I tried to prepare myself for what was going to be the blowout of all blowouts.

I heard Charles' footsteps bounding down the hall toward me. I stood up behind my desk. I saw the doorknob start to turn. My eyes widened and I drew back two clenched fists. My face was flush and my heart was trying to punch its way through my ribcage. I waited and I waited and I waited some more, fists trembling. But nothing happened. After a few minutes I sat down. After a few more minutes I calmed down. When the magnitude of what I'd just done washed over me it hit with the force of a tidal wave. If ever I needed a consult I needed one now. So I called Mommy-girlfriend.

"Mom, I can't believe what I just did."

"What happened?"

She asked the question with an easy placidness. It betrayed a belief that she knew it was bad but was certain it was fixable. Her voice carried that precise blend of concern, love and frustration that only a mother can capture correctly. Just hearing that voice, I started to feel a little better. I told her everything I'd done with the detail of a Catholic penitent and her response was perfectly balanced.

"First calm down," she said.

"Okay," I said still breathing heavily. "I'm calm."

"Alright," she continued. "Now just listen. At some point in our lives we've all done or said something that we would have handled differently if we'd just held our breath and counted to ten. You didn't kill anybody. You made a mistake. Now you have to fix it."

"I know I'm fired," I said.

"Probably, but that's neither here nor there. You need to go back to his office and apologize. What he does after that is up to him."

I took a deep breath, counted to ten and then walked the green mile back to his office. Janice acted as if none of the previous twelve minutes had ever happened. When I gestured to her that I wanted to go in she just nodded toward the door. I knocked.

"Come in," he said.

When I opened the door we both had the same expression on our faces. It read, "Are you about to start something?"

"Can we talk?" I asked. I tried to sound as contrite as I could so that he would know that I was not about to start something.

"Alright," he said.

I took a seat.

"I know there is no excuse for what I did, I guess I lost my mind a little bit and I know I'm probably fired but I just want to apologize for my behavior a few minutes ago, I'm really, really sorry."

I said it all on a single breath in one long run-on sentence. Then I added, "I'll tape the evaluation back together and sign it."

I waited for his response. He didn't say anything for several very long minutes. He just stared at me and it was the longest, scariest and most awkward pause I'd ever experienced. But eventually the creases in his brow began to soften.

"Well . . ." he began slowly, "you know Janice was the only thing that kept me from going into your office to get you. I was going to throw you out the back door of this building by your collar."

"I heard you at the door," I said. "I was wondering why you didn't come in."

"She said, 'Dr. Montgomery, you don't want to do that,'" he explained. Then he laughed. "I guess she read my mind."

"I guess," I said. "Where's the evaluation? I'll put it back together."

"It's too late. I shredded it," he replied. "I was just working on another one."

We both looked down at the papers on his desk.

"I guess I'll have to shred this one too," he added.

"That bad, huh?" I asked.

The look I received in response let me know that I definitely didn't want to see that one.

"I guess I owe you an apology too," he said. "It wasn't a fair evaluation."

"Then why did you write it?" I asked. "Why have you been on my back so much lately?"

He looked humbled in a way that I had never seen before. But I thought I might know the reason. A month before I left for school my mother and I were at each other's throats. Everyday she was yelling at me for something. We never fought and then suddenly we were fighting everyday. It was so out of character for her that after a few weeks I realized that it had to be because I was leaving. A few weeks after I settled into my new apartment, she admitted it herself.

"Candis . . ." Charles began, ". . .when you came to ask me if you should apply for that job in Far Rockaway I have to tell you . . . I . . ."

"What?" I asked.

Charles was tenuous in his response in a way that left him strangely unguarded.

"It wasn't until that moment that I realized how comfortable I'd become with your being here," he said, eyes cast just past my shoulder. "Let's just say the thought of having to go back to running this center by myself wasn't something I was looking forward to."

"But I didn't get the job," I said. "I'm not going anywhere."

Then he looked up at me with a new kind of sincerity. "Sure you are," he said. "This is the kind of place where you start your career or you end it. You've already outgrown it here. It's only a matter of time."

We'd had so many really meaningful conversations over the time we'd worked together but never one like this.

"But you keep saying you're going to retire in a few years," I said. "I can wait until then. You don't think the board would approve me as your replacement?"

"Of course they would," he said. "But you've outgrown this job too. You don't belong here anymore. If you really want to be a healthcare administrator you need hospital experience now."

We'd come to a fork in the road. It was oddly sobering to finally figure out what all the fighting had been about. We were experiencing growing pains. It was time to grow apart.

"Does this mean I'm not fired?"

"No you're not fired."

"So we just go along as if this never happened?" I asked. "No," he said. "I'm going to get you back for tearing up that evaluation."

I started looking for a new job shortly after that meeting. The first place I thought of was HHC. Working there would allow me to continue to work in the public health field. I was now certain that was something I wanted to do. But with 30,000 employees and a four billion dollar budget, HHC was also one of New York City's largest employers. Working there would also give me the chance to work in a large corporate environment.

But perhaps the most appealing prospect it offered to me was its diversity. After three years at Villanova Law School (or Vanillanova as those of us in the Black Law Student Association used to call it), I'd had my fill of being the lone dark fleck in the salt shaker. If I could land a job with HHC I could work for a large healthcare corporation without always being the person who integrated the room.

I saw an ad in the healthcare careers section of the Sunday *New York Times*. Harlem Hospital was looking for a Chief Operating Officer. As luck would have it, Donna Wilson's sister Dina was Harlem's CEO. I called Donna to see if she would be willing to put in a good word for me.

"Absolutely," she said. "I'll call her tonight. But send me your resume too. We just need to get you in here someplace. I'll circulate it. You'll get calls."

She was right. Within a few weeks, I interviewed with Shaina Green and her staff, as well as the General Counsel's office. And then I received the call that would change my life. It was from Donna's Deputy, Vonetta.

"Candis, I want to give you the heads up. Lois is going to call you. She heard that you were interviewing around HHC and she really wants you to come to Woodhull. So don't be shy when she calls. Ask for whatever you want."

The very next day, Lois' assistant called me to set up an interview. When I arrived, I met with Lois and her Chief Operating Officer. It quickly became apparent that Vonetta was right.

"I'm not sure what your title will be," Lois said. "But I know I want something higher than Associate Director because I want you reporting directly to me." It certainly sounded like I had a job if I wanted one.

"I know I can offer you 15% over what you're making now," she continued "but I'm going to ask the President if I can give you 20."

Notwithstanding such a generous offer, I still had plenty of reasons to give a second thought to working at Woodhull. Every Brooklyn-ite north of Atlantic Avenue had a Woodhull story and none of them were good. But that wasn't enough to deter me. I was full of confidence and I liked a challenge. You could tell that by the kind of men I dated. And I remembered that off-handed comment I'd made a year earlier about going to Woodhull one day to "work a little of my magic." As I sat in Lois' cavernous office being courted like a potential first-round draft pick, I couldn't escape the feeling that all of the stars seemed to be aligning to bring me to this place. Perhaps it was divine providence. So without knowing my title or salary or even what she wanted me to do, I extended my hand and said, "When do you want me to start?"

CHAPTER TWO
JUNE 1, 1998

IT'S PROBABLY BEST TO approach Woodhull from the east. Sidle through the narrow streets of Bushwick so that the menacing shadow of the J train's elevated tracks can dull your ocular senses. You'll have to dodge a cavalcade of livery taxis, city buses and an endless parade of strollers. But that will keep your reflexes sharp. Then grab a snack from the dented tin café carts that line the building (exhaust-fume flavored condiments supplied at no charge). Tuck yourself between the bins of 99¢ nick-knacks at Fad Albert's (the Walmart of Bushwick) and Woodhull's drab exterior will seem an appropriate backdrop to the compressed banality of urban living that comes to a point at the hospital's front door.

That's definitely your best method of advance. Because if you approach the hospital from the west, up an open stretch of road called Park Avenue that begins under the Brooklyn-Queens Expressway and ends one block past the hospital itself, that's when the building really slaps you in the mouth. I've been witness to the debate more times than I can count over the years. Was Woodhull always supposed to be a hospital as some within HHC contend, or was it originally built to be a federal prison as others will swear upon pain of death?

Take the ride up Park Avenue and only the prison version of the story makes sense. The structure takes up an entire city block, rising twenty stories into the air and dwarfing everything around it in a way that demands your attention. An elephantine structure monstrously situated and hideously brown, no matter how you squint, Woodhull Hospital looks like a factory. And not just any kind of factory, it looks like the type of factory to which Oliver Twist and his hungry little grimy-faced chums would have been consigned to work. No one would design the exterior of a hospital to look like that on purpose. Not unless they were in the throes of a very deep depression.

Unfortunately, that wasn't the worst of it. When I started in 1998, the entire campus was surrounded by an eight-foot chain link fence that did a remarkable job of keeping the garbage and debris circling in a constant spiral around the building. It mimicked a grotesque snow globe where old newspapers, stained coffee cups, cigarette butts and the occasional used condom swirled like imitation snowflakes.

The inside wasn't much better. All the walls on the first floor were a monochromatic white. The only visual point of interest was a single continuous frieze painted near the ceiling by the late urban pop-culture artist Keith Haring. Dozens of the black-and-white stick figures that earned the artist his fame hovered above the main floor hallways like two-dimensional apparitions. And then there was the brown brick in the visitor's elevator bays cast in the color of used coffee grounds. If someone was trying to convey that this was a place of healing, they weren't trying very hard. But it was my new home and in spite of it all, I was excited to be there.

When I arrived for my first day, I went directly to the executive suite to meet with Lois's executive assistant, Hal. Hal was a flamboyant and charismatic old-timer who'd been in the HHC system a long time. "Welcome," he said. "Did we finally get you all squared away?" He was referring to the three-week delay in scheduling my start date and my first encounter with

Woodhull's infamous Human Resources Director, Daisy Mercado.

Daisy was notorious within the walls of Woodhull because of her reputation for being "connected." In HHC-speak that translated into "untouchable." She was a career city employee who worked at another agency before moving over to HHC to serve as the Director of Human Resources at one of its hospitals. As the story was told to me, her connections couldn't keep her from being summarily dismissed from that job. But they were solid enough for her to be moved to Cumberland where she was allowed to sit for one solid year "drinking coffee and reading the newspaper" until a position she wanted opened up at Woodhull. That kind of story grows legs with each retelling, so by the time I arrived at Woodhull, Daisy's was a centipede.

I expected to start work sometime in May but I couldn't get a straight answer on the details of my employment. No one in the human resources department could tell me anything about my title or my salary and none of my calls to Daisy were being returned. That's when I discovered that when it came to getting things done, a call from Hal carried more weight than a call from Lois herself. The day after I told him why I hadn't reported to work yet I received a telephone call.

"Hello, Candis? This is Daisy. I didn't know you were trying to reach me."

Something in the voice didn't sound sincere but I played along.

"Yes I was," I said. "I still haven't received an appointment letter stating my salary or my title."

"Really?" she said. "Well, we were able to get you 20% over your last salary and I believe your title will be Associate Director."

I had a feeling that it would be best if I didn't let that go unchallenged.

"No, I believe it won't," I said.

At the time, I knew nothing about the convoluted title structure within HHC. I only remembered Lois' comment that the title of Associate Director wasn't high enough for what she wanted me to do. Her word was good enough for me.

"Lois said that wasn't the title she wanted," I said.

Still sounding like saccharine, Daisy replied, "Oh that's just the corporate title. It really doesn't matter."

"Good," I said. "Then it won't matter if you find me something else."

It turned out to be a good thing that I had the presence of mind to stick to my guns. Titles matter very much at HHC.

It was early in the morning on my first day and the executive suite was quiet. "Lois is at Central Office this morning but I'm sure she'll want to see you when she gets back," Hal said. "Central Office" was the HHC cognomen for its corporate headquarters at 125 Worth Street in lower Manhattan. "We still don't have an office for you," he added while rolling his eyes. Hal's facial expressions spoke volumes. This one seemed to offer "what else is new" as subtext. "But you still need to go to Employee Health Service to finish your physical. Have you signed up for your benefits yet?" I hadn't.

The benefits package is the reason most people accept positions in New York City government. It's arguably the best in the country. If I did nothing else I was going to make sure I took care of that. Hal's hands were moving with the swiftness of a martial arts guru pulling files and making notes. "It's not 9 o'clock yet so none of the departments you need will be open." More facial subtext. "You might as well go get some breakfast from the coffee shop. I started a file for you with some assignments. I should have it ready by the time you get back. I'll give you a schedule for the next few weeks too."

"Okay," I said.

I went back out the door I'd entered, made two immediate lefts and headed down the long stretch of hallway that I hoped would lead me back to the front of the building. One of things you were certain to encounter on a daily basis at Woodhull was someone trying to find their way somewhere. They always had the look of lost and wandering souls trying to find their way to the light. The signage in the hospital was poor, wrong or nonexistent. The absence of color on walls that seemed to go on forever provided no points of reference. Even when someone tried to give directions anything more than "that door right there" was impossible to follow.

I decided to keep walking until I reached a dead end and hoped that I would see something familiar by the time I got there. I eventually reached the entry to the surgical suite. That meant I could go no farther. But I was in luck. It also brought me to a bank of elevators so I followed the throng inside one just as the doors were closing and found myself swept off with the crush when it stopped again one level below.

It took me a minute to find my bearings. For a hospital, there was always an inordinate amount of foot traffic. The crowd around me was dispersing in every direction and as more of the walls and hallways became visible I began to feel vaguely like I'd been in these surroundings before. "I think this is the main level," I mumbled to myself. If I was right, the coffee shop was nearby. To my right was the entrance to the emergency room and I was pretty sure there was no coffee shop in there. So left it was.

The hallway was almost empty now and just as I was about to exit through a set of double doors something against the wall directly in front of me caught my attention. "Is that a dead body?" I thought to myself. It was definitely a stretcher with something long and lumpy on top of it. Whatever "it" was, it was covered by a sheet and the hills and valleys neatly corresponded with a head, torso and two feet. But no one in the vicinity was claiming responsibility for it. It appeared to be hanging out against the wall all by itself.

I drifted cautiously away from the mysterious lump against the wall and entered an expanse of space that I'd definitely seen before. I was on the main level and I knew exactly where the coffee shop was from here. As I meandered through the main lobby, I watched the people come and go. It was an undulating sea of joyless faces, some cresting with anxiety, others ebbed by pain. Most appeared ambivalent to their surroundings. Intermittent swells of commentary punctuated the moving images, consequences of the staff at the information desk having to yell through the age-tinted plexiglass.

I soon realized that part of the reason for the high volume of traffic through the main level of the hospital was that the community residents used it as a short cut. It was easier to cut through the emergency room on Flushing Avenue, make the quick left to the lobby and proceed out the side door on Marcus Garvey Avenue to catch the myriad of buses that lined up there than it was to walk all the way around the building. If the neighborhood had little regard for the care being provided within the hospital's walls they could at least appreciate its utility as a climate-controlled breezeway.

The ambiance inside the coffee shop wasn't any more appealing than it was outside so I decided to take my stale bagel and lukewarm peppermint tea to go. To be on the safe side, I retraced my steps back to the same elevator bank. When I arrived the mysterious lump was gone and in its place stood a man wearing hospital scrubs and a white lab coat. Something about his demeanor suggested that he was not a physician. He was standing in the exact spot where the stretcher had been, facing the wall with his left hand on his hip and his right hand scratching the top of his head.

The "Up" button was already lit so I joined the others who had assembled to wait for an elevator to arrive. But I seemed to be the only one noticing the show. The man paced to the end of the short hallway that led to the emergency room, stopped, turned around, paced a few feet back toward the direction he'd just come from, stopped again, looked back over his shoulder, paced a few more feet. The left hand that had been on his hip was now scratching his left cheek and he'd brought his right hand down from the top of his head so that he could gnaw on the tip of his index finger. Eventually, he made it all the way to the other end of the hallway where he turned around and began the whole routine all over again.

There were quite a few of us gathered in a space that was getting smaller by the minute. Woodhull's elevators were notoriously slow. But since everyone was facing the elevator no one was noticing "Charlie Chaplin" but me, and apparently one other person.

"Lost a body again."

The dusty little man who made the comment whispered the words so close to my ear that his breath tickled the cartilage. I flinched and gave him some space.

"Excuse me?" I asked.

"He lost a body. I know he did," the man continued.

My new companion wasn't wearing a Woodhull I.D. badge but he spoke like a person who was intimately familiar with the way things worked around the hospital.

"When it's break time around here these guys don't care what they're in the middle of. They're goin' on break. This is the elevator you take to the morgue," he said, pointing behind us. "If it's taking too long to come and it's getting close to break time, they'll just leave the body against the wall. Sometimes when they come back the body's there; sometimes when they come back the body's gone."

He was deadly serious (pardon the pun). My bewildered expression must have been amusing to him and he took it as a cue to continue to share. "Happens a lot around here," he said waving his hand confidently. "I heard one time they found a body in the Radiology waiting room, propped up in a chair, still covered in a sheet with a baseball cap on top of its head."

I guess my facial expression betrayed my suspicion that we had just left fact and were headed towards fiction. Not wanting to lose his audience, he threw up both of his hands and quickly added, "Well that's what I heard!"

By now the show was over because our wayward transporter had abandoned the hallway and at least this part of his search all together. But fortunately for me, my narrator was not discouraged. We were still waiting for the elevator to arrive and his company was the first spirited conversation I'd encountered.

"It'll show up eventually," he continued. "They always do. It's probably taking a ride on the elevator."

"Oh really?" I chided. "You've heard that too?"

"No," he responded. "That I've seen." He actually puffed his chest out a little as if with pride.

"One day I went to get on the elevator and there was a body in it all by itself," he continued. "It was late too so it was kind of spooky."

"What did you do?" I asked. Truth or fiction, I wanted to know how this story turned out.

"I knew the morgue was in the basement so I got on, pressed the button to go down and when the elevator door opened I rolled it out into the hallway. I figured somebody would take it the rest of the way."

His face was cast in earnestness even if the tale seemed too tall to be believed. He must have been out of good stories because when that one came to an end, he bid me a nice day and headed off into the distance. His departure left me the only one who hadn't given up on this elevator bank. I was all by myself when I heard the familiar ding that announced the elevator had finally arrived. I decided to take a step back when its doors rolled open in front of me. With visions of joy-riding corpses still fresh in my head, I thought it best to check its contents from the outside before I stepped in.

On my way back to the executive suite, I decided to stop by the benefits office. That's where I met Archie, the "Mayor of Woodhull." His legendary knowledge of the city's benefits system was exceeded only by his knowledge of Woodhull's underbelly. One of his many words of caution was, "Be careful who you talk about around here because everybody's related."

When I finally made it back to Hal's office, he was ready for me. "Okay, I have a file with a few assignments from Lois and your schedule for the next few weeks."

"Thanks. Do I have an office yet?"

"No," he said pausing to think. "Now that you mention it, maybe I should hold on to your assignment file. You don't exactly have a place to put it do you?"

Hal had a way of making everything seem amusing. And with all the members of the senior staff that I needed to meet, he was right. I did have little use for an office at the moment.

First up was the Chief Operating Officer, Manuel Vega. I think the best way to describe Manny is to describe our first substantive interaction. The pre-employment process at HHC was absurdly cumbersome. Some hospital networks managed it better than others. Woodhull moved at glacial speed. Part of the process required me to complete an employee physical. Most of it was completed by my personal physician but the drug-testing had to be done on site at the Employee Health Service. You would think that peeing in a paper cup would be a simple process but not so. Before I could do even that, I had to be registered in the hospital computer system like every other patient.

At the time, like all the other hospitals in HHC's system, Woodhull had one central registration area for all of its patients. We called it the "airline counter." It was a big open area near the entrance to the building that relied on a butcher shop style numbering system to manage the patient flow. You took a number, sat down and waited to be called. I made my way through the strollers and the crying babies, past the janitorial staff eating their lunch and a foul-smelling gentleman who appeared to be in the middle of his afternoon nap. As I searched for a seat I thought, shouldn't someone have made arrangements so that I don't have to sit here all day? Perhaps someone did and I just had to ask.

It was the middle of the afternoon when I went up to the window and before I could open my mouth to ask a question, the young lady behind the plexiglass said,

"Take a number and have a seat."

"I just have a ques. . .",

"Take a number and **have a <u>seat.</u>**"

I paused. She was clearly not someone to be trifled with. Still, time is money. It wouldn't show much executive-level initiative if I sat around waiting for my number to be called when, for all I knew, my card was waiting for me at the desk. I decided to risk decapitation.

"Okay, but I just want to know if I need to be here. I just joined the executive staff and I'm trying to complete my physical."

"We don't do physicals here. You have to go to EHS."

She said all of this while eating a beef patty, drinking a soda and reading Page Six of the *New York Post,* but without ever once looking up at me.

"I know. I've already been to EHS. They told me to come here to pick up my registration card. My name is . . ."

"Then take a number and have a seat."

Okay. That didn't turn out like I'd expected but I was new and I didn't want to make waves, so I took a number and sat. And I sat. After nearly two hours, Manny walked by looking as crisp and clean as white linen stationery. About 5'9 and balding in the center with shiny black hair on the sides, he glanced at me with a vacant yet whimsical look.

"Candis? What are you doing down here?"

"I'm waiting to get a registration card so that I can complete my physical with EHS."

He paused for a moment, now looking more confused than whimsical. "You shouldn't have to wait in this line," he said.

Those were my sentiments exactly.

"Let me see what I can do. Come with me," he said.

I followed him to the counter. I was encouraged. This was the Chief Operating Officer after all. If anyone could cut through the bureaucracy he could, right? He approached the same counter I'd left two hours earlier just as a patient was leaving. I started to warn him but decided against it. This was his domain. He had to know what he was doing.

"Excuse me," he said

"Take a number and have a seat."

She was nothing if not predictable. He looked at me but I'd already seen this part of the movie so I had nothing to add. He turned back to her.

"This is a member of the senior staff," he said, pointing to me.

At that moment I was really wishing he'd leave me out of it. If things didn't go well I had a feeling I'd be seeing her again. I'd never seen someone look so unimpressed. That feeling of encouragement I'd felt a few moments earlier was fading fast.

"She just needs a registration card," Manny added.

"See those people . . ." she said as she pointed out to the sea of blank faces in the waiting area. "That's what they all need."

"Yes but . . ." he didn't even get to finish his sentence before she cut him off.

"Who are you?" she asked.

It wasn't just the question it was the way she asked it. One of her impeccably drawn eyebrows was arched so severely it almost looked like a check mark. And her lips were pursed in a downward curve. She leaned forward, balancing on her right elbow, with her elaborately manicured index finger pointing up toward the ceiling. I couldn't see her left hand but I'm sure it was on her hip. The terseness in her voice left no doubt. She wasn't inquiring about Manny's identity because she was looking for a new friend. She clearly looked ready for battle, and judging from Manny's body language, neither he nor I was confident he would win. He told her his name and gingerly held up his ID card. She perused it carefully and I watched her with rapt attention.

We'd reached a defining moment. I was looking for a change in facial expressions. If we were anyplace else you would expect a clerk who had just mouthed off to the Number Two in command to be scared or at least repentant. But in that one brief exchange I learned in dramatic fashion that I wasn't anyplace else. I was at Woodhull.

Over the next thirty seconds, the three of us had this really vibrant and meaningful conversation without anyone saying a word. First she looked at him and her expression said, "So?" Then he looked at me and his expression said, "What should we do now?" Then I looked at the chair I'd been sitting in and my expression said, "Nice to see you again. Thanks for waiting for me." Manny drifted off toward wherever he'd been headed before our paths crossed. Two hours later, I took my registration card to EHS, but of course by then they were closed for the day.

Tired and weak from hunger (I didn't dare leave my place in line for something as trivial as food) I went upstairs. I thought I'd check to see if any progress had been made in finding me an office. As I rounded the corner, I encountered something that made me think, "Hmm. Here's something you don't see everyday." There was a pigeon flying down the hallway directly at me. Yes Virginia, there really was a pigeon flying on the *inside* of a hospital. I pressed myself against the wall and let it pass.

It was an "I know I didn't just see that" kind of moment to be sure, but no one else in the hallway acted surprised. They simply continued on their way to wherever they were going without commenting. It was the first of many "Twilight Zone" moments I would have there.

Hal eventually worked his magic and by late in the afternoon on my second day I finally had an office. It was located on the 10th floor inside of the Quality Management Department. The good thing about the office was that, like all of the offices located in what had previously been inpatient rooms, it had its own bathroom. The bad thing about it, at least in the beginning, was that the prevailing ambiguity about my role led everyone to assume that the location of my office was an indication of whose work I would be usurping.

I'm sure that's the reason Agnes, the Director of Quality Management, was eager to be among the first to smoke me over.

"Welcome to the 10th floor," she said cheerfully. It was after 5:00 p.m. before I was actually able to get into the office. By then the floor was eerily quiet and her enthusiasm caused an echo. "It's a shame they didn't have something set up for you before you arrived yesterday. Had I known, I would have had this set up for you myself. But that's Woodhull for you," she said in a mocking tone. "But I bet you've figured that out by now," she continued. She was feigning a bent of frustration she apparently wanted me to join her in. "Careful Candis," I thought.

It was a little early in my tenure with this organization for me to be complaining and I found it more than a little strange that she would expect me to. In the recesses of my mind I heard the echo of one of my grandmother's bits of "down South" country wisdom. "The same dog that will bring a bone will carry one." I let my new neighbor and host vent for another ten minutes while I smiled and said nothing. Once it became obvious that I was not going to be fertile ground for commiseration, she drifted back to her own office.

The next morning was Wednesday, June 3rd. Wednesdays were the days when the Senior Staff (or Executive Cabinet, whatever they chose to call it on any given day) met. I was able to put that much together based upon the pages of appointment book calendar that Hal pieced together for me. The names of the meetings changed. One week it was called Executive Cabinet, the next week it was called JCAHO Executive Team. But it was always the same people and as I would soon learn, they always talked about the same things. On this morning, it was my opportunity to formally meet the rest of the executive leadership team.

In addition to the Chief Operating Officer and the Director of Quality Management whom I'd already met, I was finally able to put a face to the piercing quality of Daisy's voice. There was Sandy Munch, Director of Nursing, and Ira Gold, the Medical Director. There were two Deputy Executive Directors – the next highest title after Executive Director in HHC. One went to Brian Mulcahy, the Director of Facilities. We met briefly as a result of my encounter with the pigeon. The other one, Francine, was not at our 9:00 a.m. meeting when it began but she arrived at some point before it ended. Francine and June, the Chief Financial Officer, I would soon learn, were the ones with all the power.

There were also other staff people who were not part of the "Executive Cabinet" but were attending some of the Executive Staff meetings – the Director of Planning, the Marketing Director, there was a Director of Community Affairs *and* a Director of Community Relations (I never did find out why there were two different people doing what sounded like the exact same job) and there was a familiar face that I was glad to see – Vonetta from Cumberland.

After everyone finished introducing themselves, Lois added her stamp of approval to my addition to the team. It was tinged with the sing-song quality of her native Trinidadian accent. "She gonna bring us a fresh set a eyez," she said. There were collective nods and smiles beaming at me from around the room, so I returned a nod and a smile of my own. As the meeting continued I was relieved to have the spotlight shift away from me.

"Ira, you need to have a talk with Lorenzo," Lois continued. "Julie thinks the press isn't finished with this story yet. The last thing we need is for somebody else to sneak onto that unit and tell the world that nothing has changed."

I made a mental note of the names so that I could ask Vonetta to fill me in later. From the serious looks on the faces around the table, whatever Lois was talking about was making everyone nervous.

"I know, I know," Ira anxiously replied. "I've talked to him already. He said he has everything under control."

Clearly Lois was not impressed.

"Um hmm," she said. "That's the problem right there. He doesn't want anybody looking at his department and you can't say nothing to him or he'll be on the phone with Dr. Ferdinand."

That name I knew. She was referring to the President of HHC and apparently he was close friends with one of Woodhull's Chiefs of Service. I figured I'd find out who it was before too long. "Well," she continued "I'm not fighting that battle today. Listen, we have Board Report in two weeks and I'm not going down there another time to get myself chewed out because of these employee performance evaluations. Get your people to get these things in on time." Heads nodded. People whispered.

"How many does Cumberland owe?" Vonetta asked.

"Cumberland is up to date," Daisy responded.

But it was strange. She seemed almost annoyed about it. As I surveyed the other equally curious looks from some of the people around the table, Brian said, "Of course the drill sergeant would have hers up to date." There were some chuckles but I didn't get the joke. Vonetta didn't seem like a drill sergeant to me. Then I surveyed the blank expression on her face and I realized that they weren't talking about Vonetta.

"I'll have to double check those numbers anyway," Daisy quipped. "I'm not sure they're accurate."

Vonetta did respond to that. "I'm sure they're accurate. Donna made sure everything was up to date before she left."

The room fell silent and Lois let out something that sounded like a grunt. But she quickly regained her composure and the meeting pressed on.

"Manny, where are we with the signage project. I'm tired of people complaining about how hard it is to get around this place," she said.

He looked up like a deer caught in the headlights, a look I would come to regularly associate with him, and he said, "I've got a vendor coming in."

"Okay good," Lois said. "Brian, Francine, where are we with the clinic renovations?"

Francine said, "I'm waiting on Brian."

Brian said, "I'm waiting on the architects."

Lois said, "Okay. Good."

The meeting went on for another half hour before Lois called it to an end. Before she left the conference room, she gestured for me to meet her in her office. I was delayed briefly by informal welcomes from the staff I'd just met. When I finally arrived at Lois' office I found her sitting at a small round conference table situated near the front of her office. The Executive Director's office at Woodhull was the biggest office I'd ever seen.

Lois had a large U-shaped desk with a credenza; a separate wardrobe on another wall for her coat and personal belongings; a full seating area with a couch and two chairs in a third corner; another couch against a far wall and a round conference table with six chairs positioned in a fourth corner just outside the door that led to Hal's office. And still there was enough empty space in the middle to hold a junior high school prom. I started calling it the "airplane hanger." June, Francine and Vonetta were sitting at the table with Lois.

"Come in, come in," Lois called out to me. "So how do you like things so far?" she asked.

I joined the ladies at the table and I immediately felt like I was sitting in someone's kitchen. "Look at all this hair this child has!" June said. Now I felt like I was sitting in my grandmother's kitchen. She always liked to fuss over my wild mane.

"So far so good I guess," I replied.

"I heard your office wasn't ready," Lois said. "You know that Brian. I'm gonna choke him one day."

"No, it was fine," I replied. "I didn't really have a need for an office until yesterday."

Francine and Vonetta had been having a conversation about Cumberland when I entered the room. With the novelty of my addition to the group over, the conversation resumed and before long it shifted from Cumberland's operations to Cumberland's now former Executive Director, Donna Wilson.

"So she didn't even say goodbye, huh?" Lois asked Vonetta.

"No."

I noticed that Vonetta kept her responses brief. She was clearly uncomfortable.

"Humph," Lois grunted again.

She, June and Francine exchanged glances among themselves while Vonetta exchanged glances with me.

"See, that's what I mean?" Lois quipped. "She claimed she loved the place so much. How come she didn't say goodbye to the staff?"

The conversation drifted downward from there. I didn't know Donna well at that point but I trusted my instincts, and what they were telling me didn't match up with the way she was being described.

"I never got that impression from her," I said. "She's always been very nice to me."

I thought it was a perfectly innocent comment but Lois, June and Francine looked at me liked I'd just belched.

"I'd better get back to Cumberland," Vonetta said. She pushed away from the table and left the room in a hurry. I was probably too naïve to be nervous about the awkward pause that followed. It wasn't too much longer though, before the conversation shifted to something else.

"Did you get a file from Hal?" Lois asked.

"Yes," I replied. "I haven't had the chance to get to it yet but that's what I planned to do this morning."

Lois had an interesting way of issuing assignments. When I finally made it to my office, a two-hour break in my schedule gave me the chance to peruse the contents of the expansion file folder Hal had given to me. It contained a folder marked "reading material," one marked "to do," and several thin booklets that I immediately recognized to be transcripts. I opened the "to do" folder first and noticed that it contained a variety of letters and memos that were addressed to Lois. Written in the top right hand corner was "Candis, Please handle - L". That's all it said. It didn't say how or by when.

This wasn't the first time I had to find my way as I went along. So I put my skills to work figuring out what each document required of me and fashioning my own deadlines based on what made sense. As more of these notated documents made their way to me in the days and weeks that followed, I set up a tickler system for myself so that I wouldn't lose track of what needed to be finished. I didn't have a secretary, but the volume had yet to reach a level I couldn't handle by myself.

As for keeping track of deadlines, it was a noble effort in which I toiled alone. I soon learned that deadlines were treated more like suggestions at Woodhull. No one in Lois' office ever kept track of when or whether tasks were completed after they were assigned.

I was grateful for the steady stream of assignments and turned them around quickly. If I happened to hand something back to Lois directly, perhaps a letter for her signature for example, she would beam like a parent whose child just brought home straight "A's" on their report card. "See what I mean," she'd say. It translated by inference into - "I told you it was a good idea to hire her." The satisfaction of a job well-done aside, my role on the executive staff was still undefined and that was continuing to make some people uneasy.

I was sitting in my office one day reading one of the transcripts that would form the basis for another one of my early assignments. One of the first functions Lois wanted me to serve was that of liaison to the Corporation's Office of the General Counsel. I knew that one of the reasons she was so eager to hire me was that she liked the idea of having an attorney on staff. It was something I knew that Charles liked about having me around as well. I left the practice of law because I believed that my law degree would be worth more outside the practice than in. In healthcare at least, that was proving to be true.

Lois urged me to introduce myself to some of the attorneys in the General Counsel's office but it was something I did with apprehension. In-house counsel can be territorial sometimes. But everyone I met seemed equally glad to have someone "in the field" who spoke their language. This particular assignment proved to be amusing to say the least. It involved a surgeon and an anesthesiologist who were sharing one of the on-call rooms the hospital makes available for physicians to rest in when they work extended shifts.

According to their partially conflicting accounts, a disagreement ensued. One was making too much noise and the other one couldn't sleep. Or one accused the other of stealing his blanket. Whatever it was, I recall it being something trivial. But apparently the circumstances weren't trivial to either of them. The disagreement quickly turned into an argument. The argument then escalated to a fist fight and before it was over, one cut the other with a scalpel. I was working with our in-house and outside counsels to navigate the hospital through the disciplinary process.

As I sat in my office reading (and then re-reading just for fun) the transcripts from the two physicians, I was struck with the unmistakable feeling that I was being watched. I looked up and sure enough there was a woman taking up the entire door frame. She peered at me with a look that under different circumstances would have caused me to hide my pocketbook.

"I heard you're working with our outside counsel," she said.

"Yes," I replied.

"That's what the Director of Risk Management does. So are *you* the new Director of Risk Management?" she asked, with a tone of unrestrained accusation.

This I knew was a loaded question. *She* was the Director of Risk Management. I refuted her query with what I thought was a reassuring smile but her disposition remained unchanged.

"So what *are* you doing?" she asked.

"Right now I'm reading these transcripts and then I'm going to eat a tuna salad sandwich. Want some?"

She didn't. After sucking her teeth hard enough to shake one loose, she turned around abruptly and left. If Lois didn't give me a clearly defined role soon I feared I would need a personal escort to my car. Fortunately, my role within the organization began to take shape soon after that.

Also buried within the confines of my expansion file folder were answers to the questions I'd made mental notes of during my first executive staff meeting. I learned that Lorenzo was Dr. Lorenzo Rendall, the Chief of Psychiatry. Sometime during the January prior to my arrival, a reporter faked a mental illness and managed to get admitted to one of Woodhull's psychiatry units. He spent the next thirty days taking copious notes that upon his release, he turned into an exposé. The article was published in an obscure local magazine. But as sometimes happens when the gods do not look upon you with favor, the article began to find an audience and that audience was starting to grow.

By the time I arrived in June, *Dateline NBC* was expressing interest in running a story. The "Julie" to whom Lois referred was the Corporation's Sr. Vice-President of Marketing and Communications. That is a position that doesn't typically wield a lot of power in most organizations, but it did for Julie. Her close ties to the president gave her muscles that she did not hesitate to flex. It didn't appear that people were terribly fond of her but most feared her so they didn't say it to her face.

"Candis, you and Lois are going downtown to meet with the Sr. V.P. of Marketing tomorrow morning," Hal called to tell me. "Be down here at 8:30 so you can ride over together."

The next day as Lois and I rode together to Central Office, she explained to me why our Marketing and Public Relations Director wasn't with us.

"Julie hates him," she said. "And I don't need any more problems with her." Then she added nervously, "This is Julie's meeting so don't say too much."

When we arrived, we were ushered into the president's waiting area which only heightened my anxiety. After a few minutes, Julie strode confidently through the door to greet us. "Come in," she said.

"We're going to meet in Dr. Ferdinand's office. He has more space than I do."

In appearance, Julie reminded me of the character Nina VanHorn on the NBC series *Just Shoot Me*. A tall thin brunette, she wore her hair in a blunt bob cut with bangs and her eyeliner was always drawn in bold. Everything about her demeanor suggested that she knew she had the run of the place. When Lois introduced me to her, Julie gave me a penetrating once over. I could tell that she was deciding right then and there whether she was going to like me or not. Lois must have sensed that she needed to play her trump card because she nervously added, "Candis is an attorney," to the introduction.

"So what?" I thought. "There's nothing legal about this." But as I saw the expression change on Julie's face, I realized that Lois knew exactly what she was doing. "Oh," Julie said. The widening eyes and sliver of a smile that accompanied that "oh" suggested that I'd just been given a pass. Just as Lois said, Julie ran the meeting, dictating what she wanted us to do and what she didn't want us to do. Her general position with the press was to cooperate as little as possible. I spoke only when spoken to and tried not to put my foot in my mouth.

When we returned to Woodhull, I barely had time to put my bag away when Hal called to tell me that Lois wanted to see me.

"I just got off the phone with Julie." Lois was grinning from ear to ear when I arrived in her office. "She seems to like you," Lois continued. "She wants you to be our sole point of contact for the press until this story dies down. I think I'm going to have Marketing report to you from now on."

Just like that I went from having no role to having responsibility for Marketing and Press. The next day Lois informed me that the Director of Strategic Planning would also be reporting to me and before long

I was responsible for managing the hospital network's contracts and letters of agreements as well. I requested permission to combine all of my new responsibilities into an office that I intended to call the Office of Business Affairs. Lois was thrilled with the initiative I took, and with her approval I finally had a purpose that seemed to make everyone else relax a little – at least for the moment.

Along the way, I managed to fit in all of the meetings that Hal scheduled between me and the other members of the executive staff. By the time I had my meeting with June, the Chief Financial Officer, it was already clear to me that more so than even Francine, she was the true power behind the throne. I'd been in Lois' office on occasions when June was actually sitting behind Lois' desk sorting the mail and making decisions on matters both business and personal. "Lois, this phone bill is overdue," she'd say. "Where's your checkbook? I'll write it out for you." The control she seemed to have made me a little nervous but I was also curious. I didn't know quite what to expect from our meeting but I couldn't wait to find out.

The CFO's office had no windows. June's desk was covered with papers but when I entered her office she gave me a warm smile that immediately put me at ease. "Sit down," she said. "So has it been what you expected so far?" So far, I'd encountered abandoned bodies, pigeons in the hallway and sworn statements that attested to physician fist-a-cuffs, so there were several ways to answer that question. I took the safe way out.

"I guess," I said.

June did most of the talking. As I listened to her, I found myself ensnared by the manner of her speech. June was tall and wore her hair closely cropped to her head, virtually identical to how Lois wore hers. Her complexion was as ebony as a starless midnight sky and equally flawless. Her diction disclosed a slight lisp but other than that she was distinctly articulate.

I'm always leery whenever I hear someone African-American described as articulate. It can so easily be taken as an insult. It's as if it should come as a surprise that we can string a sentence together without mangling syllables. Of course I knew better so that wasn't what engaged me about June. It was the fact that when she spoke she reminded me of my mother and my aunts. I always loved listening to them talk when I was growing up.

Now that I'm older I realize that it wasn't the manner of speech itself as much as it was the air of self-confidence it conveyed. Perhaps it was that same aura that drew me to Donna as well. There was something very familiar to me about these women. But as it pertained to June, it would remain a source of conflicting feelings for me.

On the one hand there was a lot about her to respect. She'd worked her way up through the ranks at HHC from a front level staff person in the finance department to the coveted spot of Chief Financial Officer. That's a position very few women get to hold. Woodhull (and now the North Brooklyn Health Network of which Woodhull and Cumberland were a part) had been generating surpluses for years. That kind of accomplishment is always credited to the acumen of the CFO.

But I also saw up close at what expense those successes came. The hospital was filthy. Bills weren't paid unless and until June personally put her thumb print on them. But of course she had her own spin on that. Her explanation also shed some light on why Donna's name drew such consternation among Lois and her cohorts.

"I had to visit the podiatrist here one day," June said. "And the doctor impaled my toe with the largest needle I've ever seen. Tears were literally streaming down my face it hurt so much. He looked at me and he said 'I ordered smaller needles that hurt a lot less but my requisition was never approved.'"

That story was the funniest I'd heard in any of my meetings with the senior staff. But I'm glad I didn't laugh because June wasn't trying to be funny. "I thought about all the money Donna spent over there at Cumberland," she continued, "while we were over here suffering. I went right upstairs and found that doctor's requisition and put it through."

I clearly took a different meaning from that story than she did. When I shared the account with Donna months later, so did she. "They controlled my budget," Donna explained. "Whatever they gave me I worked with. I never asked them for a dime extra. I chose to spend that money on the staff and the patients. June and Lois sat on their money so that they could end each fiscal year with a $20 million dollar surplus, which the Corporation would turn right around and give to Bellevue to bail it out of its deficit. Does that make sense to you?"

But what concerned me most was the degree of control I came to see June exercise over Lois. What she said, Lois did. If Lois ever challenged June about anything, I never saw any indication of it. Before June and I concluded our meeting she said something else that caused me to pause with concern. I was the fresh set of eyes after all. But I was already having serious doubts that anyone wanted to do anything about what these eyes were seeing. Nonetheless, I offered my thoughts about ways in which the operations might be improved at Woodhull.

June sat back in her chair and stared at me for a moment. Then she said, "You see, you can change things around here. You can put in a terrific new system or procedure and it will work for a while. But as soon as you turn your back, they'll go right back to the same old habits. It just won't work for long. You change things and they change right back."

I could tell that she was speaking from experience. Perhaps it said something that she'd even considered the possibility that things could be better. But there was no mistaking the point she was making. Nothing ever really changes around here so why bother to try. It sent a chill through my spine. I thought, "You are probably the most powerful person in this building. If that's how you feel, then why are we here?" I think June's words were still ringing in my ears when I went to our next executive staff meeting.

Lois jumped in with both feet. "We got our heads handed to us in Board Report," she began. I was still trying to figure out what this "Board Report" was. When I asked Hal one day if I was supposed to attend it he shook his head with dramatic affect and said, "No. And be glad you don't." I would see the members of the senior staff who did go, shuffling nervously in and out of their Board Report prep meetings. I happened to be in the executive suite the day they returned from the Board Report itself and Agnes' wig was slightly askew. In fact, she, Lois and everyone else who came in with them all looked like they'd just been in a street fight.

"I gave them a date for when we were going to bring those performance evaluations current and I'm not going back down there to look like a fool," Lois said. "So you better get with your staff and get those evaluations done."

Daisy sat in her chair with her arms folded and her legs crossed, scanning the room with a disapproving scowl. Heads nodded and people whispered. Lois pressed on.

"Manny, where are we with the signage project?" she asked.

Bambi looked up and said, "I've got vendors coming in."

"Okay. Good. Brian, Francine where are we with the clinic renovations?"

Francine said, "I'm waiting on Brian."

Brian said, "I'm waiting on the architects."

Lois said, "Okay. Good."

Suddenly, I had the strangest feeling of déjà vu. I glanced in Vonetta's direction but when she rolled her eyes and shook her head I realized it wasn't déjà vu at all. And then I realized something else. Hal wasn't at the meeting. He wasn't at any of our staff meetings and no one was taking minutes. In fact, in the three or four meetings I'd attended with the executive staff up to that point, I'd never seen any. So I had a brainstorm. I raised my hand. "Yes Candis," Lois said. "Would you like me to take minutes?" I asked.

From the expression on her face you would have thought that I had discovered penicillin. Once again she gave the room that "see what I mean" nod of approval but this time the nods weren't returned. Although Lois failed to notice it, the wind clearly shifted carrying with it an encoded message that my goodwill offering was not appreciated by my colleagues.

Ira broke the tension with an announcement. "I've come up with a model to use in our JCAHO preparations so that the staff will know how to answer questions about our plan of care." Without waiting for permission, he began handing out copies of a picture of a man holding up a globe. "It's called ATLAS and each of these arrows points to an aspect of our plan of care and if they follow this . . ."

Full of excitement, he went on for another twenty minutes and appeared totally oblivious to the fact that absolutely no one was listening to him. He finally concluded with, "So I'm going to begin handing these out. My staff and I will go around and in-service the hospital." Lois opened her mouth to speak but a yawn escaped. "Okay Ira," she said.

Before the meeting finally ended, Lois reminded us that Cumberland's health fair would be held on the upcoming Saturday and asked everyone to try to attend. As we each got up to leave the conference room, Vonetta leaned over to me.

"Are you still coming to Cumberland this afternoon?" she asked.

"I'm looking forward to it," I said.

My meeting with Vonetta was more of a formality since she was the one person on the executive team that I already knew. So my trip to Cumberland was one meeting I was really looking forward to. The staff was getting ready for the health fair and there was a general jubilance in the air, something I never felt walking through the corridors of Woodhull.

After a brief tour of the building, we returned to her office to chat. Vonetta had the kind of large physical presence that would have been intimidating if she didn't have such a maternal demeanor. She wore her hair in long dreadlocks that she was allowing to turn gray, probably in part, as a symbol of her discontent. I could see she felt more comfortable at Cumberland than at Woodhull. Her disposition was completely different. She was more relaxed and as I would soon discover, felt free to speak her mind.

"So how do you like the cast of characters?" she asked.

"They're . . . ." I was struggling to find a politically correct response, so she did me the favor of finishing my sentence for me.

"Fools. I know."

"Oh, good," I said. "So I can be honest."

We were both laughing with intense familiarity now.

"What the hell is going on over there?" I asked.

There were so many things I wanted to know now that it appeared I could finally get an appraisal from someone who also saw that the emperor was wearing no clothes. But where to start?

"Girl, who knows?" she said. "I spend as little time over there as I possibly can."

"What happened to Donna?" I asked.

Vonetta started to explain why Donna was no longer working at the network but we were interrupted by a highly animated woman in her 50's with a milky complexion, short hair and rectangular-rimmed glasses. She bounced into the room like an Easter bunny.

"Oh, Vonetta, I'm so glad you're here. I need to put your folder together for tomorrow. Remember, my dear, I have each day labeled but it only works if I get the folders back you know, and . . . oh I'm sorry I didn't realize you had company, excuse me, excuse me, excuse me. . . ."

I knew that voice.

"Candis, this is . . . ."

Before Vonetta could finish the introduction I said, "Velma. Of course."

"OH MY CANDIS IS HERE!!" Velma squealed. She grabbed me up out of the chair I was sitting in and squeezed me in a bear hug with all the might that her 90-pound frame could muster.

"Oh I finally get to meet my Candis! I feel as if we're old friends," she said with a giggle.

Then in typical Velma fashion she took over the conversation for a solid twenty minutes while Vonetta and I looked on in amusement. I'd always intended to ask Donna how someone with such a demonstrable sense of professionalism could have such a ditsy assistant. But I learned in short order from both Donna and Vonetta that as it pertained to Velma, appearances can be deceiving. For all of her eccentricities, Velma was one of the best executive assistants HHC ever produced. She wrote well, remembered everything she was told and could execute multiple tasks with minimal supervision. I also quickly came to appreciate that to know Velma was to love her. But, you had to have the full Velma experience. Talking to her on the phone took her out of a context that was very, very necessary.

Sitting in the confines of Vonetta's office, I witnessed firsthand all of the physical affectations that went along with Velma's endless sentences. Not only did she talk a mile a minute, it seemed that every inch of her body was in continuous motion. Her arms were moving, her eyes were blinking, her fingers wiggled with every syllable and she was always smiling. Velma was like a Christmas tree with all the lights flashing. She was so much fun to be around that from that day forward I made it a point to stop by Cumberland when I was having a bad day, just so that I could get a dose of Velma before I headed home.

"Velma, we were just talking about Woodhull," Vonetta said.

And just that quick, the show was over. The mere mention of Woodhull was the only time I ever saw the smile fade from Velma's face.

"Those people," she said.

She grabbed the folders she'd come into the office for and left the room as quickly as she'd entered it.

Vonetta whispered, "They're not very nice to her over there."

"Why?" I asked. How could you not like Velma?

"They probably associate her with Donna," Vonetta said. "She'd been Donna's assistant for years. And that reminds me. I've been meaning to warn you. You should keep your feelings about Donna to yourself. They're not too fond of her over there either."

"I figured that out," I said. "What's that all about?"

Once again, just as I was about to hear the full story, we were interrupted by another animated member of the Cumberland staff. But I didn't know what to make of this one.

"Hey, Von!"

"Hi Jackie," Vonetta replied. "Let me introduce you to somebody. This is Candis Best. She just joined the Cabinet at Woodhull."

Before I could respond the woman bellowed, "HEY CHICKEN! Ooh, I heard about you," she said with a wave of her hand. "I heard you're somethin' else!"

I was speechless for a moment. Did this woman just call me a capon? Vonetta must have read my mind through the look on my face. She tried to mediate before I could respond.

"She doesn't mean anything by it," she said with an anxious edge in her voice.

"Uh, uh" Jackie said, interrupting. "A good friend of mine used to say that all the time. She was a Diva girl, a D - E - E -VA. She'd walk around dragging her fur coat on the floor behind her and that's how she greeted people. 'Hey, Chicken! Hey, Chicken!' It's a term of love, girl. It's a term of love. That's what I call everybody," she said, circulating the air with sweeping arm gestures.

"Well, I'm not everybody," I said. "I don't want to be a chicken, thank you."

Jackie was still standing in the doorway. She leaned back a little to give me the once over. Vonetta was visibly nervous during the silence that followed. Then Jackie let out a raucous cackle. She plopped herself down next me and looped her arm with mine.

"I like you," she said. "We're gonna be friends!" Vonetta looked relieved but I wasn't sure how I felt.

I decided to attend Cumberland's health fair that Saturday. By the time I arrived, Lois was greeting people and Vonetta was standing by the information booth. I

walked over to Lois to let her know I was there and
before she even said hello she said, "Your *friend* is here."
I wasn't sure who she was referring to at first. But as she
gestured over her shoulder, I could see Donna standing
by one of the tables that had been set aside for guests. I
hesitated for a moment. The way Lois exaggerated the
word "friend" I knew she was making a point and not an
innocent one. But I hadn't spoken to Donna since I
started working at HHC. I still knew next to nothing
about why she was no longer at Cumberland. So I
decided to risk fraternizing with the enemy.

She saw me before I reached her. "Hi," she said
with a broad smile. "I was wondering where you were."

"Same here," I replied.

"Oh, that's a long story."

She made her way toward a quiet section of the
courtyard and gestured for me to follow, which I did. I
almost didn't recognize her at first. She was wearing a
brightly colored shorts set and a baseball cap; it was an
uncharacteristically casual look for her but she still
managed to make it look professional.

"So are you at Woodhull now?" she asked once
we took a seat.

"Yes. I've been there a few weeks now."

"Good," she said. "I was looking for people to
bring with me to Met and I thought of you but I couldn't
find your number. But I'm glad you're all squared away."

I felt the kind of stomach twinge that usually
accompanies disappointment.

"I wish I'd known you were looking for me," I
said. "This place isn't quite what I expected."

"You'll be fine," she said.

"So where are you now?" I asked. "What
happened?"

"I'm at Metropolitan Hospital. The president
asked me to be their Chief Operating Officer. I'd already
turned him down once and you can't do that too many

71

times. So when he asked me this last time I packed my boxes and went."

"Just like that, huh?" I said.

"Just like that," she said. "You'll see. That's how things go around here sometimes."

"Donna!"

We both seemed able to identify the source of that trademark squawk without having to turn around.

"Hi, Jackie," Donna said.

"Girl, you look great," Jackie responded. Then she added pointing to me, "I'm taking good care of your girl."

"Oh really?" Donna said. She cast me a knowing grin that slipped right past Jackie who was enchanted by her own thoughts.

"Oh, yeah," Jackie continued. "I'm going to introduce her to everybody. We're going to get her name out there, girl."

"Alright, Jackie, well don't let me keep you. I know you're busy," Donna replied.

"Yeah child, you know this is my busiest day." Then Jackie turned her attention to me. "Candis, stop by and see me at the D.J. booth. Uncle Arthur's going to stop by later and I want to introduce you to him."

I didn't know who Uncle Arthur was but Jackie obviously thought it was somebody I needed to meet. As she sashayed away I turned to Donna with a curious expression that she accurately interpreted without the need for further explanation. "That's a story for another day," she said.

Before I knew it we'd waded deep into summer. My new department was beginning to take shape. I now had enough responsibilities for Lois to move me to a larger office and allow me to hire a small staff. I moved into another wing of the 10th floor that was virtually deserted and took over what had been a triple-bedded inpatient room. That afforded me the opportunity to order brand new furniture - a larger desk and a conference table. I was finally starting to feel like a legitimate member of the executive team.

The 4th of July holiday weekend was approaching and the executive staff was going to spend Thursday and Friday of that week on the campus of HHC's Seaview Rehabilitation and Skilled Nursing facility on Staten Island. The Corporation was holding executive staff previews of the new million-dollar customer service training program that was being rolled out in the fall. The week had arrived for our turn.

We were midway through the first day when Sandy, the Nursing Director, walked over to Lois with a troubled look and whispered something in her ear. When Lois ran out of the room, the disruption caused an awkward and abrupt suspension of the proceedings. The presenter quickly regained her focus but when Lois didn't return after the break, more members of the senior staff, including Ira, left the room as well. Sandy returned and sat next to me.

"Hal's collapsed," she said.

"What? Is he alright?" I asked.

"He's conscious but he doesn't look good. Lois is waiting with him for the ambulance to arrive."

By now the entire room had emptied into the hallway. When I peeked out I could see Hal lying on the floor. Lois was kneeling beside him holding his hand. From what little I could see of his face, he looked scared. I wished that there was something I could do. But I felt certain that the last thing he needed was another person peering down at him when he was in such a vulnerable state.

The ambulance arrived and took Hal to the hospital before we broke for lunch. He was still there on Friday and I visited with him on Saturday afternoon. He seemed to be in good spirits but since he was in the intensive care unit, I didn't stay long. I checked in with

Lois after we returned from the holiday break to see how he was doing.

"He's back home now," she said. "He's doing much better."

I was relieved. I hadn't known him long but I couldn't imagine the executive office without Hal in it.

Another week or two passed. It was a Sunday evening when I had an eerie dream. I was visiting Hal in the hospital again but his cubicle was so dark that I could barely see him. I called out to him. I could make out the silhouette of his image but he didn't respond. It was the kind of dream that seemed to cloak me like a shroud even after I woke up. The next day when I went into the executive suite to sign my timesheet I made a point to stop into Lois' office so that I could ask her how Hal was doing. Even with the forlorn expression on her face, I wasn't prepared for her response.

"He passed away last night," she said.

I never learned the reasons behind Hal's sudden passing but his death marked a seismic shift for me and Woodhull. After that, any levity I had toward my work environment seemed to pass away with him. The fault line exposed itself shortly after Hal's funeral. The minutes I'd drafted from our meetings did not go over well with the executive staff.

I knew how to write minutes. There were no editorial comments but they did clearly state who promised to do what. Since due dates were rarely discussed at our meeting, I was forced to put "update to be provided at the next meeting" next to nearly every entry. Since that was pretty much the extent of my interaction with the rest of the executive staff, I have to believe that the minutes had something to do with what prompted Lois to call me into her office that day.

I thought she wanted an update on some of my projects. But when I sat down her expression was atypically stern. Her trademark megawatt smile was gone and it took the dimples that usually framed her face with it.

"Your colleagues are starting to complain about you," was how she began.

It was the kind of sentence that irrevocably alters the remainder of a meeting. I felt the warm sensation that an unpleasant surprise will bring, rising to my cheeks.

"Really," I said.

"Yes," she continued. "They say you make them feel stupid."

She had the rest of the meeting to herself after that. Fortunately, there wasn't much more to it. She cautioned me to moderate my tone and I left.

As I walked back to my office my mind was spinning with reenactments of the various interactions I'd had with my colleagues. I was trying to identify what I could have said or done to prompt the warning I'd just received. But as I thought about how little constructive work I'd actually seen take place during my first eight weeks, my disposition shifted from anxiety to irritation. Lois used our only substantive supervisory meeting to date to discuss what people were saying. But that was all she wanted to talk about. There was no discussion about what was or was not getting done – not just by me but by anyone. And there never would be. For the first time, I began to think that I might have made a serious mistake coming to Woodhull. It would not be the last time.

DESPITE MY ERODING CONFIDENCE in my boss, I tried to fit in. But the more we worked together the more I saw how big the difference was between my style and Lois'. The lack of accountability was maddening to me, but that wasn't really my affair. However, Lois had other leadership peculiarities that eventually did impact me directly. The first time I experienced it, it was purely as a spectator. The only other person on the senior staff that I made any meaningful connection with besides Vonetta was Sandy, the Director of Nursing. She didn't say much in meetings. But I noticed that whenever she did speak, what she said seemed to make sense.

We would talk on occasion. When my curious mind wanted something clinical explained, I gravitated toward her rather than Ira for an answer. Ira was always willing to explain something. He welcomed any opportunity to talk. The problem was that once you got him to start talking you couldn't get him to stop. Sandy always gave me succinct explanations and she welcomed an exchange of ideas. It appeared that our discussions were the only times she had the opportunity to do that. Unfortunately for her, she was the Director of Nursing in name only.

Before becoming Executive Director, Lois had been the Director of Nursing at Woodhull. For all intents and purposes, she still was. She was constantly circumventing Sandy and working directly with the nursing staff at all levels. I could appreciate that she had long-standing relationships with these people and I don't think there was anything malevolent in her intent. But intentional or not, her actions made Sandy insignificant. As a white woman and an outsider to HHC, Sandy already had two strikes against her trying to run a densely ethnic nursing department comprised of nurses who had worked for the Corporation for decades.

What Lois may have viewed as her way of keeping in touch with the front lines, the staff exploited as an opportunity to treat Sandy like she wasn't there. It was an unworkable situation that Sandy chose to accept. When Lois began doing the same thing to me, I did not.

Once Lois informed me that she wanted the Director of Strategic Planning to report to me, I accepted it as I would any assignment. I thought that projects that fell under the purview of Planning would come to me and I would pass them along to Elliot, a thin, pale, and thoroughly forgettable man. He rarely seemed to have an opinion unless he was sure it was shared by everyone else in the room. He reminded me of cooked spaghetti – not firm enough to stand up straight and would stick to any surface he was thrown against. When I noticed that I wasn't receiving timely responses from him I asked him why. He responded with, "I was working on something for Lois."

Unbeknownst to me, she was still giving him work to do directly. She would send us memos jointly which would annoy me. But she was the boss so that was an error in protocol to which she was entitled. It became a problem when I received an assignment either from her or directly from Central Office with deadlines that I was expecting him to meet. More often than not he wasn't meeting them because according to him, he was "working on something for Lois." So one day I spoke to her about it.

"Lois, would you prefer to have Elliot reporting directly to you again?" I asked. "It really doesn't matter to me if you take him back." She appeared shocked that I would ask such a question and it showed in her voice.

"No," she said. "Why would you say that?"

"Because it's difficult for anyone to report to two people and obviously it's impossible for Elliot to do it. The work I ask him to do isn't getting done. He's always busy doing something for you."

This is where it got interesting. First she denied it.

"I'm not giving him anything to do," she responded, now almost hostile.

She was still my boss, so I probably should have dropped the matter. Charge that mistake to youth. I didn't.

"So you didn't ask him to prepare a presentation you had to make last week?"

"Oh a – well yes but . . . ," she stammered.

"And he's not writing your holiday greetings to the staff?" I continued.

"Well what do you want me to do?!" she asked in a huff.

"Either take him back or give the assignments to me so that I can keep track of what he's doing. Then I can make sure all of the work gets done," I said.

"No, I don't want him back," she said. "Fine. I'll give the work to you then."

But she didn't. To combat my growing levels of frustration, for respite, I began to run to Cumberland more and more. One day Vonetta and I were talking. I knew she'd been with HHC for more than thirty years, so I hoped that she could answer a nagging question I'd been mulling over. "How in the world did Lois ever get to be a CEO?" I asked her one day. I don't know whether it was because the question came out of the blue or because of the level of angst in my voice, but Vonetta laughed for a long time before she answered.

"Well," she began. "Lois spent her nursing career here in Brooklyn as far as I know. I definitely remember her when she was a staff nurse here at Cumberland. That was when Cumberland was still a hospital. She went over to Woodhull with the rest of the nursing staff when this hospital closed and that one opened." Apparently, Lois didn't build her reputation by being the best or the brightest. She built it by always being available. I've touted the often overlooked value of being dependable in every career development presentation where I've been invited to speak. Lois could be the poster child for how far dependability can take you.

"If there was a shift uncovered that no one else would take, she would do it," Vonetta added. "And people liked her."

I could attest to that. If nothing else, Lois was a charmer. You only had to watch her in action at one of Woodhull's "Town Hall" general staff meetings to see that. She never used a podium. She'd walk up and down the aisles with a microphone in her hand like Oprah did in the old days and the staff ate it up like ice cream cake.

She was warm and approachable and very visible. There was always an employee waiting for her car to pull into its space in the morning or waiting for her at her car before she went home at night. And she listened to whatever they had to tell her. It didn't seem to matter to them that their complaints rarely if ever got fixed. That they could tell her directly and feel that she genuinely seemed to care was enough for them.

Vonetta continued to narrate Lois' curriculum vitae for me, supplementing it with those valuable anecdotal tidbits that the paper version always leaves out.

"Woodhull used to have a terrific Nursing Director. I mean she was old-school. That department ran like clockwork when she was in charge. Lois worked her way up the ranks and she and another nurse – what was her name?" Vonetta paused to probe her memory but it wouldn't give up the name. "Well anyway," she continued. "They were both being groomed to replace the Director whenever she retired. Now as I heard it . . . ."

Vonetta's voice took on that subtle shift in tone that rumors have a way of shaping.

"The Director really wanted the other nurse to be her successor, not Lois. But that woman left to go to another facility. So Lois moved up another rung and she became the Nursing Director's deputy. Then the Director got sick. Lois was there. So she became the Acting Director of Nursing. But her boss never came back."

"What happened?" I asked.

"She died. And Lois got the job permanently," Vonetta explained.

According to the rest of the story, Woodhull then went through a series of Executive Directors and found itself without one just four months before a Joint Commission survey. Once again, Lois was there. So she was appointed Chief Operating Officer. She led them through the survey without causing any major embarrassment and the rest was history.

It was so typical of city government. Municipal employment is one giant lab experiment for demonstrating every type of management decision an organization should *not* make. Number One on the top ten list is promoting people to leadership positions for reasons that have nothing to do with their capacity to lead. I had plenty of family and friends who worked in New York City government over the years. When I joined HHC they sent me to work with volumes of sound advice. Of course, the two most memorable quotes came from my mother.

First: "The City likes to promote people to their level of incompetence." Second: "The ass you kick going up the ladder will be the very ass you'll have to kiss coming down."

Ultimately, Lois became the CEO of a $300-million-dollar healthcare network because she was an unobjectionable person who was in the right place at the right time. Give credit where credit is due. She could be a charming, engaging and likeable person to most. She had a beautiful smile and while that may seem like a trivial attribute to mention in a professional profile, it is one that can go a long way toward making people feel at ease. But the ability to make people feel at ease can be a legitimate means of persuasion or a Trojan horse.

After Hal's death, Lois decided that she wanted a search committee to find his replacement and she put me on it. Representing Human Resources on the committee was none other than Archie, "the Mayor of Woodhull." He already had a reputation for speaking his mind, whether it was appropriate to do so or not. He was probably not the best person for me to be making friends with at the time but I responded to his candor.

Once, while we were waiting for a candidate to arrive for an interview I remember him saying, "Just because a person is nice, it doesn't mean they should be running a hospital." I knew I was going to pay for laughing at that one. But even the very exercise we were participating in was proving his point.

The production that ensued to find Hal's replacement was so elaborate that when we finally hired someone, four weeks into the job she came to me and said, "You know, after the interview process I went through I really thought I was going to be doing something important." Two weeks after that conversation, she quit.

I began to put out feelers myself about other jobs in the Corporation, but both Archie and Donna cautioned me about how it would look if I left Woodhull less than six months after I started. So I resolved to stick it out. But I stopped trying to fit in. Despite Lois' warning about "not making people feel stupid," as I saw things that I thought could be done better, I offered my opinion. Sometimes I just couldn't help myself. Some of the behavior I observed was mind-numbingly dumb. Self-censorship doesn't come easy to young executives who haven't had their wings clipped yet.

Late one evening, one of the patients set their room on fire (don't ask) so all of the senior staff came in. After the situation was brought under control, a group of us were down in executive administration. It was about 3. a.m. and Lois was flittering around the office trying to find the right number to call Councilman Ruiz, the city councilman covering Woodhull's district, and a man to whom she was wedded by fear.

She was going over and over what she was going to say to him. I watched this for a few minutes while I mentally debated whether I should open my mouth. Finally I said, "Don't you think you should call Dr. Ferdinand first?" I had to mention the president by name because I think if I had said "your boss" she still would have called the Councilman.

Fear influenced Lois almost as much as June did. Nowhere was this more apparent than in her relationship with Councilman Ruiz. He was mixed up in everything that had to do with Woodhull. He came to the hospital's Community Advisory Board meetings and the meetings would go on for hours. She was terrified of him and she surrendered almost total control of the hospital to him when it came to any decisions she thought he might be interested in. The entire office knew that if he called, he was to be patched through to her directly no matter where she was or what she was doing, even if she was at a meeting with Dr. Ferdinand.

But my reservations about Lois' pliability were cemented during one of the last days that I was still welcome in the inner sanctum with her and June. They were having one of their daily chitchats discussing mundane matters. Lois was walking over to the conference table where June and I were sitting and she casually said, "Oh June, I did what you told me. I washed my hair with Tide this weekend."

Then June responded, "Good now you can. . . ."

The conversation didn't trail off, my mind did. I just sat there. I'm sure my mouth was hanging open while I tried to make sense out of what I'd just heard. I recall someone saying something about stripping the perm out of her hair. Whatever the reasons were, they seemed to make perfect sense to the two of them.

The strangest feeling came over me. It was straight out of science fiction. It mirrored the moment when the hapless visitor slowly realizes that he's the only human in a room full of aliens. Confusion gives way to doubt, then doubt to disbelief and finally disbelief to fear. All I could think about was how to make a graceful exit without letting them know that I had "discovered the truth." I waited a few minutes then innocently excused myself and left the suite to take the elevator back to my office. I was engaged in a private conversation with myself all the way there.

Woodhull's reputation remained in the bowels of public opinion during this entire period. I suppose the hospital didn't accomplish much because nobody expected much of it. Everything I witnessed from the inside told me that the people working there weren't expecting much of themselves. There was no way to separate that from the caliber of the leadership to which they were subject. The only thing Lois ever seemed truly confident about was nursing. Everything else, she deferred to June or Francine. If it was an area that neither of them was interested in, then it was a free-for-all.

Whatever the reasons for Lois' dependency on those members of the senior staff that she trusted, it was clear that none of them were helping her to grow as a leader. Every other decision she made was made and then changed based upon who got to her last. As a consequence, every other member of the executive staff was looking for their own way into her head. Everyone was pulling her in different directions. It was impossible to keep your footing in that environment.

It was like being back in high school. Everything ran by gossip. But while everyone on the leadership team was feeding that engine, no one was watching to see where the boat was going. With each passing week I found myself stumbling over another piece to the puzzle of why Woodhull was so dysfunctional despite the fact that the CEO was so popular. What I witnessed was someone who was easily manipulated by the people she trusted or the people she feared. That list was so long that it made it difficult to know who was actually steering the ship at any given moment. From every vantage point it looked like chaos.

I thought about all of this as I walked down the hall. When I carefully considered the nature of the relationship that Lois had with all of the people who influenced her in general, and June in particular, it revealed a frightening picture. The people who were actually making the decisions didn't have to be accountable for any of them because they operated in the shadows. Few knew who they were. It was the definition of absolute power and we all know how that turns out. By the time I'd reached the elevator I'd come to the conclusion that if one person could get the CEO of a $300-million-dollar healthcare enterprise to wash her hair with laundry detergent, she could get her to do just about anything. My final thoughts as the elevator doors closed in front of me were, "We're doomed."

CHAPTER FOUR
SPRING, 1999

FROM JULY OF 1998 through March of 1999, I tried my best to go along so that I could get along. But it was a lost cause. By Spring Woodhull was waist deep in preparation for a survey by the Joint Commission on the Accreditation of Healthcare Organizations (also known as "JCAHO"). The survey would take place in October. JCAHO surveys are accreditation reviews that every hospital in the country must participate in at least once, every three years. With pressure now being applied, the work environment went from the absurd to the ridiculous. Lois appointed her driver to be a co-coordinator for survey preparation. We had roaches the size of matchbox cars patrolling the hallways and mice so brazen that they would forage for food in broad daylight, anywhere in the hospital that suited their fancy.

On top of that, despite nearly a year of threats, complaints and generalized embarrassment, we still could not complete a task as simple as making sure employee performance evaluations were submitted on time. To avoid a JCAHO citation, 98% of the evaluations had to be submitted within whatever timeframe we stipulated in our policies. We set the timeframe! So you would think that would stack the deck in our favor. But Woodhull still couldn't get above 83% and the entire corporation knew it.

I remember one meeting vividly. Lois was once again attempting to exert some authority about the evaluations. Francine wasn't in the room when the meeting started and the rest of the cabinet was going around in a circle giving opinions and suggestions about how to improve the numbers, as if the solution lay somewhere outside of the room. "I've had it with this," Lois said. "I'm not going down to Board Report another time to get my head handed to me about these evaluations. You'd better get on your staff to get these evaluations in on time," she said. By now I had heard this speech so many times I could lip sync it right along with her.

Just as I was about to doze off, Daisy leapt to her feet, pointed at Lois and then swept her finger around the room at the rest of the Cabinet. With a shrill and ominous tone she said, "If I'm going down, you're all going down with me!" Then she stormed out of the room. Lois said nothing. The rest of the executive staff said nothing. Everyone just sat there, stunned. After that performance, I suppose Lois felt she had to do something equally dramatic.

"I want you all to come in this Saturday and bring those evaluations up to date," she said. Then she left the conference room as well.

I wasn't concerned. First, because I didn't mind working on Saturday, second because I had a small department, and third, because all of my evaluations were already done and submitted. So, I sat back and watched the rest of the cabinet react, as they murmured among themselves about not wanting to come in over the weekend. A few minutes after Lois left the conference room, Francine came in, late as usual. I watched as one of the other senior staff members filled her in on what she'd missed. They'd just gotten to the part about coming in on Saturday when Francine stood up and announced, "We're not coming in here on

Saturday." Then she left the room. I don't know who said what to whom after that but I know this – no one came in on Saturday and they never did get to 98%.

I learned about the differences between formal and informal leadership authority as an undergraduate business major. Some leaders are anointed by the group – that's informal leadership. But just as often, companies and divisions within companies are led by people who no one but their bosses can stomach. Nonetheless, they have formal leadership authority by virtue of the position they hold.

No matter how they reach the top of the pyramid, however, once in a position of leadership these people have the power to influence others. The greater the breadth and scope of the position, whether it's formal or informal, the greater that power becomes. It never ceases to amaze me when professional athletes or entertainers get caught doing something foolish and then when asked about how their actions might influence their young fans, they respond, "I'm not a role model." Of course they are. However a leader comes into their position, once they choose to take up residence in it they have an obligation to accept the responsibility that goes with it.

At Woodhull, I was beginning to see the dangers inherent in faulty leadership and it led me to draw my own conclusions about the most dangerous type of leader. Contrary to what some may believe, it is not the maniac or the zealot or the evil genius. As impressionable as people can be they will run from a maniac. The intensity of the zealot will repel the masses from them and the evil genius cannot cultivate a following because let's face it – no one likes a genius until after they're dead. The most dangerous type of leader is the charismatic person with a weak mind.

A person with charisma will always draw a crowd. But if that person is weak, they will eventually become the puppet of the maniac, the zealot or the evil genius. Not sometime – every time. It's guaranteed. The weak-minded leader is leading people but is being led by individuals who most people would never follow. It's like leaving a loaded weapon in the cafeteria of a prison. Someone is going to pick it up and use it. And whenever a powerful person is weak enough to be manipulated by someone else, you can be certain the person doing the manipulating will have dishonorable intentions. After all, only people with dishonorable intentions use manipulation as a tool. Like those criminals in the cafeteria who find the loaded weapon, they *have* to use it. It's what they do.

From my perspective, Lois' primary focus should have been holding her people accountable. But her primary interests seemed to be about every other trivial concern. To my keen but naïve sensibilities, it was an unpardonable crime. I was on a mission from God after all. We're supposed to be changing things around here, I thought. I still didn't get it. She was telling me everything I needed to know. Fitting in was vitally important to her and I wasn't fitting in. Rather than conforming, I didn't even try from that point on. Instead, I started to retreat.

I once dated someone who called me a Vulcan. At the time I thought he was just being sarcastic because I knew how to break up without crying. But in retrospect, I realize he was being quite insightful. I did tend to sum people up rather quickly as either "logical" or "illogical" and if you fell into the latter category I responded like Spock. My mind processed it this way, "You are behaving irrationally. I have work to do. We can resume contact when you start to make sense. Good day."

I suppose that's how I treated most of my colleagues during the balance of my first year at Woodhull. For me that was the end of it. I just focused on doing my work and spent as little time around the senior staff as possible. And since I wasn't thinking about them, I assumed that they weren't thinking about me. But life among humans doesn't work that way. I also failed to appreciate my inability to mask my feelings when I thought things didn't make sense. After one meeting Vonetta pulled me aside and said, "Girl, everything about your body language is screaming that you don't want to be here." I really had no idea it was that obvious, but even after she brought it to my attention I doubt I did much to change it. I realize now how distracting that must have been to everyone else.

As the weeks turned into months it became increasingly clear that I was the odd man out on the leadership team. I noticed that there were more and more senior level meetings being held without me. At first I didn't care because my work was always done well and on time. At the time, I believed that was all that really mattered. But eventually, the less you're in the loop, the less work you receive. I should have been worried about being fired, but I wasn't. I was more concerned about my brain turning to mush. There were plenty of people at the hospital collecting a check for counting paperclips all day but that was not why I came to Woodhull. If my fresh set of eyes were no longer needed, I would take them elsewhere.

By the spring of 1999, I was so disenfranchised that rumors began to circulate that I was going to be fired or let go with the next round of layoffs. It was time to plan an exit strategy. I called Donna. We'd both agreed that for the sake of professional appearances, it would be best for me to try to make it a year. But by March, I was so desperate to leave, I didn't care what it looked like. So she arranged for me to meet Harry Galick, the Director of Human Resources at Generations +, the HHC Network where Donna was now Chief Operating Officer.

We had our first meeting within a few weeks and bonded immediately. But in typical HHC fashion it took until the summer before we could arrive at a date for my transfer. In the interim, things grew increasingly sour. By that point, Lois and I were clearly at odds which gave everyone else on the Cabinet carte blanche to give me the cold shoulder. By the time we held our network retreat in June, I was so unhappy and so uncomfortable that I was ready to resign without a job.

I called Harry on my cell phone from the retreat and told him that with or without an offer I was leaving North Brooklyn. Fortunately for me, my transfer had finally been approved. When he told me that I could officially tender my resignation it felt like the happiest day of my life. It wouldn't last.

I gave four weeks notice so that I could finish every assignment that was still outstanding. Candis and Woodhull were not a fit. While I had many strong opinions about Lois' leadership style, few of them good, she was still the one in charge. There is a management axiom called "Loyalty, Voice or Exit." I'd voiced my opinions. It was clear that this was not going to become a leadership team I could ever feel loyal to and mean it, so it was time to exit. I did everything in my power to do so in a dignified and unobtrusive manner.

As much as people at Woodhull loved to gossip, I said little about why I was leaving or how I felt about the people I was leaving. I don't think I was ever disrespectful to Lois although I can't speak for her perceptions. In short, I can't think of anything I could have possibly done during my thirteen months at Woodhull that would have justified what happened next.

Two weeks into my four-week notice, Daisy called to tell me that four weeks would not be required. In essence, she was saying that as far as they were concerned I could leave immediately. My transition document was just about finished, so I told her that I would make the upcoming Friday my last day. I could use vacation time to bridge the gap between my last day at Woodhull and my scheduled start date at the Generations + Network.

I was working directly with Donna concerning my assignment, but as my start date drew closer I still didn't have confirmation of where I should report. The network needed some help at Harlem Hospital in their Human Resources department because they were also going through a JCAHO survey that year. So I went to Harlem a week before I was scheduled to start and interviewed with their CEO and their Chief Operating Officer. I remember the CEO asking me if I left Woodhull on good terms. "I think I did," I replied. I certainly believed that to be true. Whatever my personal feelings about Lois, I did whatever she asked me to do.

Later that week I met with Harry. Silver-haired with a slender build, he always displayed the same laid-back demeanor. Some thought it was too laid-back. It took forever for things to move through the human resources department. But he had been in the system a long time and had figured out that the key to survival was to bide your time and lay as low as possible. We got along well from the very beginning so when we sat down to chat I was expecting more pleasantries. His demeanor never changed no matter what he was talking about. That's why I wasn't prepared for what he was about to tell me.

"So how did your interview go?" he asked.

"Fine I guess. It was pretty straight forward."

"Well, we have a little bit of a problem," he said.

Every cell in my body seized with tension.

"I don't think it's going to be anything to worry about," he added. "But I just wanted to give you the heads up."

I could feel heat rising to my face. I tried hard not to appear nervous.

"The thing is," he continued, "there's been a lot of conversation about your transfer. A lot of calls are coming in over here about you." I didn't need to ask where the calls were coming from.

"And what are they saying?" I asked.

I felt the warmth in my cheeks shifting from nervousness to anger. Lois would have to tell a bold-faced lie if she even implied that I didn't do my job and I said as much to Harry.

"No. No one is talking about your work," he said. "They're saying you're not a team player."

I thought, okay. I don't think that's true but I can fix that. He wasn't finished.

"They're also saying that you're difficult to work with."

And I thought, that's not fair but I can fix that too, what else? I still wasn't concerned. I had yet to hear anything that amounted to more than idle gossip of a variety that would probably dissipate before my arrival.

Then he added, "And they're saying that you don't like Hispanics." A heavy fog rolled in from the mountains.

Tammany Hall is not a building. It is a monument from the past. At gateway to the period and place that first taught America how to whittle race and ethnicity from a club to a cantilever. The concept of a cultural group banding together for political leverage may not have originated in colonial New York. But Tammany Hall can be credited with turning the practice from an art to a science. And in New York, while scandal may have demolished that particular structure, the archways have remained intact. Every arch has a flagpole and with each new wave of immigrants, flags are raised and lowered and raised again.

Ethnic politics have coated every artery of governmental appointments in New York since the

Indians and the Dutch first sat down to do business. It's a fact of life in the city– you learn to love it or you leave it. But for the group that sees its flag being lowered to make way for another, the changing of the guard is never easy (a point of contention to which New York holds no monopoly). No matter how many eloquent speeches the experts deliver about the many benefits of a more heterogeneous society, there will always be people who resist that kind of change.

They are the ones who through brute force or the force of their net worth, find a way to maintain pockets of isolated space reserved exclusively for their kind of people. Unfortunately they set the wrong kind of example. Quests for a more diverse landscape that would otherwise be motivated by notions of sensitivity and fairness are instead poisoned by the attitude of an ill-advised contingent of the few, that "it's our turn now." That kind of thinking rarely plays out well.

But bring diversity down off the stage and into everyday lives and all it really represents is one group saying to another, "Hey, I matter too." It's difficult to argue with that. So the task of actually carving out equal time in the spotlight is left to that vast majority comprised of the rest of us. And it is a clumsy two-step of a dance, even with the best of intentions. Part of the price of admission is accepting that toes will be stepped on until grace can be achieved through practice and commitment. Until then, all you can do is ease cautiously to the dance floor, push and pull, lead and be led until you reach that uneasy peace that gradually becomes easier with time.

HHC has a large dance floor but its dancers are largely self-taught. So it produces as many clods as it does coryphées. The way the dance played out at Woodhull during Lois' tenure was decidedly awkward. For example, Lois was Caribbean of African-descent leading a hospital with a large Hispanic population in a district whose city councilman was also Hispanic and proud of it. The compromise as it pertained to her appointment to CEO meant that her Chief Operating Officer had to be Hispanic. This is not conjecture on my part. I was directly informed of this expectation by more than one person who was in a position to make sure that it happened. It was a push of sorts. There are very few Hispanic executives in healthcare, so perhaps it was a necessary push. But Lois chose to select someone like Manny, whose managerial skills were woefully inadequate and every other interested party seemed content to go along with that. There are better ways to dance.

At the moment that I was sitting across from Harry, however, none of that really mattered. I didn't know how I ended up in the middle of the dance floor during that particular number. And even if I did, my side of the story was one I would never get to tell. Whoever was making phone calls knew exactly what they were doing when they started that particular rumor. The Sr. Vice-President for the Generations + Network was an émigré from Puerto Rico named Luis Morales.

The gossip was spreading corporate-wide compliments of an unexpected source – Shaina Green, the Sr. V.P. for Planning. I remembered her from the collaboration meetings I participated in while I was still at the Fort Greene Center and from the day she interviewed me for a job with her division. Beyond that our interactions were few and far between.

There are some people who remind me of animals for some reason, like cats or ferrets. Shaina reminded me of a round, brown Tweety-bird. She was shaped like a bubble around the middle with a caramel-colored complexion and cute little Tweety-bird facial features. And just like Tweety-bird she never stopped talking.

In the summer of 1999 she was talking about me, and her topic was "Why no one in HHC should hire

Candis." For reasons that to this day remain a mystery to me, she actively inserted herself into the debate of whether my short HHC career should continue or end in flames. And this too is not speculation. I learned about her participation in the rapidly escalating smear campaign because Donna received one of the calls that Shaina placed, a call in which she specifically told Donna that she should not hire me.

Over the years, I came to learn that this sort of behavior was actually rather typical at HHC. I was only one in a long line of casualties. Every corporation has its share of corporate gossip. But what would amount to a "buzz" anywhere else took on the character of a locust swarm at HHC. Once it got started it didn't usually stop until there was nothing left of the subject but a bony carcass.

The people at HHC loved telling war stories about how this Executive Director was led away in handcuffs or that one was caught on tape in a compromising position with his secretary. There was never a dull moment working at the Corporation because there was always someone sitting on the front porch telling stories and counting carcasses.

Harry was a "life-er," although mostly in other parts of city government, so I suppose he thought that he knew how this worked. He put his hand on my shoulder.

"Don't worry about it," he said. "It'll pass. Go on home and enjoy what's left of your vacation."

So I did. Two weeks went by. My start date was scheduled for July 12, 1999. But I'd heard nothing from anyone at Gen + since my last meeting with Harry. Somewhere around 8:00 p.m. on the night before I was supposed to start work, my telephone rang. It was Harry.

"How are you enjoying your vacation?" he asked.

"It's been great but I'm ready to get back to work," I answered. "Do I come to your office tomorrow?"

There was a prominent pause in our conversation. I knew that meant bad news.

"That's why I'm calling," he finally said. "You can't report to work tomorrow."

My cheeks concaved from the air that seemed to have been sucked from my lungs.

"What?" That was all I could get out.

"This thing with you and Woodhull hasn't died down the way I thought it would," he said.

I couldn't mince words now.

"Harry, do I still have a job?"

"I don't know."

He promised to call me when he knew more and then hung up. I was sick to my stomach.

I tried to reach Donna during the week that I should have been at work, but she was out of town on vacation. When she finally called me back I was beside myself. She on the other hand was actually laughing by the time I finished filling her in on everything that had transpired. When I told her what Harry said about not knowing whether I still had a job, she nonchalantly replied, "And you believed him? I'll see you Monday."

In the one-week delay between when I was supposed to start and when I actually did, a senior staff position opened up because someone resigned. Once I arrived at Metropolitan Hospital it was like emerging from a bad dream. I had tangible proof that I wasn't crazy. Executive staff meetings actually *did* have minutes! People were expected to deliver on their responsibilities and if they didn't there were consequences. At Woodhull everything moved at the speed of refrigerated peanut butter but at Gen + everyone was on hyper-drive.

For the first few weeks I was almost paralyzed with fear. I was now the Network Associate Executive

Director for Ancillary Services. That meant that I was responsible for the Laboratory, Radiology, Pharmacy, Respiratory Therapy and Food & Nutritional Services everywhere in the network where those services were provided.

I went from responsibility for a staff of four to a staff of over one thousand. I had never been in charge of anything like that before. It was the first time in my life I was afraid that I couldn't handle a task I'd been given. But I also knew that it wasn't just my reputation on the line. Donna took an enormous risk on my behalf. It was only after I started at Gen + that I learned just how far out on a limb she'd gone for me.

Luis, my new Sr. Vice-President, told Harry that I was not to be hired. And he said the same thing to Donna when she returned from vacation. Once I'd settled in, she replayed their conversation for me.

"You should have seen him," she said. "He marched into my office, waving his arms in the air. 'She's not coming to work here and that's final!' Then he stormed out. I was right on his heels. By the time he sat down at his desk, I was leaning over the other side," she said.

When the HHC networks were reorganized, the decision was made to eliminate the Executive Director title at the diagnostic and treatment centers. Donna was the last holdout. It was only because of her reputation and the fact that Dr. Ferdinand seemed to like her so much, that she was able to stay at Cumberland as long as she did. But in the end, she had to give up the position and she didn't like it. She took the opportunity to remind Luis of that fact as she peered down at him from in front of his desk.

"I came here with nothing," she said. "And I never asked you for anything. I just did whatever I was told to do. Well, I'm asking now! So Candis *is* coming here even if all she does is make my copies. And she's coming here with her title and her salary in tact." Then she went back to her office. And he wasn't on her heels.

I learned in our years together that when Donna whipped herself up into a froth like that, most people just got out of her way. Even her bosses! I don't know why she went to bat for me the way she did. At that point we barely knew each other. In fact, in all the years since I don't think I ever asked her directly why she did it, but I know her well enough now to hazard a guess. She knew how character assassination worked at HHC. It was like the gladiator games. If you didn't get up, the lions would eat you. If that transfer hadn't gone through, no one else would have touched me. My career at HHC would have been over before it began. She must have believed that she knew just enough about me to know that I couldn't have done anything to deserve that. In the end, I guess that was all she needed to know.

Needless to say, failure was not an option. So until I had something better to hang my hat on, that would have to be the motivation that kept me going. I saw very little of Donna during my first month at my new home. She later told me that she did that on purpose. "Everyone was watching to see if I was going to have to prop you up," she said. I would have to sink or swim on my own.

Donna may have been able to convince Luis to let me start working at the Generations + Network, but that didn't mean he had to like it. For the first three months that I worked there he wouldn't even look at me. When it was my turn to report at senior staff meetings, his jaw would visibly clench. It was beyond awkward. I walked on egg shells with every word I said.

CHAPTER FIVE
WINTER, 1999

I STARTED MY NEW job before the person I was replacing left, so I was able to shadow him for two weeks. I realized how fortunate I was that the schedules worked out that way after my very first day on the job. Just getting around to the facilities was an accomplishment unto itself. I think we went back and forth between the hospitals twice that first day alone. By the time we met up with Donna at Lincoln Hospital that afternoon, I literally collapsed into a heap in the conference room. I couldn't keep my head up. I had to rest my forehead on the conference table. Donna laughed at me. "Not like Woodhull, huh?" she asked. Not at all.

I walked into the position knowing absolutely nothing about the areas for which I was now responsible. This was the position that taught me the difference between managing and leading. Prior to that point in my career, I'd enjoyed being a hands-on manager – pitching in to do whatever needed to be done. I still believe that in the early stages of a management career you should know how to do whatever it is you're asking your staff to do. And every once in a while you should be willing to roll up your sleeves and help because you send a message to your staff that you're not asking them to do anything that you aren't willing to do yourself. In my experience it's a message that spreads quickly and builds a lasting rapport.

But this new job meant that I was responsible for Lab Technicians, Radiology Technicians, Pharmacists, Respiratory Therapists and Nutritionists. These are all licensed staff positions and while their department directors held these licenses, I did not. Micromanaging was not an option. No matter how badly they might have needed help, I couldn't fill a prescription or shoot an X-ray. I had no choice but to learn a new way to lead. It was the best thing that ever happened to my professional career.

Little by little I started to gain a foothold. Even my relationship with Luis began to turn around. There was a dizzying array of projects going on within my division when I arrived. I was responsible for bringing computerized order entry to all of the network facilities. Instead of writing laboratory and X-ray orders by hand, the physicians would order them in the computer so that the results could be returned directly to the electronic medical record. At the same time we were also consolidating all routine laboratory work for the network with Bellevue Hospital, so that they would process those lab tests going forward. The physicians hated the plans. So, in addition to making sure the projects stayed on schedule, I had to find a way to keep the doctors from staging a revolt.

We were also bringing computerized technology into all of the Radiology departments. When I started in July, the network only officially included Metropolitan Hospital on First Avenue in Manhattan and Lincoln Hospital in the South Bronx, as well as any off-site clinics they operated. But Harlem Hospital was also being integrated into the network. By October their ancillary services were added to my portfolio as well.

All of these complex projects had to be completed within a short timeframe and our progress was being observed with keen interest throughout the Corporation. I noticed right away that one of the things that drove Luis was competition. He liked being the first to do everything. So as I started delivering these projects on time, his frostiness toward me began to thaw.

I was feeling more comfortable in my own skin with each passing day. I was beginning to earn my own reputation rather than having to struggle under the weight of one that had been thrust upon me. This meant that Donna and I were now free to spend more time around each. I could finally find out the whole story behind why she left Cumberland. I was also eager to hear her version of the story behind the rift between her and the senior staff at Woodhull. I asked her about it one day when we were having lunch in her office.

"What's the deal with you and Lois?" I asked.

"What do you mean?"

"They didn't seem to like you very much over there. For the first few weeks after I got there, they couldn't get through a meeting without bringing your name up and they weren't giving you compliments."

She laughed. I wasn't sure how she would take the next question I wanted to ask but she didn't seem to mind the inquisition so I decided to risk it.

"Is it true that *you* wanted to be the Executive Director at Woodhull?"

I watched her expression carefully to see if I'd gone too far. But her smile never waned. She didn't hesitate in her response either. In fact, she almost seemed glad that I asked. It was as if she knew there were some distorted stories floating around and she wanted to set the record straight even if it was only with me.

"I'll tell you what happened," she said boldly. "I didn't want to go to Cumberland when they sent me. But I know how to be staff. When the president says he has an assignment for you, you go. I've done it over and over with this corporation. I got there, I did my job and it wasn't easy. It took a lot of work to turn that place around. Then as soon as things started to look up . . . the visits were going up, the patients were happy, they told me there weren't going to be anymore Executive Directors at the D & TC's and I had to go to work at one of the hospitals. I didn't want to have to leave again."

There was just a hint of vulnerability in her voice and demeanor as she talked about not wanting to leave. Even in the short time we'd known each other, it seemed out of character for her. "I even offered to report to Lois if it meant I could stay. No one ever mentions that!" she said. And just like that the vulnerability was gone. "But since they were determined to eliminate the Executive Director title at Cumberland, the only way I could stay was to be the Sr. Vice-President of the North Brooklyn Network. So I asked Dr. Ferdinand to give me *that* job if it was the only way I could stay. *That's* how it happened," she said defiantly.

So this was the source of the undercurrent between Donna and Lois. Cumberland was part of the same network as Woodhull even before there was a North Brooklyn Health Network. In the beginning they both reported to the Sr. Vice-President who ran Bellevue Hospital. The decision to break North Brooklyn out on its own was made not too long before I arrived. But at that time, it was a network without a Sr. Vice-President. So with both Lois and Donna sitting as Executive Directors in the same network you had what amounted to a kingdom with two queens. Two grown women cooking in the same kitchen is a setup for somebody to get cut.

I didn't know Dr. Ferdinand or the history surrounding the formation of the network system. But I knew enough about how these two women managed their operations to know that it would never have worked. And that's how Donna ended up being shipped off to Metropolitan Hospital.

When I became responsible for the ancillary services at Harlem Hospital, it brought the number of departments that I was responsible for to 15, divided among three hospitals. In addition, I also had to keep track of any ancillary services that existed at the more than 30 outpatient clinics in the network. The first thing I did was to ask Donna for permission to restructure my division. Rather than have each department director report to me directly, I wanted to appoint a network director for each of the ancillary services in the division. That person would then be responsible for all of their services at all of our facilities. I was certain the new structure would make all of us more effective. She approved my plan without delay.

The relationship that grew between Donna and me was the antithesis of what I had with Lois. Mostly because Donna was everything Lois was not. She expected you to perform and let you know in no uncertain terms if you weren't getting the job done. She gave clear direction and her opinions were her own. But she was willing to let you experiment. She gave you credit when your ideas worked and provided unwavering support and protection when they didn't. I'm not sure I would have fully appreciated how fortunate I was to be working for her had I not spent the previous thirteen months at Woodhull. That fact alone made me appraise my time at Woodhull as a worthwhile learning experience, even if I didn't get to change the world.

CHAPTER SIX
JANUARY, 2000

As WE MOVED INTO 2000, I wouldn't say the work became easier but I was certainly more confident in doing it. I was fortunate to have terrific managers who made my job easy. But they still had expectations of me. They needed me to be knowledgeable enough to provide the support they needed when they needed it. I had to learn fast but I also had to respect what they knew and give them the space they needed to do their work.

After Donna approved my restructuring plan I was able to identify a network director for Radiology, Pharmacy and Food Service by pulling each from one of the hospitals. Carlos, the Radiology Director, came from Metropolitan and he quickly became the "teacher's pet." If I gave my network directors two weeks to complete an assignment, Carlos did it in one. But if he was the angel on one shoulder, my Pharmacy Director, Mitch, decided he would be the devil on the other.

Mitch ran the Pharmacy Department at Lincoln and had been in the Corporation for more than twenty years. I'd already learned through experience that when you are a young executive, charged to supervise managers who are older than you with more years on the job, at least one of them is going to test you. Mitch stepped up to that plate within my first few weeks on the job. I would come to see him and he'd make me wait in the outer office until he was ready. I would request information from him that I needed for Luis or Donna.

He would respond directly to them rather than giving the information back to me. The day that I received a memo from him informing me of the two-week vacation he was taking rather than requesting approval for it, I decided that the time had come for us to have a little chat.

When I arrived at his office at the appointed time, the secretary buzzed him on the intercom. I was already standing in the door to his office when I heard him tell her, "She's just going to have to wait. I'm in a meeting."

He was startled when he looked up and saw me smiling at him. And I could see his face flush with color when I said, "Yes. You're in a meeting with me."

His guest left quickly and I sat down in his place. I've never been one for small talk when large matters need to be discussed.

"Mitch, it seems that you're struggling with having to report to me." His face lost all expression.

"No I'm not."

"Oh, I think you are."

I went on to recount the examples of his conduct that I thought were inappropriate. I could see his facial muscles tighten as he readied a response in his mind.

"Now I don't know what the source of the problem is," I said. "I don't know if it's because I'm younger than you or that I haven't been with HHC very long or that I'm a woman. Maybe *you* wanted this job."

He quickly interrupted me.

"I never wanted that job! It was offered to me before and I never wanted it."

"Whatever," I continued. "What I do know is that whatever the problem is, it's *your* problem. You're either going to get over it or you're going to be getting yourself over to the retirement office. We'd hate to lose you but I'm sure you'll have a great party. You have a lot of friends." Our relationship improved markedly after that.

Donna supplied me with my Director for Respiratory Therapy. Hugh was a stern man who had transferred from another HHC network and was working with the Nursing Director at Lincoln. He took his responsibilities seriously and I never had to tell him something twice. For the laboratory I was able to hire Marie, a young lady who had worked for me as an Assistant Director at Woodhull. She vowed that she was going to follow me wherever I went for as long as she lived. And finally, there was Miles LeVeille, the Director of Food Service at Metropolitan, who everyone affectionately called "Mr. Miles."

Marie began her career at Met and she used to talk about Mr. Miles constantly when we worked together at Woodhull. So from my very first day, I felt as if I already knew him. He proved to be every bit as delightful as she'd always described him. A classy gentleman in his early 60's, he'd worked at Metropolitan for more than 10 years after a distinguished career with the Marriott Corporation.

And he continued to distinguish himself at Met because of his ability to make any event we held at the hospital feel like it was catered by a five-star hotel. Dietary aides rarely come with etiquette training but Mr. Miles could train the roughest characters on how to serve meals on fine china with the refinement of a white glove restaurant. We loved him and he loved to please.

When Hugh took responsibility for the Respiratory Services at Harlem he discovered a manager there named Juan. Hugh made the mistake of bragging to me that Juan was smart, energetic and could write well. Hugh was using him to manage quality control for all of the network's respiratory services. After meeting Juan, I realized that the entire division could benefit from his talents so I stole him from Hugh and made him responsible for managing quality improvement for the entire Clinical Support division (my division's new name). With that decision my new team fell into place.

I recognized almost immediately that I'd put together a group that made hard work fun. The hectic pace of being responsible for services at three different hospitals left little time to be idle. There were many times when just making it to the different meetings was the major achievement of the day. There was always a fire to put out. But having a team of individuals who could solve problems quickly and who were accustomed to performing at a high level, created a singular kind of job satisfaction. It made all the extra effort more than worthwhile.

Along with enjoying my new staff, I was actually enjoying my colleagues as well. Everyone seemed to be at the top of their game. My very first friend among my new colleagues was the Network Associate Executive Director for Facilities Management, Jack Feliciano. Stocky, mocha-faced, and full of machismo, Jack was the penultimate "man's man." Whatever you needed from him, he delivered. That also made him one of Donna's favorites on the senior staff. His larger-than-life persona made him the star of one of the funniest memories of my time at Gen +.

I shared my office suite at Met with Nancy Carver, the network's Chief Information Officer. Cheerfully blond and obsessed with the Atkins Diet, Nancy started a month after I did. We became kindred spirits because she, like me, arrived from another network with a cloud over her head. She had been the CIO at the North Bronx Network and their Sr. Vice-President, John Fortunado, decided that she wasn't what he was looking for. But he couldn't just let her go. This was HHC of course.

"When I met with Harry I found out that John told Luis I didn't get my work done on time and he had to get rid of me," she told me one day. "That wasn't true.

I couldn't believe he would say something like that. I cried all the way home."

Just about every project I was working on had a technology component, so Nancy and I were joined at the hip for about a year. One day she and I were visiting one of the satellite clinics with our staff to prepare for one of the computerized lab conversions. We were only conducting a walk-through so we asked the driver to wait, but when we returned the driver was gone. It was the middle of the summer and easily the hottest day of the year.

There we were on 125th Street in Harlem melting all over the sidewalk. Nancy pulled out her cell phone and called the transportation office to find out what happened. But transportation reported to Jack Feliciano. So calling the department directly instead of calling her colleague was her first mistake. Nancy and Jack used to have sparring matches from time to time so perhaps she wanted to avoid him. She may have believed she could use her network title to strong-arm his staff instead. If she did, that would count as her second mistake.

Throwing your weight around as a network executive worked with some departments but it never worked with any of Jack's staff. His people didn't listen to anybody but him. It didn't matter who you were. It could have been Donna, Luis or the mayor himself. They weren't taking orders from anybody but Jack Feliciano. When calling the transportation department didn't work, Nancy decided to call Jack's office. But she couldn't get through so she called her secretary and had her secretary call his secretary. I watched her go through these machinations for nearly fifteen minutes while the rest of us were creeping up on a case of heat stroke.

One of the things that Jack and Nancy used to fight about was getting in contact with each other. Included among the list of departments that fell under Jack's purview was Telecommunications. He took great pride in the fact that the cell phones he issued to all the senior staff came equipped with two-way radios. For some odd reason Jack felt strongly that this was the only acceptable way for us to communicate with each other. But Nancy preferred to use the phone. Why they chose to draw a line in the sand over that, I will never know.

Nonetheless, I was slowly liquefying into a pool that was gathering at my feet. I needed a resolution to our transportation dilemma and quickly. So I decided to try chirping Jack on the two-way radio.

"Jack, pick-up. Over."

He responded so quickly you would have thought that he'd been waiting for my call.

"What's up Candis? Over."

"Where are you? Over."

"In my office. Over."

I could see Nancy out of the corner of my eye. She was turning red and not because of the heat.

"But Nancy just called your office. She's trying to reach you. Over."

"I know but she won't use the two-way so I'm not talking to her. Over."

At this point I had to put my hand over her mouth to keep Jack from hearing the curse words that Nancy was hurling in his direction.

But before I could say anything else to him, he said, "My drivers don't have time to be sitting around all day waiting for you guys!" We had a problem.

Now, he was pissed. Even though Jack and I had a good relationship, I knew he might not be willing to help me now because he knew I was with Nancy. I had to think fast. So in my most helpless, girly voice I whined in one continuous sentence, "J a A A C C k k, I don't know what happened with the transportation but we're standing out here and its s o o o o hot and we've got to get back to Met and I don't know what to d o O O o o!"

I didn't hear anything at first. But I wasn't concerned. After a few seconds, he asked where we were. He was still trying to sound authoritative, but, I could hear his veneer cracking under the weight of my feminine guile. And now I was in character. I took a deep breath, let out an exaggerated sigh and said, "We're in front of the Renaissance clinic on 125th Street. Please hurry. I'm feeling a little lightheaded." There was another pause but I knew I had him.

With the defeated voice of a hen-pecked husband he said, "I'll send somebody out to pick you up."

I don't know how he did it but Jack had a van there in 97 seconds. I was laughing. The staff with us was laughing. Everybody was laughing except Nancy. She was appalled. She looked at me like I had betrayed the entire female race. She actually yelled at me. "I can't believe you did that!!"

I don't perspire, I sweat. And I don't like to sweat. It's not very ladylike. I would have said anything to get out of that heat. By this time the door to the van was open and I could feel the air conditioning tickling my pores. I placed my bags in the van, looked over my shoulder at Nancy and said, "You can be a feminist in the heat all by yourself. I'm getting in this van. Do you want a ride or not?"

There was no shortage of funny stories like that at my new home. I ran into Ira at the HHC Christmas party the year I left Woodhull and he asked me how I liked working at Gen +. "I love it," I said.

"Yeah, but I bet we have more fun," he replied. He managed to sound just like an eight year-old.

"We have fun," I said. "But we also get our work done."

By the spring of 2000, Woodhull seemed like a distant memory and so did any remnants of the accusations that I was going to be trouble. Once all of the laboratory consolidation projects were completed my counterpart at Bellevue and I were invited to make a presentation to HHC's Board of Directors. It was the kind of attention that Luis loved. He usually would have made the presentation himself, with the people who actually did the work feeding him what to say. But Donna insisted that we be allowed to do this presentation. After it was over, she practically hugged me to death.

"You just don't know how proud I was of you," she said. "That presentation was flawless." Donna rarely got excited about anything. I'd never seen her like this before and at first I didn't get it. Did she think I would freeze? But that wasn't it. "Just about everybody who'd spread that gossip about you last year was in that room today," she said. "You just shut every one of them up." But the icing on the cake was still to come. Shortly after we returned to our offices at Met she came into my office with a look of disbelief on face and shut the door.

"You're not going to believe this," she said. "Luis and I were just talking about the presentation and how well you did. And then we started talking about how well the radiology project is coming along. He looked at me with a straight face and said, 'You know, I'm so glad we hired Candis.'" If there'd been a fly in the room it could have flown right down my throat. Donna had her hands on her hips. She was laughing but through a face still creased with disbelief. Of course she couldn't let him get away with that.

"WE? WE? What we?!! After all the hell you gave me about hiring that child?" she said. Watching her reenact her displays of disbelief was even funnier than the comments themselves. "And do you know he had the nerve to look at me like he didn't know what I was talking about?" she said. I laughed as hard as she did but I didn't care how he reached his conclusion. After everything I'd been through, I'd take a compliment from Luis any way I could get one.

One of the ongoing complaints we received from the Executive Director at Harlem was that the directors with network responsibility were neglecting Harlem in favor of the other two hospitals. The network structure meant little to the staff who had dedicated responsibilities at only one hospital. Each hospital had its own culture, its own identity and they wanted that identity respected. I decided that I and each of my network directors would spend Fridays at Harlem in an effort to address their feelings of neglect. That made Friday the one day of the week that we knew we would all be in the same place at the same time. So we started having weekly divisional meetings there over lunch.

I quickly began to look forward to those meetings. Even though there always seemed to be more work than time to complete it, on each Friday afternoon that we spent together we found something to laugh about. Sometimes it would take nothing more than the lunch itself.

"I know I gave you until next week to finish the first draft of your departmental strategic plans," I said during our first Friday lunch. "But I'd like to know how it's coming along. Everyone received the format from Juan right?"

"Here is mine," Carlos replied with an irrepressible smile as he handed his crisply bound report to me. "I finished it already."

The team was accustomed to this by now. And they regarded him more like you would an eager little brother than a suck-up, everyone that is except for Mitch.

"Big deal," he said. "Did you do mine?"

"Why do you have to be so angry all the time?" Carlos replied.

We were all gathered around the table, laughing as usual at the banter between them. But, Mr. Miles had no time to join in. He was too busy. We benefited greatly from having him as a part of the team. He made sure our first lunch together was a hot meal with servings from the five major food groups. We had fresh fruit, rolls, fish, scalloped potatoes and for the vegetable – Brussels sprouts.

I have to admit, somewhat reluctantly, that I can revert to the level of a pre-adolescent when it comes to my food. I'm not all that fond of fuzzy water (aka "carbonated"). I don't like lumps in my Cream of Wheat. I won't eat lima beans, and I absolutely loathe Brussels sprouts.

It took a great deal of restraint but I managed not to scream. Mr. Miles worked so hard on arranging the lunch. And the relationship I had with all my directors had grown to the point where they were quick to respond if they even suspected that I was unhappy about something. I didn't want to upset him over something so trivial. Besides, it would be difficult to explain why a grown woman was having full-body convulsions over a vegetable. I took a deep breath so that I could summon a calm voice without appearing medicated. "I don't like Brussels sprouts."

I thought I'd done a respectable job of masking my internal hysteria. When I say I don't like Brussels sprouts I mean I don't like anything about them. I don't like the way they smell. I don't like the way they look and I don't want them cohabitating with anything else I'm expected to eat. But despite my best efforts, my body language must have been broadcasting my feelings. Before I could say anything else all five of my staff members were tripping over each other trying to be the first to take the little slimy green balls from my plate.

The following Friday we ordered from the Korean soul food place across the street. But Mr. Miles would not be appeased until he had the opportunity to make up for what he was convinced was an unforgivable crime – serving his boss a vegetable she hated. So we tried again. The staff brought up plates for each of us and he fussed over them like an expectant father as they set the table.

"I ordered your plate special to make sure it didn't have Brussels sprouts on it," he said. His word was good enough for me. The food service staff put plates before each of us topped with plastic covers. The one in front of me had my name on it. And Mr. Miles was peering over my shoulder when I lifted the lid. There was chicken, rice - and Brussels sprouts.

"No. You must have the wrong plate," he said. I wasn't concerned. I trusted that he'd figure out what went wrong. He grabbed another plate and took off the lid - more Brussels sprouts. At this point we each pushed our chairs back from the table and all eyes were on Mr. Miles. He was starting to look a little bit manic. Lids were flying everywhere as he personally searched for that elusive plate without the Brussels sprouts. But the little buggers were everywhere. I'd never seen him so mad and neither evidently, had his staff. They ran away after the unveiling of plate Number 5. As lid Number 7 hit the floor I heard his Haitian accent trailing off in the distance as he ran down the hall after them.

Some variation of this routine happened every time we had a lunch prepared by the Harlem Food Service department. No matter what Mr. Miles said, no matter how carefully he planned, every single week without exception, there were Brussels sprouts on my plate. I would have attributed it to intentional sabotage if it had been happening to anybody but Mr. Miles. His staff loved him too much to ever do him in like that. Every week he vowed that the kitchen staff would get it right. And every week we'd have to keep an oxygen mask nearby to make sure he didn't lose consciousness from the outburst that ensued when they proved him wrong.

But then again this was Harlem Hospital. It was a place that often rivaled Woodhull when it came to dysfunction. The only difference between the two hospitals was that Harlem had a fabled history. Woodhull did not. Harlem Hospital was the first hospital in New York to hire an African-American physician. It was one of the first hospitals to have an African-American CEO. Even Princess Diana paid a visit to Harlem Hospital.

On its worst day, it was still considered a jewel to the residents of that community. The employees, particularly the old-timers, were fiercely proud and protective of its legacy. So you could usually prevail upon that pride to coerce them into doing the right thing when all else failed. And even when that didn't work, you had to give them credit. When they messed up they did it with style.

For instance, when we first arrived we discovered that the secretary for the Laboratory's administrative office had this unique illness that meant that she couldn't come to work on Mondays. Unless of course Monday was a holiday and then she couldn't come to work on Tuesdays. When Marie and I confronted the Lab Manager about why he had allowed this to go on for so long he said, "But she's really good."

"How can she be good? She's hardly ever here," I retorted. When the secretary did make it to work, she rarely got there before 11:00 a.m. But he had an answer for that too.

"But she stays late to make it up."

"How would you know?" Marie asked. "You don't stay past 5 o'clock yourself."

I tried to help him see the flaw in his reasoning. "Her job is to support lab administration," I said. "If the office closes at 5:00 p.m. and the vendors she's supposed to contact close at 5:00 p.m., it doesn't matter if she stays until midnight. She's not helping anybody." He looked as if that had never crossed his mind. But from the sheepish look on the secretary's face, I could tell that it had definitely crossed hers.

But in fairness, Harlem's staff was not alone in the network in their ability to engage in behavior too bizarre to be believed and too outrageous to be believable fiction. It was at Metropolitan Hospital where we discovered that one of our laboratory technicians was drinking the chemical reagents we used in the lab equipment. He had a drinking problem and his supervisor knew it. I'm guessing that maybe he couldn't risk being caught sneaking alcoholic beverages on to the premises yet again. Whatever his motivation, he apparently decided that the alcohol content in these chemicals was worth the risk that their toxicity might pose to his vital organs.

Staffing was the one consistent obstacle we faced at HHC. When you were allowed to hire you couldn't find good people willing to take the job and if you had people willing to take the job you weren't allowed to hire. Luis always wanted to look good so he took the pre-emptive position of saying no to everything. That was except for political appointments. There seemed to be no limit to the number of six-figure salaried executives he was willing to hire if he thought it would enhance his political connections. But ask for a clerk who might actually do some work and the answer was always no.

There were lots of firsts for me at Gen +. When I saw "Board Report prep meeting" on my calendar it marked another one. I was excited by the prospect of finally getting to see what all the fuss was about. As it turned out I wasn't going to find out after all. I was invited to the prep meeting because they needed information from my division for the report, but, I wasn't going to be attending the actual Board Report itself. Getting to peruse the Board Report binder for the first time, however, only piqued my curiosity. It was the size of the Yellow Pages.

Donna chaired the meeting with Sasha, the Network Associate Executive Director of Quality Management. During the two weeks that I shadowed my predecessor before he left, I got to know him really well. I liked him right away and one of the things I liked most about him was his bluntness. Most people feel the need to be politically correct when describing a person to someone they don't know. He was not of that ilk.

For instance, as we were reviewing the list of the departments I would be responsible for and he was describing the Chiefs of Service that I would be working with, he described one of them by saying, "He looks like he should be on a street corner selling watches from underneath his raincoat." When I finally met this particular Chief, I almost burst a blood vessel trying to keep from laughing because that's exactly what the man looked like.

But my predecessor saved his most pointed comments for Sasha. Among the other contemptuous depictions he used to describe her, he stated in no uncertain terms that he thought she required psychotropic medication. She was a tiny blond with a thick Middle Eastern accent and Donna liked her for some strange reason. She once tried to explain Sasha's outlandish behavior by telling me that she had been a princess in her country before the royal family was overthrown. "Yeah?" I said. "Well I'm a princess in this country. So I'm not impressed."

You could hear Sasha's stiletto heels clicking down the hallway at breakneck speed. The chief role of Quality Management is to point out what's wrong with everyone else's department, which is bad enough. But Sasha would try to extend her reach by insinuating herself into the process of how you should fix it. Luis loved her which meant she had sovereignty throughout all the hospitals in the network.

Once Harlem Hospital joined the network, Gen + was preparing for a JCAHO survey every year. It turned Sasha into a Tasmanian devil spinning from hospital to hospital, wrecking havoc as one survey ended and the preparation for the next one began. Thanks to the early warning I received courtesy of my two-week orientation, I made it a point to establish my division as a Tasmanian devil-free zone during my first vigorous encounter with Sasha. After that we settled into an uneasy truce.

The winter gave way to spring and we began ramping up in earnest for Lincoln's JCAHO survey. My team and I moved our offices to Lincoln full time as did any of the network staff that wasn't already based there. This meant that Donna had to move too. The set-up at Lincoln meant that we didn't get to see each other as often. But I did happen to be in the executive suite one afternoon after they returned from a Board Report. They had the same disheveled look that Lois and her crew used to have after each of their Board Reports. Donna discretely motioned for me to meet her in her office. So I slipped in while Donna stood in Luis' doorway in an apparent attempt to calm him down. When she finally returned to her office, I didn't even wait until she'd finished closing the door.

"What happened?" I asked.

"This was the worst Board Report I've ever been to and I've seen some pretty bad ones," she said.

"Details, details!"

"We knew we were in for it. We had some really bad OB/GYN cases to go over this quarter. I tried to tell them how to write up the cases to minimize the damage but they don't listen. Dr. Ferdinand ate them alive. He finally got so fed up with the answers he was getting that right in the middle of the meeting he told Luis that he wanted the Chief of the Service fired!"

"Are you serious?" I asked.

"I wouldn't kid about that. Everyone was stunned. He didn't even go into executive session," she said.

"What's executive session?"

"That's when the Board sends everyone out of the room so that they can deliberate in private. That's how they would usually handle something like that. Or else they'd wait until the meeting was over and tell the Sr. V.P. in private, but not this time. Dr. Ferdinand ordered her dismissal right there in the middle of the meeting, in front of everyone."

"So now Luis has to tell her?" I asked.

Donna stared at me blankly.

"Tell her? She was in the room when he said it! It was so sad. Everyone was staring at her. She looked like she'd just been hit in the head with frying pan."

Coincidently, I no longer had any desire to attend Board Report after that.

Taking on Harlem Hospital meant working with its Executive Director, which proved to be an experience unto itself. Donna's sister Dina was pushed out of her position as Harlem's Executive Director in 1999. She was replaced by a psychologist who had worked with Luis and Dr. Ferdinand in the past. He was originally from Chicago, which may have explained why he acted like a gangster so much of the time. He was notorious for cursing at his staff during meetings. Even he and Donna had a loud and rancorous argument that culminated with her throwing him out of her office and threatening to pay $5 to have his legs broken if he ever spoke to her again in a way she didn't like.

I suppose an altercation between us was inevitable given my tendency never to back away from a good fight. But that certainly wasn't something I was looking forward to. Despite my successes, I was still raw from my experience with Lois and very sensitive not to be perceived as a troublemaker. But, it would appear fate had conspired against me.

He called on the phone one day and the first thing I heard after I said hello was, "DIDN'T I TELL YOU. . . ." It went downhill from there. I took the receiver away from my ear and held it a full arms length away from my body, but, I could still hear what he was saying. That's how loud he was yelling. When he finally let me respond, my first thoughts were inspired by that great American philosopher and fellow Brooklyn native – Bugs Bunny: "Of course you know, this means war."

It took no time at all for me to forget that I was speaking to someone who outranked me. I gave as good as I got. That telephone conversation didn't last long. And he never called me again after that. Instead, he wrote me up weekly and sometimes daily. If I sneezed he wrote a memo. If he thought I looked at him oddly, he wrote a memo. One week he complained that my directors never spent any time at Harlem and the staff was being neglected. The next week he wrote that they were spending too much time at Harlem and the staff was being smothered.

He wrote so many memos that one day the secretaries in Donna's office asked, "What the hell is going on with you two? We had to start a separate file just to hold all the memos he writes about you." Fortunately for me, people were already looking at him sideways when they passed him in the hall because of his antics. So if his condemnation was the worst that was being said about me, I was fairly certain that no one was listening.

Lincoln was surveyed in the Fall of 2000 and did exceptionally well. Despite the hard work, I was sorry to see the survey come and go because that meant that my team wouldn't be based at the same hospital anymore. The fact that we were now spending more time together only created more opportunities for me to have a front row seat for the amusing exchanges that always seemed to occur, especially between Carlos and Mitch.

I was in the executive suite one day retrieving mail from my mailbox when Mitch walked up. We were talking to each other while I rifled through the envelopes when I came across one that looked like it was holding a greeting card. I couldn't think of what it could be. It wasn't my birthday. I opened the envelope and there was a Boss' Day card inside. I'd never received a Boss' Day card before. I opened it and when I saw Carlos' signature, in a mocking tone I showed the card to Mitch and said, "Now you see. Look at this. Carlos was the only one to remember me today. He's so special."

I was only joking. I didn't even know it was Boss' Day. But Mitch turned red as a tomato. He whipped out his two-way radio and clicked "Group Send" so that all of the division directors would hear him at the same time.

"Emergency! Emergency!" he shouted. "Meet me in Carlos' office right now!"

Then he ran out the door like his britches were on fire. I ran out behind him.

"Wait, Mitch! Wait! I'm not mad. I was just kidding!" But he couldn't hear me. His little legs were moving so fast I could barely keep up with him in my high heels.

Responses were coming in from all over.

"What's the matter?"

"Never mind!" he yelled. "Just meet me in Carlos's office! WE'RE GONNA KICK HIS ASS!"

By the time I caught up to Mitch, the group was outside Carlos' office, looking at Mitch like he had lost his mind. He looked like he'd lost his mind too. His hair was standing straight out from the sides of his head. I slipped past him to get between him and Carlos while Mitch passed the card around to the others.

"Look at this! Look at this!" he said.

Even after they read it, they still didn't seem to care the way Mitch did. Meanwhile, Carlos was standing up behind his desk trying to look confused. Mitch shouted at him.

"You just had to be the star didn't you? You couldn't let us in on this?!" Carlos tried his best to look innocent. But I know I saw just a hint of a grin as he coyly replied, "I didn't put your names on the card?"

It was customary for the president of HHC to come to the hospital at the end of a JCAHO survey so that he could participate in the exit conference with the Joint Commission surveyors. Immediately after Lincoln's survey was over, he asked to speak to Donna. She called me to her office as soon as he left. Lois was retiring and he wanted Donna to go to North Brooklyn to be the new Sr. Vice-President.

She gave an Academy Award-winning performance in her various attempts at refusal, but in the end she agreed as everyone else knew she would eventually. Then Luis announced that Harlem's Executive Director would be taking Donna's place as Chief Operating Officer for the network. That meant that I and everyone else who had been reporting to her, would now be reporting to him. That was the day I knew I was going with her.

I'd learned so much during my eighteen months at Gen +. And now I was eager to take what I'd learned back to Woodhull so that I could finish what I started. I learned that hard work could be rewarding and fun. I'd learned to lead as well as manage. But watching Donna up close taught me other valuable lessons as well.

If you spent enough time around Luis and Donna to witness the kinds of decisions they made, you wouldn't need a MBA to figure out that Luis should have been reporting to Donna and not the other way around. But she never once acted like she believed that. She always paid him the respect due his position. To my knowledge, they never had a cross word. I know there had to be days when his behavior was frustrating to her, but, she never showed it publicly. Watching her made me see how I could have managed my relationship with Lois differently. And the lesson wasn't wasted.

Of all of my directors including Mitch, my "Peck's bad boy," only Hugh was struggling in his relationship with his staff. I started receiving letters of complaint about him within a few months of his arrival. But he was so good at his job that I filed them away without mentioning the letters to him. But one day at his request, I attended a meeting with him, his Department Director at Lincoln, and the Assistant Director there. Hugh had been complaining to me about the Department Director and from what little I'd seen of the man, I wasn't impressed with him either.

When we sat down, Hugh and the Department Director sat across from each other with stone-like faces. The Assistant Director, a man with a soft-spoken demeanor, decided to break the silence and began to speak. "They're both nice guys," he said. "I know they both mean well. I'm sure if they would each try to see the other's side maybe . . ."

I leaned forward. The Assistant Director's head was now pointed down toward the table. So I wasn't sure if I was witnessing what I thought I was witnessing. But when he looked up there was no mistaking it. The environment that Hugh had created within the department had brought this man to tears. He was practically balling. It's hard to dismiss an encounter that makes a grown man cry. It was time for me to take a closer look at Hugh's relationship with his staff. When I returned to my office I pulled out the letters and read them again. Then I asked Hugh to come see me.

"Hugh," I began. "I want you to listen to me carefully." I needed to say that because I knew he was a very proud man and I didn't want him to miss the point I wanted to share because he was feeling defensive. "You have my complete confidence," I said. "I know how dedicated you are to these departments."

"Some of these guys are sloppy in their practice," he said. "I can't tolerate that."

He couldn't restrain himself and I didn't try to stop him. "I don't expect you to," I said. "But there's *what* you do and there's *how* you do it." "You don't have to compromise your standards, but, try taking a deep breath and counting to ten before you approach the staff if you're not happy with something they're doing. If you approach them while you're angry, they're only going to focus on *how* you spoke to them. Then they'll use that as an excuse to disregard everything you say." That seemed to strike a chord with him. He began to relax in his seat and quietly mull over what I was saying.

"You're starting to generate letters . . . ." Hugh intercepted my comment before I could finish it.

"That's just sour grapes," he said.

"You're probably right. I'm willing to believe that, but, I won't always be your boss. Whoever you report to next may not have this context. Take it from me. You don't want rumors to be what shapes your reputation in this corporation." He sat silently for a few more moments, and then said he understood.

When it was time for me to make my departure, my team took me to Carmine's Restaurant for a farewell dinner. As I looked around the table I felt an unfamiliar sadness. I was sure I'd never be so fortunate as to have a team like this again. They each went around the table taking turns sharing their reflections on what it had been like working with me.

Juan said, "I've never in my life had a better boss."

"I have," Mitch added as if on cue.

Marie said, "I don't have to say anything. I'm going with her."

Then Hugh spoke. "I know you don't think I listen to you but I do. Now when I go to speak with my staff I hear your voice, like an angel on my shoulder."

I thanked them for their support and for the beautiful Mont Blanc pen they gave me as a goodbye gift. We dug into the family-style portions of pasta for the second time and continued to replay the most humorous highlights of our time together. I was thoroughly engrossed in the dinner conversation when the waitress tapped me on the shoulder. "Excuse me, Miss. Your dining companions ordered this especially for you." It was a steaming plate of Brussels sprouts.

CHAPTER SEVEN
JANUARY, 2001

THERE WAS MORE THAN a little irony in the fact that I was returning to the North Brooklyn Health Network with Donna Wilson. And it was an irony that was missed by no one. Donna's first challenge was to put her new team together. She hit Woodhull like a tsunami. Donna may have been under the same cultural constraints as Lois but she had no intention of putting up with "Bambi" for a Chief Operating Officer. Manny was traded to Gen +.

Vonetta had retired a few months after I left in 1999, as did Velma. There was a woman counting paperclips on the senior staff when I arrived in 1998. Lois hired this woman after she was fired from another HHC facility and sent her over to Cumberland as Vonetta's replacement. But for some unknown reason, just before Lois retired, she fired the woman and blamed it on Donna. Lois' Machiavellian CFO June, retired a year earlier. Francine sent word to Donna that she wanted to be the network's new Chief Operating Officer. When Donna declined the offer, she retired as well.

With all the movement, word quickly spread that Donna was conducting a bloodletting. But in truth, she only actually fired one person – Daisy. Daisy made the mistake of telling someone that Donna could not remove Manny from his position. But Donna does not take kindly to people telling her what she can and cannot do. It was classic political satire. After years of rumors about Daisy's well-placed connections, when pressed,

126

they turned out to be highly exaggerated. When Donna went to the usual suspects with her intentions regarding Daisy, not one person lifted a finger to save her job.

Even though I was only responsible for a small department when I left Woodhull, I still felt like I was leaving unfinished business. So I returned on a mission to finish what I started, even if I wasn't exactly sure what that was. The first thing that struck me was how little things had changed in the time that I was gone. Brian finally received the drawings from the architects to renovate the ambulatory care clinics, but in the eighteen months that I was gone they'd only gotten as far as putting glass blocks in one of the waiting rooms.

I wasn't the only person from Gen + that Donna brought back with her. Gretchen came to Gen + from Central Office about a year before we left. Luis approved the transfer, I suspect as a favor to someone. Then he tried to give her to Donna as a Special Assistant. There was only one problem. Donna didn't want a Special Assistant.

Since Luis already had one, Gretchen floated around as a Special Assistant of Special Projects. She attended the Executive Cabinet meetings, but, she didn't sit at the table. However, she did get to have an office in the executive suite. That proved to be her undoing. Since she was taking some of her direction from Luis, she appeared to think that empowered her to circumvent his secretary, Ava.

Donna and I kept our distance as the two of them started marking their territory. We couldn't even lay bets on who was going to come out on top because the odds were too heavy – in Ava's favor. Gretchen seemed to be the only one who didn't know that. Every time she made a snide comment to Ava, Ava acted like she wouldn't or couldn't respond. Gretchen would sneer and the rest of us would wince. "This isn't going to be pretty," Donna said.

We knew Ava was planning something, but, she was as cool as a cucumber about it. No one knew what it was. Then one day I came into the suite to retrieve my mail and I saw moving men packing up Gretchen's office. When Gretchen arrived to work that morning she discovered her office had been relocated to a dark corner of the 9th floor, courtesy of Ava. Luis kept his door closed that entire day. So, when Donna told me that Gretchen begged her to take her to North Brooklyn, I must say I wasn't very surprised.

Maura was also running from someone. While neither of Gretchen nor Maura had been on the Executive Cabinet at Gen +, at least Gretchen was in the room. Maura couldn't even see the room from the position she had. When Donna liberated Maura, her promotion was tantamount to an Olympic-level triple jump. She went from being a social work supervisor to being a member of the executive staff with responsibility for Case Management and Social Work.

Donna's return meant being reacquainted with some of her former staff as well. One was a woman named Rhonda, who Donna had been responsible for bringing to HHC several years earlier. I'd had limited interactions with Rhonda during my first tour of duty. But she seemed to be very interested in knowing what role I was to play now that I was back.

"So are you going to be the Chief Operating Officer?" she asked me on my first day back at Woodhull.

"I don't know," I said.

Shortly after that, Rhonda met with Donna and asked Donna to give her a position that would put her "at the table." So Donna gave her a shot at stardom by putting her in charge of Cumberland.

The rest of the Cabinet were old timers – Agnes, Ira and Brian were still there. Elliot was promoted to my old position when I left, so he was now on the Cabinet. Sandy, the Director of Nursing, had left under suspicious circumstances. The new Nursing Director was someone who'd come up through the ranks of Woodhull's nursing department. Then there was Wayne, the Administrator for Psychiatry.

He was an interesting character. When the Psychiatry department had their ears boxed by that reporter's expose back in 1998, they needed to find somebody to blame for all of the horrible things he wrote. Since they weren't about to lay the blame at the feet of Lorenzo, FoF ("Friend of Ferdinand"), Lois made the administrator the goat. Wayne was hired to replace him a few months after I arrived.

I remembered Wayne to be a nice guy, but not much else. He was tall and pink and looked good in a suit. As I came to work with him more closely it was clear that he believed himself to be CEO material. It was also clear that he believed the only qualifications one needed to be a CEO was to be tall and pink and look good in a suit. He got under Donna's skin early and never seemed to be able to find his way out.

Rounding out the Cabinet were Daisy and June's replacements. Tom, the new CFO, was very tall and even pinker than Wayne. He had red hair that blended seamlessly into his complexion. With his horn-rimmed glasses, he looked every bit the bean counter. The first time I laid eyes on him I thought he had to be the most boring guy on the planet. He was anything but. He and Donna butted heads early and often because he had a habit of double-checking everything she asked him to do with Central Office before he did it. He was definitely courting a head wound with that approach. I so enjoyed how adroitly he bobbed and weaved to avoid the hatchets that Donna seemed to hurl at him on a near weekly basis. But he and I got along famously.

The Human Resources Director was a bright young man who had been the Director of Labor Relations. We were excited about his prospects. But less than a month after we arrived, his background investigation turned up some problem with his taxes which forced him to resign.

"That is so stupid. What a stupid thing to do," Gretchen ranted when she found out. "How could he fuck things up like that? We really needed him!" I was fairly certain that he was a lot sorrier than we were. Donna tapped a woman named Yvonne who had been assisting Harry at Gen +, to be the new Human Resources Director and she rounded out the team.

My physical return to the network followed Donna's by two weeks. The original crew may have wanted to see me go a year and a half earlier, but, they were anxious for me to come back - for one reason and one reason only. They were desperate to know what it was like to report to Donna directly and they were scared. Because of my unique history both with Woodhull and Donna, I was the only one on the new Cabinet who didn't need an orientation to either. So they asked me to conduct one.

Yvonne put together a lunch for the new team and I agreed to share my thoughts. Brian was the first to speak up. "What was it like working over there?" Every face at the table was staring at me like a hungry baby chick waiting for a worm.

"Well, the pace was fast," I said. "Donna is used to having people who respond to her requests the first time. There was, I guess you might call it, a healthy level of competition among the senior staff when it came to our performance."

Then for some odd reason Rhonda felt the need to interject. "I don't really think it was competition. People just wanted to get their work done," she said. I looked at her rather oddly but declined to verbalize what

I was thinking, which was, "Were you there?" The curt tone and contorted body language that accompanied Rhonda's abrupt interruption proved to be a harbinger of the type of relationship that would develop between us.

Donna now had her new team and I needed to put together a team of my own. She gave me responsibility for all the Ancillary Departments that I'd had at Gen + and added the administrators for the clinical services. What she did not give me was the Chief Operating Officer title. But I remembered the lesson I'd learned from my old boss Charles, and focused on the work instead.

Returning to North Brooklyn from Gen + meant going from six direct reports, five of whom were men to fifteen direct reports, thirteen of whom were women. Working with a staff comprised primarily of men is a very different experience from working with one comprised primarily of women. Testosterone is always on the move. It has territories that it wants to conquer. Estrogen needs an audience. It wants to be heard and felt. It wasn't until my return that I discovered my decided preference for the testosterone approach.

My staff at Gen + never seemed to need much from me. Our one-to-one supervisory meetings usually lasted no more than ten minutes. They gave me updates and let me know if they needed me to intervene on an issue. More often than not, they wanted to handle things themselves. Beyond that, they wanted to get back to work and I let them.

But now I found that my one-to-one meetings were approaching an hour. The women wanted to talk at length about <u>everything</u>. It was killing me. On top of that, my physical environment had changed. I had a huge office at Metropolitan Hospital with a wall of windows. The office was located in a tiny two-office suite that I shared with Nancy, the Network CIO. Since both of us spent so much time traveling from hospital to hospital, we were rarely there at the same time. In short, it was a calm and peaceful environment.

When I returned to Woodhull, I was assigned an office with no windows in an executive suite that included five other offices including Donna's. Gretchen was next door to me, Brian was across the suite, and Maura was next to him. In addition, all the timesheets for the hospital's middle managers were located in the executive suite. There was no end to the noise and the foot traffic. Within the first month I was out for four days with the worst flu I'd ever had, and I never get sick.

And then there was Jackie. Our return meant that Donna and I would both be reunited with her. Donna's new role and new location gave her a logistical sand barrier. But I had to make a decision about how to handle our "friendship." For the first few months after I arrived at Woodhull in 1998, Jackie swept me into her world and we were "good friends" just as she said we would be. It tends to be true that with people who are as over-the-top as Jackie, most of what they say usually ends up amounting to gross exaggeration.

But when Jackie said she knew a lot of well-connected people that she was going to introduce me to, she wasn't exaggerating. She did know a lot of well-connected people. The "Uncle Arthur" she wanted to introduce me to that day at the health fair turned out to be Arthur Tillman, the U.S. Congressman for the district. She not only introduced me to him, but also, to his son David, who was a member of the State Assembly. "She's part of the family now," Jackie told David on the day that we met. He and his wife became close friends of mine, something for which Jackie deserves at least part of the credit.

But I soon discovered that there was a cost to Jackie's largesse. The people that Jackie knew made her attractive to be around for those who wanted to be around the people she knew. So this group became her entourage. They ran errands for her and accompanied her to events. As high a regard as I have for myself, I have never wanted to have an entourage. I certainly didn't want to be a part of someone else's. But it didn't take long for Jackie to find things she wanted me to do for her as well. Her most frequent request was for me to write a letter or memo for her because she said she liked my writing style.

The first time she asked me, I wrote the letter without giving it a second thought. After all, it was a harmless enough request for one friend to ask of another. But in no time at all, Jackie was calling me to give me an assignment every other day. I soon had enough of that. "I'm not your damn personal assistant!" I snapped at her one day. Unfortunately, you had to talk to Jackie like that sometimes to get her attention.

"Eeewww!!!" she squealed. "Why are you talking to me like that?" She actually sounded wounded. "I only ask you because you write better than I do," she said. "Jackie, there is nothing wrong with the way you write and your writing will only improve with practice."

Then there were all the places we had to go so that she could introduce me to all of the people I "needed to know." Being so new on the political scene I took her word for it. So even though I would prefer a root canal to a cocktail party, I agreed to go at first. The problem was that these events were usually fundraisers of one sort or another, but Jackie never wanted to pay to get in. It would only be once we got there that I discovered her plan was for us to find a way to slip in.

She didn't find this the least bit embarrassing, perhaps because nothing ever embarrassed Jackie. On the other hand, I was mortified. I would pull out my checkbook, my hands quivering with shame and Jackie would say, "Put that away girl! Put that away! We're not paying. I'm gonna find somebody to get us in here. Hold on a minute."

But those were minor matters. My biggest dilemma when it came to being friends with Jackie was that everywhere she went she rolled in like a Nebraska dust storm. We'd be in the board room at Central Office for example, a place where you'd be expected to comport yourself with at least a measure of decorum. And there would be Jackie yelling out, "HEY CHICKEN!" to whoever she thought she knew that happened to pass by. The woman did not have a discreet bone in her body. I would melt into the corner of my chair, trying to position my body so that it would say, "I'm not with her" to whoever was now staring in disbelief in our direction.

Of course that never worked because if you were with Jackie, everybody knew you were with Jackie. She'd loop her arm into my arm so that she could whisper about people throughout the event. Only Jackie didn't know how to whisper. So whatever she said everyone around us heard and everything she said was inappropriate. That was Jackie – wildly inappropriate, all of the time. It just got to be too much.

I found myself having no choice but to put some distance between us in the months before I left in 1999. And I certainly wasn't about to open that can of worms back up now that I'd returned. I felt bad about it. I really did. And I'm certain she calls me everything but a child of God to this day because of it. But so be it. Jackie is a dish that must be stirred with a long-handled spoon.

In truth my new responsibilities left me with far less time to socialize than I'd had before. I had a team to assemble. My new role was the merging of responsibilities that had previously been divided between Francine and Manny. Divided is probably too generous a word to use. Even though he had been the Chief Operating Officer, Manny had three departments reporting to him, Francine had twelve. The first of my new department heads to meet with me was a young lady named Chrissy.

Before I arrived, Donna laughingly informed me that people were walking on eggshells in anticipation of their first meetings with me. But if that were true nobody told Chrissy to be scared. The first words out of her mouth were, "Your first name is Candis, right?" I said yes. Then she gave me a wide smile and said, "That was the play name I gave myself when I was little." I have to admit it disarmed me. I figured a person had to be extremely confident, a little kooky, or perhaps a bit of both to greet a new boss she'd never met so casually. I liked her right away.

Marie was true to her word. She was expecting her second child when I left Generations +, and she spent her entire maternity leave checking in with me to make sure I'd found a place for her on my new Table of Organization. I had. Francine had organized the clinical departments into service lines but once Donna and I arrived we realized that they were not functional.

In most hospitals there is a Director of Ambulatory Care who is responsible for all of the outpatient services across all the clinical departments. The inpatient services are typically run by Nursing. With the service line model, the administrator for Pediatrics or OB/GYN for example, would be responsible for the management of both the inpatient and the outpatient services for their department. Despite their titles, Francine's department directors had nothing to do with the inpatient service. We'd had some success with the service line model at Metropolitan Hospital so Donna said, "If we're going to do it, let's do it right." That was all she had to say. I moved people around until I found the right fit for each of the services.

That pretty much defined our first year back. There was a lot of moving around with everyone trying to "get in where they fit in." In my first meeting with my managers I shared my philosophy on healthcare management.

"Always remember that as administrators we don't generate a dime of income. Our role is to make it easier for the clinical staff to provide services. That's where we earn our keep. So I don't ever want to see a Chief of Service writing a memo to request more toilet paper. That's your job." In truth, that was something I learned from Charles, but, I still found it to be sound advice. The rest of the lesson was all me.

"Here's how I work. When I give you an assignment I expect it to get done and done promptly. How you get your work done is up to you. I do not check up on my staff. If I don't hear from you I assume it's been taken care of. So if you find that something or someone is prohibiting you from doing your job, you need to let me know quickly. Moving barriers out of your way is my job." Marie was grinning. She'd heard this speech before.

"And one more thing," I said. "You will find that I am fiercely protective of my staff. But that does not mean that I will not hold you accountable. Just make sure that if you've messed up in some way, you tell me before somebody else does."

I still missed my old team. In the beginning I had serious doubts about whether I could replicate the kind of well-oiled machine that we had at Gen +. But with a few more moves, adds and changes, I found that my new group began to gel. I was not getting that same feeling from the executive team. There was something flaccid about our meetings. Even at Gen + there were some of us that got along better than others, but, it never emerged as rifts. That leadership team was a team. But with this group, it seemed more like a collection of cliques and individuals.

Perhaps Donna noticed it as well. As we approached the spring she decided to have everyone on the senior and middle management staff assessed by a Myers-Briggs Personality Type Consultant for a management retreat. Most of us had never gone through the experience before. For me, it was an epiphany. I found out that I was an INTJ which stands for Introverted, Intuitive, Thinking and Judging. As I learned more about this particular type of personality, it explained so much about why I was responding so dramatically to the change in my environment. Sharing the information I received with my staff seemed to create A-HA moments for them as well. Here's how Wikipedia[1] describes an INTJ:

> INTJs are very analytical individuals. Like INTPs, they are more comfortable working alone than with other people, and are not usually very sociable, although they are prepared to take the lead if nobody else is up to the task. They tend to be very practical and logical individuals with a strong individualistic streak and a low tolerance for political correctness, spin or emotionalism. The INTJ mindset in regards to other people could be summed up as: "If you don't want to be called an idiot, don't do stupid things."

Substitute "Candis" everywhere it says INTJ and you could tattoo that quote on my bicep. It doesn't get any more accurate than that. And at no time in my life was that more true than when Donna and I first returned to Woodhull. It turned out that one of the facilitators for

---

[1] http://en.wikipedia.org/wiki/INTJ

the retreat was himself an INTJ, so he used that type frequently in his examples. Hearing him describe how INTJ's respond to certain situations and more important, why, was akin to having a religious conversion experience for me.

It explained why I reacted to others the way I did and why I was generating the reactions that I was receiving. Learning this about myself and sharing it helped me to get closer to my new staff. Unfortunately, it didn't help in my relationship with some of my colleagues nor did the retreat bring the Executive Cabinet any closer to each other. I decided that this wasn't really my concern. So I focused on one thing and one thing only – getting the job done. And we were facing an awesome task.

Imagine showing up for work at a Widget Factory only to find that the entire plant is located at the bottom of the ocean. We spent the first few months on the shore trying to convince the incumbents that you can't build widgets under water. But every time Donna would try to bring that fact to their attention, the Woodhull faithful would look at her like she was speaking Aramaic. Two of the loudest voices of dissent belonged to Ira and Lorenzo, who in addition to being Chief of Psychiatry, became the President of the Woodhull Medical Group, P.C. within a year of our arrival. This was a separate professional corporation that employed all the network's physicians and technical staff.

Ira had been connected to HHC in one way or another for his entire medical career. He was a medical resident at Kings County Hospital and remained there as an attending until he came to Woodhull to be its Medical Director in 1995. The description that most people who know him would probably agree on is that he is an avid cyclist, an enthusiastic advocate for asthma care education, and someone who never met a microphone he didn't want to grab. Donna was convinced that he suffered from Adult Attention Deficit Disorder.

It was a curious phenomenon to watch. If he couldn't dominate the conversation he quickly lost interest. First he would fidget. I suspect that was probably the result of his attempt to find an opening to interject himself into the conversation. If he couldn't find an opening after a minute or two, then he would pull out a pen and start doodling. He collected ornate fountain pens with calligraphy tips, so doodling could occupy him for ten to fifteen minutes at a time. He might look up once or twice to check for an opportunity to regain control of the discussion. But if he couldn't find a way back to center stage by the time he'd lost interest in doodling, he would put his pen away and fall asleep.

It wasn't until I returned in 2001 that I actually identified the pattern. Once I did, I noticed that he never deviated from it. It could be a staff meeting with a few people or a presentation in the auditorium with several hundred. If he didn't have the microphone, it was fidget, doodle, and sleep every time. You could set your watch by it. Sometimes he would even snore.

During all of 2001 and throughout the early part of 2002, Ira and Lorenzo were the lead spokesmen of the "you can make widgets under water" campaign. If you pointed out that the productivity of our Widget Factory was way below what other factories were producing, Lorenzo would argue passionately that you were wrong. But I really enjoyed Ira's responses in the early days. You could confront him with a very specific and detailed fact like, "You can't be productive under water because your tools keep floating away." And Ira would respond, "Yes, but if you forget about that, we're doing really well."

This was the environment we returned to. But as ridiculous as it was, it was also the kind of environment where Donna did her best work. Where Lois spent most of her time blowing air bubbles with the rest of the staff, Donna came in, extended a few courtesies to be polite, and then announced, "We are moving the factory to dry land." End of discussion.

I was accustomed to her directness by now. In fact, it was one of the things I loved most about working for her. I think one of the reasons why our relationship grew so close so quickly was that we were very similar in that respect. After our eighteen months together at Generations +, we developed a shorthand in our ability to communicate with each other so that few words were needed. All I needed to know was which parts of the factory I was responsible for moving. She told me and I went to work.

We were approaching what would be my third Joint Commission survey at that point. So I was by then, fully indoctrinated into the peculiarities of HHC's "Fall Madness" (HHC surveys always took place in the fall). It was always a difficult adjustment for physicians or administrators who'd worked at private hospitals to endure an HHC Joint Commission survey. I doubt there is a hospital system in the country that prepares for these surveys the way HHC does.

This part of the Corporation's history dates back to the late 80's and early 90's when a few of their hospitals (Woodhull being one of them) actually lost their accreditation status temporarily. Being accredited is a requirement for billing Medicaid and Medicare, so a loss of accreditation can be financially devastating. But in truth, that is also why it's highly unlikely that any hospital would ever lose its accreditation permanently, unless it really wanted to close. The real injury comes from the humiliation. Public hospitals have enough image problems without having to climb out from under that rock.

So the Corporation created a culture around JCAHO survey preparation that was strikingly similar to the way a host city prepares for the Olympic Games. It happened every year like clockwork. Only the players changed. They conducted practice reviews that they called "mock surveys." The staff from the Regulatory Affairs division at Central Office recruited staff from HHC hospitals that were not being surveyed, to pretend that they were Joint Commission surveyors. The mock surveys were always brutal. The results were supposed to be confidential, but, nothing was ever confidential at HHC.

Donna decided not to wait until the HHC mock surveys would occur in 2002. Toward the end of 2001 she hired a private consultant to come in and conduct one. Once the results were in, there were a few people missing "from the table." Donna negotiated for Agnes to transfer to another HHC facility. Gretchen was named the Director of Quality Management in her place. The only other Quality Management Director I'd ever worked closely with was Sasha. So anyone would have been starting the race uphill as far as my feelings about QM Directors were concerned.

I loved Operations because I liked the feeling of actually accomplishing something. If it's broke just tell me what and where and get out of my way. I'll get it fixed. In hospitals, (or least in HHC hospitals), Quality Management exists to tell you what's broke and to put that information in reports of varying lengths and configurations. From my point of view that's pretty much all they did. So my attitude about Quality Management was going to depend heavily on the attitude of the person leading it. If the Director was an open, positive and engaging person, I would welcome their input. It's difficult to see all the things that need fixing in an area that you work in everyday.

But we didn't get that kind of Director, we got Gretchen. Now that she had a defined role, she could not wait for her turn to report at our weekly Cabinet meetings. It always started with a deep sigh as if from exhaustion. She had a frizzy mane of blond hair streaked with gray that she would wipe dramatically out of her face with both hands, only to have it fall right back in the way again. "Well . . ." she would start with a labored tone, "here are the latest reports from my staff and . . ." She would hand out the reports with a pained expression. "It's bad. It's really, really bad. I don't know what we're going to do."

Her reports didn't leave much of an opening for discussion. Instead, we would continue around the table. Yvonne would report on where we were with performance evaluations. For the entire first year after we returned, I laughed every time she reported. Woodhull went from 85% to 99% on the timeliness of performance evaluations in the very first month after Donna arrived. That problem ceased to be a problem immediately. The more vexing challenge we faced was in the quality of the evaluations, not how quickly they were completed.

At our first Board Report after returning (I was now a reluctant participant in the meeting), a board member made an astute observation that we had to take as a "follow-up." A follow-up was equivalent to a "punt" on a question we couldn't answer at the moment. The question was, "How can a network with over 2,000 employees have 1,900 rated outstanding and only three that need improvement?" The question became even more difficult to answer when we learned that our network had one of the worst records for absenteeism in the Corporation.

There were those who you could tell were struggling to come up with something to report on at Cabinet meetings. Wayne could report on the same upcoming psychiatry survey for three weeks in a row. Elliot was primarily interested in people supplying him with information to cut and paste into the planning reports that had to be sent to Central Office each month. Brian had figured out that the way to deflect attention away from the renovation projects that were grossly behind schedule, was to make sure that he had folders to hand out to everyone. They were full of color copies (because he was also responsible for the print shop). And I'm certain that they went right into the recycling bin after the meeting was over.

Donna's most pressing concern, however, was Nursing. After the JCAHO consultant's devastating report, Donna had also decided to let the Nursing Director go. Finding a replacement was proving to be difficult. We managed to lure one of the Deputy Nursing Directors from Lincoln Hospital. She agreed to come over as an Interim Director for three months, and everyone loved her. But we couldn't convince her to take the job permanently. Then Donna hired Nigel. He'd been the Director of Nursing at Harlem when Donna's sister Dina was the Executive Director, and Dina thought highly of him. When the "Chicago Gangster" took Dina's place, he and Nigel locked horns immediately. Nigel was eventually fired. But if Nigel lost his job because he couldn't get along with "Al Capone," I certainly wasn't going to hold that against him.

As we came closer to the end of our first year, I developed a renewed respect for how awesome an undertaking it was going to be to "make magic" at Woodhull Hospital. I had plenty of reasons to hold Donna in high esteem. When I arrived at Gen + the staff adored her. So I was taken aback by the amount of resistance she was still receiving at Woodhull, even as we neared our first anniversary. If I thought this was going to be an easy assignment I was very much mistaken.

When I moved back to Brooklyn in 1998, I found myself living less than two blocks away from the first place I'd ever lived as a child. My parents bought an apartment at 21 St. James Place when it was still a hole in the ground. And although we moved to Queens when I was four, there were still plenty of people and lots of memories that kept me coming back. Moving back to Clinton Hill meant coming full circle for me. I'd even thought about attending Emmanuel Baptist Church, the church where my sister had gone to nursery school and the place where we both spent many summers before and after we moved away. That was the intention, but I hadn't quite gotten around to it.

Then 2001 arrived, and I was finally ready to start the research for my doctoral dissertation. I'd decided to write about ethnic variations within the Black community. What better place to start than at a Baptist church? Emmanuel was one of three churches that graciously consented to allow me to distribute my research questionnaires. I approached the project like a scientist. I was going to find subjects, collect my data and move on. That was the plan at least.

But for some reason, I found myself returning to Emmanuel. Part of it was familiarity. Attending services there allowed me to reunite with some of the friends I'd grown up with and women who were like second mothers to me. I tried to dismiss my feelings as owing to nothing more than nostalgia. I had chosen to be on the self-study track for my spiritual growth which was fine except for one small problem. I wasn't really studying.

Then one day on my way to work I passed a billboard that read, "God doesn't call the qualified, he qualifies the called." The quote branded itself in my memory. But I had no idea how much it would come to have meaning in my own life. At that point I was simply plodding along, failing to see how events in one part of my life connected to the other parts of my life. I couldn't see it, but I could feel it. I couldn't identify what I was feeling yet, but I was definitely feeling something.

The new year didn't offer any false promises but it brought change nonetheless. New York had a new mayor and a new mayor meant a new president for HHC. Dr. Ferdinand had managed to hold on to the top spot through two different administrations at City Hall and that allowed him to become the longest sitting president in the history of the Corporation. But his luck ran out with Michael R. Bloomberg.

After much speculation, Mayor Bloomberg appointed Dr. Andrew Chang to be president, a physician who had his own history with HHC. He'd also been a medical resident at Kings County Hospital; and he was responsible for Harlem Hospital's medical affiliation contract with Columbia University at the time of his appointment. The significance of his appointment for Woodhull became apparent when during one of his first public addresses, he repeatedly referred to the good old days at Kings County when he walked the halls with "his best friend Ira Gold."

Dr. Chang came into office with a lot of grand ideas that boosted his public profile. Within the Corporation, however, he was making the Sr. Vice-Presidents nuts. He wanted new corporate-wide protocols for chronic disease management. He wanted all of the hospitals to have MRI machines and computerized registries to track patients with specific kinds of medical conditions like diabetes and asthma. Bellevue was getting a brand new ambulatory care pavilion, Coney Island a new bed tower, Jacobi a new hospital and Kings County, a new campus.

His initiatives involved these elaborate productions that he called "collaboratives." They included quarterly meetings with hundreds of people and all of these things cost money - money that the Corporation didn't have. But when that minor detail was raised he would respond, "We need inspired leadership." Translation: "Not my problem. Handle it! Handle it!" Eventually, the Corporation's CFO had enough and after more than twenty years with HHC, we lost him to the private sector. What I didn't know was that one of our new president's "grand ideas", a project he dubbed the Ambulatory Care Redesign initiative, would turn out to be just the spark that Woodhull needed.

By the time we entered 2002, my team seemed to have found a comfortable stride. But the significance of Woodhull's upcoming survey was missed by no one. No matter how many mock surveys we had with summary reports that set off the fire alarms; no matter how many cabinet meetings we had where Gretchen reported, "This is bad. This is really bad. God this place is awful. I don't know what we're going to do"; no matter how long it took to complete a task as simple as painting the lobby, there were still a surprising number of people who thought that Woodhull was better off before Donna and her crew arrived. A horrendous Joint Commission survey would be a perfect way to prove it.

It was time for some dramatic action. The never-ending renovations to the ambulatory care clinics were causing Donna considerable angst. Brian was holding project status meetings every Friday for the ostensible purpose of keeping things on track. We just couldn't tell what track they were watching. Donna called me into her office.

"These renovation projects we've got going on all over the place are starting to make me nervous," she said. "I need you to get in this. Start attending those Friday meetings for me. See if you can give Brian some help to move things along. We can't go into a survey with construction tarp all over the building."

"I'm on it," I replied.

When my boss asked me to take care of something that's what I did. If the assignment took me into someone else's area, that was of no concern to me. I locked on to the target like a heat-seeking missile. Once that happened there were only two places for everyone else to be, in my path or in my vapor trail.

Brian had to that point been unable to deliver any projects on time. It was looking like the three ambulatory care clinics that needed to be completely renovated by the summer, would be no different. Per Donna's request, I began attending the weekly renovation project status meetings, initially just to observe. It didn't take long for me to identify the source of the problem. Woodhull had next to no positive inertia. So any obstacle no matter how small would stop forward progress in its tracks. Once that happened it seemed like no one knew how to press start again. Entire schedules could be stalled indefinitely because one person decided that they didn't want to relocate their office.

As a case in point, a decision had been made months earlier to give a section of the 9th floor over to the Chemical Dependency department so that they could expand their outpatient clinic. I wasn't a fan of the idea of moving the program to that location, but, as Donna used to say, "I know how to be staff." So once the decision was made I assumed it would move forward. Every week at Donna's Executive Cabinet meeting Wayne would report, "We're ready to move in just as soon as the space is ready." But the move never happened.

So at my first renovation project meeting I was eager to learn why a project that required no construction at all couldn't seem to be brought to conclusion.

"Brian, do you know when my people will be able to move in?" Wayne asked.

"The space isn't vacant yet," Brian replied. "As soon as it's vacant we can get it cleaned and ready within 24 hours."

Wayne said okay and Brian was poised to move on to the next agenda item when I stopped him.

"So when is the space going to be vacant?" I asked.

I thought it was a simple question, but, it seemed to stump the group like *Final Jeopardy*. Nobody responded as I watched vacant stares bounce back and forth across the room like ping-pong balls.

"Well . . . ah", Brian said. "I don't know. It's the medical residents. They won't move."

"What do you mean they won't move?" I asked.

Then Yvonne chimed in. The residency program came under the purview of Human Resources.

"We sent letters to the Chiefs about consolidating their on-call rooms in the 9-100 unit," she said.

Brian was visibly relieved at having some verbal support. "We worked out the new room assignments and everything," he said. "But they won't move."

"Did you give them notice of when they had to vacate?" I asked.

"Yes. They were supposed to be out three weeks ago," he said.

"So what's the problem?" I asked.

Brian shrugged. "They won't move."

Somehow we'd just entered an Abbott and Costello routine.

"Well move them!" I said.

Brian blushed but there was no audible response. Clearly I was missing something and I really wanted to know what it was.

And then a funny thing happened on our way to the shoreline. When Donna first announced that we were moving the factory to dry land, most people gave her the sort of glassy-eyed stare that could best be translated into, "Yeah, right. What the hell do you know?" Woodhull was definitely a "this is the way we've always done it" kind of place when we first came back. Needless to say, nobody packed for the move right away.

But there was this small group. They seemed to linger in the corner after the meetings with a strange look on their faces. It suggested a composition of both fear and hope. Eventually, one by one they would approach, always alone when no one was looking, careful not to be spotted by the others. They'd grab us by the arm and ask with an almost inaudible whisper of anticipation, "Are you really going to move the factory to dry land?" When we responded affirmatively, they would express a palpable sense of relief. "Thank God! I knew you couldn't build widgets under water," they'd say. "But I didn't want to say anything because I thought I was the only one. What do you want me to do?"

And that's how we built a little army. These were usually people who hadn't been at the hospital very long, so they still found it frustrating when their tools floated away. But there were also a few old-timers who were willing to try working a different way. Whenever we discovered these little troopers we gave them a rope and told them to start pulling. And they did. One of those people was Brian's deputy, Dana. I knew she was something special right away.

149

"Well, Candis . . ." she said. Her first few words were tentative. But Brian didn't seem to mind so she continued. "We've tried to move them but they give the facilities staff a hard time. My staff gets stuck in the middle."

"What do you mean by a hard time?" I asked.

Dana seemed so relieved that someone was finally asking the right questions.

"We brought them boxes. We offered to move their things. But every time the housekeepers knock on their doors the residents say that they're sleeping and tell the staff to go away."

"Do the Chiefs of Service know this?" I asked

"Yes. They know," Brian answered.

I wanted to make sure all the bases had been covered. Dana handed me a copy of the notices that had been plastered all over the unit. Judging from the date on the bottom, the occupants had indeed known for weeks. Brian was looking as frustrated as Dana, which I found amusing since at that point his title was higher than mine.

"And each Chief knows where their new rooms are?" I continued.

"Yes they know," said Yvonne. "We went through the room assignments with them over and over again. They don't like it because all the services are getting fewer rooms, but they know."

Now, even Brian was feeling empowered. "The problem is, practically every resident has their own on-call room right now. You should see it up there. They've turned them into apartments. They've got microwaves and refrigerators. I found a couch in one of the rooms!"

"Who let them do that?" I asked.

Once again, I thought it was a simple question. But after watching Brian's recently acquired air of empowerment seep out of him like the air in a punctured bicycle tire, I thought it was best not to press that particular issue. It didn't matter. I had heard enough anyway.

"Okay. Here's what we're going to do." I explained that we were going to send the notices around one more time. We'd give them until midnight Thursday. "On Friday at 8:00 a.m., I want a locksmith and two housekeepers up on that unit," I said. The blood drained from Brian's face.

"I don't want my staff to get yelled at," he said. "Who's going to make the residents leave if they don't want to?"

"I am," I said. "I'll meet your staff up there."

He agreed with an expression that read, "Better you than me." I made sure to inform all the Chiefs myself that I would be personally supervising the relocation. Interestingly enough, the hallways were as quiet as a country chapel by the time I arrived. The entire unit was empty, cleaned and ready for occupancy by noon. When I arrived at that afternoon's project status meeting, I pushed Brian to the side and started handing out assignments. And he let me. He'd managed to survive twenty-plus years in the Corporation in large part by being pliable. I guess he decided that it was easier (and safer) to be in my vapor trail. It was a bloodless coup.

After three years of planning, I took one look at the designs for the ambulatory care clinics and knew immediately that they were inadequate. What we needed to do was gut the entire space and rebuild from the ground up. My new plans for the clinics were going to cost several million dollars. But thanks to the thriftiness of June and Lois, we were sitting on quite a little nest egg. I went to Donna with my idea. I'd redrawn the architect's plans myself on some tracing paper they'd given me. I finished my presentation and readied myself for any number of questions I thought Donna might pepper me with. But there weren't any. All she said was

"Go for it. I'm sure as hell not giving this money to Bellevue." I loved that woman.

I went over the new plans for the medicine clinic with Cora White, my service line administrator for Medicine. "You don't have enough chairs in the waiting room," she said. Cora was one of the last additions to my team. A down-to-earth administrator, she'd worked her way up through the system, rising from a medical records clerk to the administrator of our largest service. She didn't mind rolling up her sleeves to get her hands dirty if that's what it took to get the job done. Those are the people I pick first when I'm assembling a team.

"Patients don't come here to wait," I said in response. "They come here to be seen. If we've got more than 40 people in the waiting room, we're doing something wrong." I was determined to bring an end to the days of having mob scenes in the waiting area where people brought their breakfast and lunch to the clinics with them.

The old Woodhull team couldn't manage to spruce up the clinics in three years. We tore the space down to the studs and rebuilt it in six months. The brand new medicine clinic opened in June of 2002. The Pediatrics and OB/GYN clinics were up and open by August. We'd fixed the physical environment. That left the inner workings to be tackled and that job proved to be much more formidable. I decided to take a walk through the new clinic during the second week after we reopened in the new space. When I arrived I thought we were in the middle of a police action. There were people everywhere. We didn't have enough chairs in the waiting room and it looked like we didn't have enough chairs in the building.

As I waded through the sea of forlorn faces I passed Rhonda, Cumberland's Administrator, standing against a wall with a smirk on her face. "Is it always like this?" she asked smugly. "This is so chaotic I feel uncomfortable being in here."

"Well, you could always leave," I replied.

I called Cora to come down from her office and we both scratched our heads while we tried to figure out what went wrong. I soon discovered that it always looked like that, even though they now had twice the space they had before. But I was beside myself with frustration when I went into the back and found most of the exam rooms empty except for the physicians who were reading the daily paper while eating their breakfast. We were definitely doing something wrong.

I returned to the executive suite just in time to see Rhonda leaving Donna's office, her now trademark smirk firmly implanted on her face. "Rough day in the medicine clinic I hear," Donna said. I took a seat across from her desk.

"She couldn't wait to tell you, could she?" I said.

"It looks like we're getting this just in time," Donna said. She handed me a memo inviting both of us to the first leadership meeting of the Ambulatory Care Redesign initiative.

"Is this that project Andrew is planning?" I asked.

"Yes. According to our president, patients will be in and out of our clinics in 60 minutes – start to finish," she said with a bemused grin.

"This I've got to see," I said.

The windfall of managed care transition grant money that HHC received fell into that category of gifts that inspired the saying "be careful what you wish for because you might get it." The final version of the legislation grouped the grant funds into specific categories with strict requirements for how the money could be used. The funds in some categories evaporated over night. In other categories, we couldn't think of enough ways to spend it. Dr. Ferdinand used some of the funds for that customer service training initiative in the fall of 1998; a training that turned out to be a colossal waste of time and money. If we had rude clerks it wasn't because they didn't know how to be nice. They chose not to be and we weren't giving them much reason to act any differently.

Dr. Chang's new Ambulatory Care Redesign project managed to fit within a category that still had money to burn, so burn we did. The Corporation hired consultants to manage what would be a two-to-three year project. Each redesign "collaborative" lasted nine months and involved training hundreds of people on how to collect data and manage change. I was skeptical, but, I was also desperate. So we entered Woodhull's medicine clinic in the first round.

If there was one lesson that came out of the collaborative that made it worth the cost of admission, it was the emphasis on picking the right people for the team. I personally selected each member of the first group more for their energy and attitude than for their technical skills. Cora and a young man from the IT department became the team leaders. The consultants also recommended that the team have a champion on the executive staff. There was no question about who that was going to be.

It was a bold move to pick our busiest clinic to be the first one in the project. Most networks picked Pediatrics because that service was smaller and easier to manage. But I've always been one for jumping into the deep end of the pool.

The collaborative was organized with precision. Each one required four major gatherings where all of the redesign teams throughout the Corporation would meet and compare notes. In between each gathering, the teams had a number of goals to accomplish. First they had to collect statistics on how their clinics were functioning currently. Then they had to design a new model that would make the clinics operate more efficiently. Then they had to test this new model.

The training that the teams received was extremely valuable in helping the groups to stay on track. Even more important, it gave them previews about what to expect from their co-workers when the time came for them to test their new models in the clinic. I kept a close watch on what they were doing. It was just as the consultants had predicted. The test team created a cocoon for their sessions. They had their own registration clerk, their own nurse and their own physician. It was as if their patients were operating in a parallel universe.

At the same time, the rest of the staff in the clinic had been carefully scrutinizing this strange group of people moving around them, collecting data and having meetings in the clinic conference room. In the beginning the bulk of the staff, from clerks to physicians, was braced and ready to resist any attempt to change how they worked. You could hear the complaints echoing through the hallways.

But when no one asked them to do anything differently, their resistance turned into curiosity. Of course, they wouldn't admit it at first. But, you would see them from time to time peeking into the conference room when the redesign team was having a meeting or casting surreptitious glances toward the exam rooms where the pilot tests were being conducted. The consultants also trained the team to be on the look-out for the informal leader of the resistance.

To our surprise, their recommendation was not to ship this person out. To the contrary, they suggested that this individual would turn out to be the star of the project. I was sure the consultants made their first misstep with that advice. They'd never met Niecey. "They better not come over here with that mess!" she'd say loudly. "Always wasting money reinventing the wheel. If they want to throw money away, throw it my way."

But the medicine clinic redesign team was undaunted. They saw eight patients during their first pilot session. They broke for lunch as a team and were finished with all their patients by the time the clinic was supposed to close at 4 p.m. That was enough to get anyone's attention. The morning clinic sessions always spilled over into the lunch hour and overtime was a way of life. There were a lot more peering eyes when the second pilot test got under way. But when Niecey passed the exam rooms all she said was, "Humph." She still wasn't impressed.

By the fourth pilot, however, the redesign team added a second group to the project and the buzz was beginning to spill out into the hallways. They regularly reported to me on their progress. Part of my job was to remove any barriers they were encountering. I could do that in my sleep. I was in my office one morning when Cora stopped by to tell me a story. She was glowing like a halogen light bulb.

"I just came from the medicine clinic," she said. "You're not going to believe what Niecey just said to me." I'd had enough encounters with Niecey to seriously doubt that there was anything she could say that would surprise me. "She came walking up to me in the clinic," Cora said, her glow undiminished. "And she said, 'Ms. White, you know your teams are being held up because all their patients have to go to the nursing station to get their vital signs taken before they go to the exam room. We can take vitals.'" Niecey was a Patient Care Associate and she was absolutely right. They could. Cora now had my full attention because Niecey wasn't finished giving advice.

"If you put a scale and some equipment in the exam room you can cut the nursing station out altogether," Niecey said. "Put a PCA on the team and it will save you a lot of time." Cora's smile was blinding me now. I was still wearing my poker face but Cora had one more quote to share before she was done. Before Niecey returned to her duties she turned to Cora and said, "By the way, Ms. White, you can put me on the next team. I don't mind." Cora won that poker game because I folded. I was now smiling as hard as she was.

"Can you believe it?" she said. "Girl, I think we're about change something in here. I'm so emotional I don't know what to do next."

"I do," I said. "Get that child a scale and some equipment and put her on a team!"

By the third collaborative gathering, Cora and the Woodhull medicine clinic were the Belles of the Ball. The initiative as a whole was proceeding relatively well for HHC, with some groups doing better and some doing worse. But Woodhull's medicine clinic was performing so well you would have thought they were a plant. The consultants raved about the team and they loved Cora. Her shoot-from-the-hip style doesn't work for everyone, but, if you wanted results you wanted Cora. And her staff loved her for it.

The collaborative had reached the stage where the teams were supposed to present their final models to their executive champion for approval. Then they would develop a schedule for rolling the plan out to the entire clinic. That part of the project was supposed to take three weeks. But the entire medicine clinic held a team meeting. I believe Niecey was their spokesperson. They had a simple message they wanted Cora to deliver to me. "We don't want to wait three weeks to roll out this new model. We're ready now."

So they did. In the process the medicine clinic started a minor revolution at Woodhull. Their dramatic turnaround sent out some sort of sonic pulse that reverberated throughout the building. I had Chiefs of Service and department directors from all over the network asking me when redesign was coming to their area. The surface changes were obvious. The clinic sessions now started on time and ended on time. They were actually able to close the clinic for lunch so that every employee could take their lunch break. Overtime disappeared.

But whatever we changed happened at the cellular level. And it was those subtle changes, I believe, that made what was happening in the medicine clinic so infectious. We never said a word about customer service. As it turned out, we didn't have to. The staff was polite to the patients because they were polite to each other. They liked working together. It's amazing how much more productive staff become when they actually look forward to coming to work. That was the "stuff" that the rest of the hospital wanted a little bit more of.

I contacted Central Office to see if we could accelerate the timetable and bring more clinics into the program. But they were still moving at the speed of government. The moment I hear the word "can't" I stop listening. If Woodhull wanted redesign, we were going to give them redesign. For the first time in history, we were getting calls from other hospitals in the Corporation to ask if they could take tours of our clinics.

The Dental clinic, the Eye clinic, Pediatrics, Women's Health, even the Radiology Department - they all organized redesign teams. The energy the teams were generating was palpable. And that gave me an idea. I went to Donna.

"You know these redesign teams are really taking off," I said.

"I know," she said. "They can't believe it at Central Office. Not little old Woodhull."

"I was thinking," I said. "What if we created a redesign project for the inpatient service?"

Donna looked intrigued. "They certainly need something," she said.

Important work gets done in ambulatory care. Patients are *made* well on the inpatient service; they *stay* well in the outpatient service. And thanks to our increased efficiency, business was booming for the network. But a hospital's bread and butter will always be its inpatient service. Outpatient services may be noble and necessary, but for some reason when they're attached to a hospital, they always lose money – at least in New York. So, inpatient revenues are what pay for outpatient services.

But it was Woodhull's inpatient service that continued to earn the hospital its deplorable reputation in the community. We needed to find a way to send that sonic pulse that the staff was generating on the ground floor up through the elevator shafts. At Donna's suggestion, I went to Nigel first to talk to him about my idea. The nursing department had never warmed to the idea that my administrators had managerial functions on the inpatient units as well as the outpatient clinics. It was a constant tug of war for control. But Nigel and I got along pretty well. And despite his promises to Donna that he had the cure for what ailed the department, Nursing was still struggling now almost nine months after his arrival. He looked weary when I met with him. "At this point," he said, "I'm willing to try anything."

With his blessing, I prepared a presentation for the Cabinet. It was really more of a formality since the bulk of the work would be split between Nigel's staff and mine. But half way through the presentation it was clear to me that I was not connecting with my colleagues. The presentation was being met with an unmistakable frigidness. After I finished, I went to Ira. "Was there something wrong with the presentation?" I asked.

"I don't know," he said "It definitely seemed like no one was listening to you."

I left Ira no more enlightened than when we began our conversation so I went to Donna next. Unlike Ira, she had an explanation. "I think most of the Cabinet just didn't care," she said. "Once you said the project wouldn't cost any money, you lost Tom. Yvonne's only interested in the HR angle, and what did you expect from Wayne and Elliot? No, I'll tell you where the cold shoulder came from."

"Don't tell me. Let me guess," I said, "Gretchen and Maura."

"You got it," she said. "And you're going to love this. Gretchen came to see me right after the meeting ended. She said, 'I think you need to talk to Maura. She's feeling very hurt'."

"Hurt?!!"

Donna put her hand up to stop me before I could continue. There was more.

"Right. For what?" Donna said. "That's what I wanted to know. Apparently, Maura's feelings were hurt that you didn't come to speak to her about the project first. She's doing all that work with the case management rounds and your presentation didn't acknowledge her."

"Is she serious?" I asked. "Case Management is only one small part of the inpatient service."

Donna was getting angry just thinking about the conversation again. "I know it!" she said. "I told Gretchen 'No. I'm not going to speak to Maura. If you want to help her, take her this message from me. Tell her I said to pick today to grow!'"

It was ridiculous but not surprising. I'd worked in the same suite with Maura for almost two years at that point and I'd learned a lot about her in the process. Many mid-level managers struggle with the transition to executive leadership because they don't know how to delegate. They tend to be overly involved in the decisions their managers make. That described Maura to perfection.

She was one of the most intrusive managers I'd ever observed. Even after Donna had all but the timesheets for the executive staff removed from the suite, there was still a constant parade of people coming in and out. We had Maura to thank for that. Morning, noon and night there'd be one group inside her office and another one waiting in the wings to be next. I remember thinking it odd. She only had a hand full of managers who directly reported to her so who was she meeting with?

I soon learned that she held supervisory meetings with her managers *and* all of the staff who reported to them. It rendered her managers impotent. Maura's office wasn't large so she usually had to leave the door open to accommodate the number of people inside. You could see her department directors sitting in their chairs with slumped shoulders, looking like wilted lettuce while she held court. And even if you didn't see her you could always hear her. She was very loud. That's how I knew she verbally berated her staff. She saw nothing wrong with speaking to them like they were children. Everyone has their own style. That just happens to be a style that I abhor.

One of the things I always drilled into the managers who worked with me was the expectation that they be respectful to their staff at all times. You can be stern without being rude. People will only do so much out of fear and they absolutely cannot grow. But you didn't have to spend a lot of time around Maura to figure out that, more than her limitations as a manager her biggest problem was that she needed to be the center of attention. Maura was a television with only one channel. It had to be all Maura, all the time.

We'd just passed the eighteen-month mark of our return, and while my own staff had come together as a team, the Executive Cabinet still hadn't. At best we were co-existing. Gretchen and Maura became a tag team almost immediately. They in turn absorbed Wayne and Elliot through osmosis. Rhonda seemed to have formed some sort of relationship with Gretchen, although, I'm not sure they ever became friends. She quickly alienated herself from the rest of the Cabinet as all of her reports turned into weekly variations on the mantra "no one pays attention to Cumberland."

Outside of that merry band of revelers the rest of us functioned autonomously, only interacting if circumstances forced our paths to cross. Each of us considered "our team" to be the members of our own staff, not each other. That was as true of me as anyone. But as my responsibilities continued to grow, I think my team came to personify Gulliver among the Lilliputians. Unbeknownst to me, "Clinical Operations" and its fearsome leader became both loathed and admired.

"There go the Dolls," Donna said. My weekly service line meeting was just breaking up. It was larger than usual because I'd invited Bobby the Radiology Administrator and a few other members of the Clinical Operations division to attend. I knew it was Donna speaking before I turned around because she was the one who gave that nickname to my all-female crew of service line administrators. "I get such a kick out of watching your people," she said.

"Oh yeah? What's so funny?" I asked.

She was needling me on purpose. She knew I was like a mother lioness when it came to my staff. Nobody could talk about them but me. We were standing in the small hallway that led from the executive office conference room to her office and we were watching my staff as they mingled in the suite on their way back out into the world.

"All kidding aside," she said. "That's one thing everyone always gave you credit for at Gen +. You know how to put a team together. Your people like to work together and they love working for you."

"You think so?" I said.

The comment caught me by surprise. It wasn't something I'd given any thought to of late. But that casual observation reminded me that despite my concerns that I would never find another team like the one I had at Gen +, this Woodhull group was shaping up nicely.

"What do you do to them?" she asked, still grinning.

"What do you mean what do I do to them? Now you're just being funny."

"No, I'm serious. Look at them," she said, gesturing in the direction of group. "Your people don't just walk in and out of room. They strut peacock-style."

Donna had a talent for artful phrasing. But through the laughter, her remarks did cause me to take another look at "my people." They were in the process of leaving the suite just as another group of Maura's staff was filing in. The difference in their demeanors made for a striking contrast. There was Maura's group, shoulders bowed, forcing their faces into plastic grins. They shuffled into her office like weathered garden gnomes called before the royal court to do another dance of the sycophants.

And then there was my group, heads up, shoulders back, infused with gaiety. Their arms swung as they walked like they were off to conquer the Philistines. Looking at the two groups side by side I thought, "They do look a little like peacocks don't they?" It wasn't arrogance. It was confidence, although, the difference between the two is often missed by people who are lacking the latter. If my staff thought that they could conquer the world then I could rest easy that my message was getting through to them loud and clear. That's what they were supposed to think.

By the time the fall arrived, the network was limping but momentum was building nonetheless. There were still pockets of resistance here and there but their voices were getting weaker and weaker. There was simply too much to marvel at. Three new clinics, a new lobby, and Donna didn't stop with the physical plant. She went all out for employee-related celebrations. The staff mobbed the line at our first employee appreciation barbeque like refugees from a war zone. After that she said, "We have to do something for these people. I don't think they get out much."

So we started having events. Lots of events. We held our own "Showtime at the Apollo." We hired a live band, my Dolls were the Apollo Dancers, a member of the housekeeping staff dressed up as Sandman and yours truly played KiKi Sheppard. We had a spa day with free massages and manicures, a relaxation room and even held a pep rally leading up to the Joint Commission survey itself. Donna didn't mind spending every dime of the surplus we inherited as long as we spent it on patients and staff. Between the events and the continuing buzz that our redesign teams were generating, it was a formula that more and more of the staff began to respond to. Many were responding, perhaps most, but not all.

In the midst of the countdown to Joint Commission, Donna found herself with an uncomfortable dilemma that she was being forced to confront.

"You've got to help me," she said to me late one afternoon.

"Okay. What's the matter?"

I couldn't tell whether she was joking or not. There was a chuckle in her voice and a smile on her face but concern was lurking behind her eyes. I never took my eyes off of her as I sat down.

"You've got to help me do something with Angela," she said.

She definitely had a problem on her hands and it was one of her own making. Donna hired Angela Highland to run a small grant-funded program at Cumberland a few months before she left in 1998. Lois fired Angela within a few months after I arrived and it was one of the few times that I could defend, at least in part, the decision she made. I knew Angela only in passing then, and from what I encountered she seemed like a delightful person.

But she ran into trouble because she fancied herself a scholar. And she liked to show it with overly erudite responses to every question whether the question was directed to her or not. Somewhere down the line, she rubbed someone the wrong way at Central Office. That is something that is easy to do and almost always fatal. I distinctly remember a conversation Lois and Vonetta had about Angela while I was in the room one day.

"Tell Angela to keep her mouth shut when she goes to those meetings downtown. They're not interested in what she has to say. Just tell her to collect the information and come back. Don't say anything." I'm sure Vonetta delivered the message. But Angela either couldn't or wouldn't heed it. She was gone within the month.

I think Donna believed Angela was fired because of their friendship and not because of anything Angela had done. So she decided to bring her back. Angela joined the Cabinet within weeks of our return in 2001 but without a defined role. I knew from personal experience, that was a recipe for disaster. I never shared what I knew about the reason for Angela's dismissal. There didn't seem to be any point at first, partly because Donna had already rehired her and partly because what I heard, I was in no position to verify at the time. But the facts soon verified themselves.

I knew why Donna and I were having this conversation at this particular moment in time. As the survey drew closer, we were having more frequent meetings with the Chiefs of Service and we'd just come from one. Donna was discussing how she wanted to handle the process of preparing for the survey. Someone as academic as Angela could not resist the opportunity to be involved in a discussion like this. The survey process is dictated by the voluminous standards that the Joint Commission releases and refines on an annual basis. Spouting regulations brought Angela to orgasm.

We were just about to adjourn the meeting when Angela raised her hand. I saw it. I know Donna saw it. But by the look on her face, Donna was trying to figure out a way to pretend that she didn't. She said, "Okay, thank you everybody." She was so close, but, she wasn't fast enough. Angela interrupted. "Excuse me, Donna. I just want to say something." I could see Donna's coffee-colored complexion flicker with crimson.

"Yes Angela," she said. The impending dread seemed to curl her vocal chords.

"Well . . ." Angela began. Always articulate and visually expressive, this would be the only hesitation in her discourse. "These were all excellent points that everyone brought up. But it's important to remember that the JCAHO standards were promulgated in such a way that we have to make sure that we review them differently than we did before. There was an advisory opinion that I copied last week and I really think that we should all review it. We have to reorganize our thinking processes to make sure that WAA, WAA, WAA, WAA, WAA."

I tried so hard to hold on. I knew I wasn't the only one who thought that Angela sounded like the adults in a Charlie Brown cartoon when she spoke at a meeting. I'd polled people. We all agreed that she was speaking English, but, nobody ever knew what she was talking about. So people stopped listening to her. That only made it worse. She was very sensitive. I think the problem was that she didn't like being without a defined role so she tried to create one. And she could be quite obstreperous in making her point if she thought people weren't taking her seriously. Slights were met with even longer, more rambling, more confusing recitations.

I don't know whether it was the pressure of an approaching survey or the fact that it was late in the day. This had been going on for months but for some reason at this particular meeting, Angela took everyone over the edge. She was still talking.

"And you know, we really need to pay attention to WAA, WAA, WAA, WAA, WAA." Meanwhile, I watched everyone around the table. As Angela continued to speak everyone else in the room began to lie back in their chairs, their necks started to get limp and their eyes were rolling up into their skulls. It was like watching a cascading epileptic seizure. Donna saw it too.

Now sitting in her office all I could do was stare at Donna. Her laughter wasn't convincing. There was a discernable level of desperation threading through her voice.

"Come on. I've never asked you for anything before," she said. "You've got to help me."

"Donna you know I'd do anything for you but help you do what?" I asked.

"I don't know," she said. "Give her some direction."

"Give her some direction! Are you kidding?"

"I can't believe you're going to turn your back on me like this after everything I've done for you!" she said.

Desperation or no desperation, it was now getting funny, even though we knew we shouldn't be laughing.

"Donna, you know she's not going to take direction from me."

"I'll get on my knees if I have to," she said.

And she actually started to bend a knee. We were both laughing so hard we were crying. But we couldn't avoid the unavoidable forever.

"Donna, ask me anything else. You know there's nothing I can do about this." Just like that, the laughter was gone, for both us. Angela's strained relationship with the rest of the Cabinet and the Chiefs had passed awkward long ago. I knew Donna didn't have any options left and so did she. This called for a decision that only she could make. She made it, but, it couldn't have been easy. Nobody likes to hurt a friend.

We were moving toward the shoreline slowly, but we were moving nonetheless. But now weeks shy of the survey, between running my departments and the renovation projects, I was burning out. It all came to a head one Thursday afternoon. It was such a trivial thing looking back on it. We were deciding on additions for the new lobby. Brian mentioned that he wanted to move the command center for Hospital Police up to the corner that had previously been occupied by the Gift Shop.

I thought it was a terrible idea to waste such prime space. Everything in the lobby should have something to do with Patient and/or Guest services. The command center could go anywhere. I thought we had agreed that we were going to move the information desk to that corner and outfit it to look more like a hotel reception desk. I was sitting in the conference room when someone happened to mention in passing that Hospital Police had just finished moving into the "old Gift Shop."

I can't remember ever losing my temper the way I did that day. To this day, it is one of the few actions that I deeply regret. I stood up and walked around to Brian's office. His office was empty, but, he had his own conference room and that door was closed. Without knocking I threw the door open so hard that he, Dana and the two other members of his staff who were also the room, actually jumped back in their seats. "I TOLD YOU THAT HOSPITAL POLICE WAS NOT MOVING INTO THE LOBBY!!! HOW DARE YOU MOVE THEM WITHOUT SPEAKING TO ME FIRST!"

For once, Brian mustered up an ounce of courage and tried to stand up to me. "Don't yell at me in front of my staff," he said. It was a meek response but considering the fact that steam had to be coming out of my ears, it still took a lot of courage for him to get even that much out. He didn't say anything else and I was getting madder by the moment.

"YOU KNOW WHAT? I'VE HAD IT WITH YOU!" I yelled.

I stormed out of his conference room and headed straight for Donna's office. Her door was open and I rarely knocked so she didn't react immediately to me coming straight to her desk. That was until she saw the wild look in my eyes. Then she sat back in her chair, way back. I wasn't yelling, but I was clearly still very angry.

"I have had it with Brian. I want him fired right now!"

Her response was unperturbed both in tone and expression. She folded her arms across her chest and said, "Four weeks before Joint Commission? I don't think so. Brian's not going anywhere."

"Then I'm not going to any more renovation meetings," I said. "That's it. I'm finished!"

"Okay," she said.

I stormed out of her office.

My parents happened to stop by for lunch the next day. When they went into Donna's office to say hello, she walked up to my mother and said, "You know that daughter of yours came marching into my office yesterday and I thought she was going to kick my ass. What do you do with her when she gets all riled up like that?"

I was so embarrassed. My parents just shook their heads. My mother casually waved her hand like she was swatting a fly and said, "Oh, we can't do anything with her when she gets like that. We just sit quietly and wait for it to pass. Fortunately, it doesn't happen often." My father was standing right beside my mother nodding silently in concurrence. There was not a voice in the room that would come to my defense.

It was an odd and humbling experience. Having my boss and my parents discussing my behavior while I was standing in the room made me feel like we were in the middle of a parent-teacher conference. I found myself drifting toward a distant corner with my hands in my pockets, kicking at imaginary rocks.

I must admit, I was born a handful. From an early age my older sister was as close to an ideal child as a parent could ask for. For the most part she did whatever she was told. According to my mother when my sister was a small toddler, not more than two years old, my mother could dress her and then sit her in the middle of the bed with a book and these instructions,

"Sweetheart, I want you to sit here and read this picture book while Mommy gets ready. You stay right here, okay?" And my sister, looking like a caramel-colored cherub, would smile back at her with pudgy, dimple-imbedded cheeks and big brown eyes and say, "Okay Mommy." It didn't matter whether it took my mother 15 minutes to get ready or 45 minutes (and knowing my mother it was closer to 45). When she returned to the bedroom she would find my sister right where she'd left her, sitting in the middle of the bed, reading a picture book.

But when it was my turn, things didn't go so well. I don't profess to remember exactly how I handled the situation at two years old. But judging from what I know about myself and everything my family has told me about my personality even at that tender age, I believe the scenario played out thusly.

My mother dressed me, sat me in the middle of the bed with a book and gave me the same speech she'd given to my sister seven years earlier. I looked at the book, and then I looked up at her and smiled. But I'm sure I didn't say anything. My mother may have interpreted that smiling silence to mean "Okay, Mommy." But what I was actually thinking was, "I didn't ask you for this book. In fact, I see four or five things in this room that I find infinitely more interesting than this book and I'm going to get into every one of them as soon as you round that corner."

I know for a fact that when she returned to the bedroom, she found me coated from forehead to foot in petroleum jelly and baby powder. It didn't take too many more interactions like that for my mother to decide, "I need to deal with this one differently." I was truly blessed to have been born to my parents. Had it been any other couple, I'm certain that I would have landed on the back of a milk carton years ago.

When the next renovation meeting took place, I was in my office signing requisitions. Sometime after it was over, I heard a knock at the door. It was Dana.

"Can I come in?" she asked.

"Sure."

Before she could say anything else I offered her the apology that I'd been too embarrassed to give to Brian directly.

"I have to apologize for my outburst yesterday. It was so unprofessional. I don't know what got into me," I said.

"I figured something had to have really upset you. I've never seen you lose your temper before."

"It doesn't matter what it was. There was no excuse for that," I said.

"I understand" she said. "I just came to ask you if you would please reconsider coming back to the meetings."

"No." I was adamant about that.

"We just get so much done when you run the meetings," she said. "We really need you there."

Her pleas softened me a little but not enough.

"Dana, there aren't that many projects left. You can handle them. If you need me for something just call me or send me an email. I'll always help you if I can, but, it's time for me to pull out of Facilities' work and focus on my own."

I wasn't sure whether my pulling out of the meeting would have an impact or not. But something miraculous happened. It didn't. They no longer needed me. Between the hidden stars we found like Dana and the ones we added along the way, Brian discovered that addictive quality that accompanies actually getting projects delivered on time. His team gathered momentum and they never looked back. I wasn't the only one who benefited from working for Donna. She definitely had an impact on him as well. He wasn't the slacker on the Cabinet anymore and he liked how that felt. You could tell.

There were still plenty of people who resented the push to dry land. I had a saying I used to repeat to my staff often in the early days. When you enter a chaotic situation you have to remember that some people are benefiting from the chaos. Those are the people who fight change no matter how obvious the benefits are to everyone else.

That was half the battle. The other half had to do with perceptions of loyalty. No matter how inept I thought the prior administration had been, there were plenty of people who still thought that Lois was the best CEO Woodhull ever had. Not surprisingly, the largest group of loyalists was clustered among the nursing staff. She was one of their own. It was to be expected. We were never going to win some of them over. A few left, but, the ones who remained would have loved nothing better than to see the hospital crash and burn during the survey, and they kept busy stirring up trouble.

It did not help that despite our high expectations, Nigel had not managed to win over the majority of the nursing staff. Donna called him into her office as our countdown to the survey continued. "Nigel, when I hired you," she said "you told me that I wouldn't have to worry about Nursing anymore. It's been almost a year and all I do is worry about Nursing."

He wasn't solely to blame. The biggest problem we had was instability. We couldn't keep nurses. They'd start, stay a month and then leave. The morale was in the toilet. Nigel had no problems recruiting nurses when he worked at Harlem Hospital, even with his reputation for leading with a firm hand. We thought that perhaps that's what Woodhull needed. Apparently it wasn't. Being the Chief Nursing Officer is a pressure-cooker position in any hospital. He joined us with less than a year to go until the survey, with a demoralized staff and fragile leadership underneath him. I'm not sure anyone could survive that kind of pressure.

I remember wandering into Donna's office shortly after one of her meetings with him. The situation was coming to a head. We received word that half the ICU nursing staff was planning to quit right before the survey. Nigel assured Donna it wouldn't happen, but, she wasn't encouraged. I was leaning in the doorway that separated the vast expanse of Donna's office from the office of her assistant, Mimi. When Donna saw me she couldn't contain her frustration.

"Nigel has got to go!" she said. "I can't take it anymore. I could do better running that department by myself. Mimi, get Yvonne on the phone!"

I gestured for Mimi not to pick up the phone. It was probably not the time for sarcasm, but, there are some set-ups that are just too good to pass up. I folded my arms just like Donna had at me a week earlier and I made no attempt to repress the grin as I spoke.

"Three weeks before Joint Commission? I don't think so. He's not going a-n-y-w-h-e-e-r-r-r-e-e."

The look Donna gave me at that moment was priceless. She was so mad I think she would have spit at me like a camel if she wasn't such a refined and distinguished charm school graduate. Instead, she just glowered at me for a minute. She didn't like it, but, she had to admit it. I got her good that time.

"Get out of my office," she snarled. The only thing missing from that statement was the word "bitch" but judging from her expression it was on the tip of her tongue. I obliged without delay. My good deed was done for the day.

It was only a matter of time now. Gretchen had practically lost her voice from criticizing so much. We feared we'd have to put her on suicide watch soon. There were lots of doubts. Donna and I talked about it often as the clock wound down. Despite Nigel's assurances to the contrary, the rumors proved true and those ICU nurses walked out two weeks before the survey. To add insult to injury, they transferred to another HHC hospital. For the life of us we couldn't understand how that network's human resources department could process the transfer when they knew that we were heading into a survey and they weren't. But there was no time to dwell on that. In the final days before the survey we reached a point where we had to have faith in the power of things unseen, because everywhere we looked we saw problems.

We were the first of the HHC hospitals surveyed that year. We held our breath, prayed that the attention to the staff, the momentum from our achievements and the preparation was enough. It was. To our amazement and the shock of the free world, Woodhull scored a 98. Two other HHC hospitals scored 98 that year, but, we were the first. Since it was the last year that the Joint Commission issued scores with the survey results, it also meant that no other hospital would ever score higher.

WE'D BROUGHT THE WIDGET Factory to a point where the top few floors were drying out and the results were showing. I saw it as a major hurdle leaped. Perhaps a more accurate analogy would be that I had finally given birth because I was starting to feel the effects of post-partum depression. Or perhaps I was just tired. Swimming under water requires effort. Running under water requires a lot more. And so much of the job was thankless during the first few years.

I could respect the people who, not liking the way things were changing, decided to leave. But very few people did. Most of the disgruntled just dug in their heels, probably because they had no place else to go. Nobody came to Woodhull to recruit. Instead, with every three tugs we made toward land there were two tugs back into the water. I would uncover practices that were so unprofessional that I wondered how they could ever have been implemented in the first place.

The word "embarrassed" doesn't seem adequate to describe how I felt when, after having been responsible for Woodhull's laboratory for nearly two years, I discovered purely by chance that there were no supervisors in the building on the weekends. They just carried beepers in case somebody needed them. I went ballistic and changed the practice immediately. But as I had to rather awkwardly explain to Donna, "That's not something I would have even thought to check!"

And then there was just the bizarre. We once had an employee call a Code Blue -- the code for the trauma team -- on another employee only to find out the employee wasn't dead, he was sleeping. Then there was the time that an employee fell in the basement and instead of calling for a stretcher, they dialed 911. The paramedics could barely contain their laughter as they came into the hospital to transport one of our employees up one flight in the elevator to our own emergency room.

And the patients themselves could be a highly effective source of torment from time to time. One ICU patient decided that he wanted to take a cigarette break within the confines of his room. Only he failed to remove the oxygen cannula from his nose before he lit up – literally! When the nursing staff heard a loud "poof!" accompanied by a flash of light that shot through his window blinds, they rushed into his room and found him sitting upright in his bed, cigarette still in hand and white plumes of smoke wafting from his scalp. His eyes were all you could see of him and they were as big as baseballs. The rest of his face was covered with soot.

Once the survey was over, it was back to the mind-numbing reality of the amount of work that still lay ahead of us if we really wanted to change things. The adrenaline rush had subsided and the aches and pains were rising to the surface. And to be perfectly honest, I was still more than a little annoyed that I hadn't been appointed Chief Operating Officer yet. I doubt Donna would have disputed that I was already functioning in that capacity. I knew the reason why the appointment hadn't happened, but, I took little comfort in that. It was the first time I started thinking about leaving. I couldn't find enough motivation in simply doing the work.

By July, Donna once again found herself doing a little housekeeping. This time it was Cumberland.

Rhonda was responsible for half of the network's ambulatory care services and I had the other half. The service line structure meant that my Dolls had to work with her when their services intersected with Cumberland or any of the clinics under Rhonda's supervision. As I took over more and more departments like Managed Care and the Appointment Center, it meant Rhonda had to interact with more of my staff. If I hadn't been able to tell before, my staff let me know just how much the mention of my name made Rhonda's blood boil.

One day Jasmine, the service line administrator for Pediatrics, came to me. "Ms. Best, can I talk to you?"

"Sure."

"What's going on between you and Rhonda?" she asked.

"I don't know what you're talking about." I really didn't.

"The way she talks about you, it makes me uncomfortable having to go over to Cumberland," Jasmine continued.

"Is she threatening you?" I asked.

"No," she replied. "I just think it's unprofessional."

"Jasmine, let me ask you something. Do you ever hear me saying anything about Rhonda?" Her response was right on the heels of my question.

"No. Never. We all talk about how one-sided this is."

"My point exactly. Whatever the problem is, it isn't between Rhonda and me because I'm not participating. I don't give it any thought. Neither should you."

The moment my Dolls really began to come together as a team was the day the administrator for Medicine, the one that Cora eventually replaced, went to work for Rhonda. I was not impressed with the woman's work ethic and I was quite direct with her about it. I think the fact that she and I weren't getting along was what made her attractive to Rhonda. Donna tried to warn Rhonda about hiring this person. She saw the same things I saw. But since Donna rarely told her staff how to handle their affairs she relented when Rhonda insisted on hiring the woman. A year later, Rhonda was forced to fire her for the same reasons that I had listed in the woman's performance evaluation.

That fiasco, along with the fact that the ambulatory care services that reported to me were outpacing the ones that reported to Rhonda, led Donna to have another one of those conversations that she didn't like having. When it was over, Rhonda had a clearly discernable reason to hate me. She was going back to her old job as the Director of Managed Care, a department that mercifully was being given back to Finance. And I was given all of Rhonda's old responsibilities, including the running of Cumberland. But Cumberland was a big place that had to have an on-site administrator. Since there was no one else to do it, I had to go. I dreaded the idea. Run a diagnostic and treatment center? Been there, done that. But Donna didn't tax without reward. When I went, I went as the network's new Chief Operating Officer.

CHAPTER TEN
FALL, 2003

FOR ONE SOLID YEAR after the survey, it felt like no one on the senior staff had the energy to do anything more than put one foot in front of the other. But the time had come for us to emerge from the fatigue-induced coma that had blanketed us since the survey ended. There were a few more changes to the leadership team that had not been anticipated. Tom, my red-headed buddy who ran the network's finances, announced that he was retiring. Donna promoted someone from his staff to take his place, but within a few months that person was lured to the private sector. He really regretted having to abandon her so soon after his promotion but he had no choice.

"Donna, please don't ask me to stay. I need the money," he said during the meeting where he submitted his resignation. It was hard to fault him for that.

But fortune was turning in our favor. The Woodhull P.C. had recruited a young man to run their finances, and as it turned out Donna knew him by reputation. He'd worked for HHC before.

"He's not going to be happy working for the P.C.," she told me one day. "I'm going to offer him the CFO position with us."

He accepted, and with Simon we gained a young, bright and very enthusiastic addition to the team who was eager to learn. I was happy to see that my run of having CFO's that I worked well with was not going to end. There was only one loose string. The previous

CFOs had also served as the network's Chief Information Officer – the person responsible for all of the network's technology projects. Donna was concerned that Simon was too new to the executive level to give him that responsibility as well.

"Let me have it," I said.

I'd learned a lot from Nancy when we worked together to bring all those technology initiatives online at Gen +. I really enjoyed it. I'd even helped Tom bring the Pharmacy ordering system online when I returned in 2001. It was one of the projects that we bonded over.

"Hmm, the Corporation has never had a COO/CIO before . . . ," she said as she mulled it over. "But that's no reason not to do it. Okay."

The decision had to be approved by the Corporation's Chief Information Officer but Donna wasn't concerned about that. For one thing, my reputation for getting things done had now almost completely erased the scuttlebutt from the Lois era. More important, no one in Central Office had the stomach for tangling with Donna once she made up her mind about something.

The new responsibilities were just the jolt I needed. In the meantime, Donna decided to engage a consulting group to work with the Woodhull P.C. The administrative side of the network was finally starting to show signs of life and it was becoming more and more apparent that the physician side of the equation was not keeping up. Although, I'm sure the physician leadership would have said that the opposite was true. Kerry Rand and Associates had done work with one of the other networks in HHC and came highly recommended. They began their work with us by interviewing a cross section of the hospital's leadership and key staff, both administrative and clinical.

I'd almost forgotten that the consultants were on the premises when Donna called me into her office. She'd just completed a phone conference with Kerry Rand himself and he told her some things that she wanted to share.

"I just received the results of the focus group interviews," she said.

"What did they say?" I asked.

"Kerry made a point of asking me about the pep rally we did for Joint Commission."

"Really?"

"Yes. All the events we did in fact. The Showtime at the Apollo, the pep rally, the Gospel concerts – we haven't done anything like that since the survey ended," she said.

She was right. I'd almost forgotten all about them.

"Apparently the staff really misses them," she continued. "According to Kerry, they're still talking about it."

I was surprised that those events had made that much of an impact on the staff.

"We have to bring some of it back," Donna added. "I told Kerry it wasn't that we didn't care. We were just too tired to keep that going."

"Amen to that," I said.

"That wasn't everything though," she continued. "Your name kept coming up during the interviews."

I wasn't expecting that.

"Okay," I responded with a laugh. Since she was laughing too it didn't seem inappropriate. I'd been mentioned a time or two in the numerous letters that had been written about the hospital administration since Donna returned to North Brooklyn. The mention I enjoyed the most was the one that referred to me as the "Terror Queen." I knew I'd developed a reputation as a person to be feared, but, since no one could tell me why

I never really took it seriously. Especially, since I had a lot more people trying to get into my division than trying to get out.

But this consultant *was* taking it seriously and he wanted to meet me to talk about it.

"Kerry said that every once in a while he finds young executives that he likes to work with," Donna continued. "When I told him about you and all your degrees, all the departments you have and how involved you were in the work we've done since we came back, he asked me if he could work with you directly. He thinks you're interesting."

I agreed immediately. I'd already met the consultants who did the interviews. And I remembered Kerry from the introductory retreat we held. Our first discussion after the interviews was really something more than a meeting. I think he was trying to figure me out. I'm certain that both he and Donna thought it would be a tough sell to get me to voluntarily tackle the perceptions that were floating around about me.

Kerry had an impish quality to him. But I found him to have an honest and engaging style with a penetrating wit that I was drawn to immediately. As someone who really likes to get to the point, I marveled at his laser-like ability to zero in on the central issue of whatever we were discussing. He earned my respect quickly so he had my full attention.

He told me early in our interactions, that his wife was a psychologist. You could see her influence in the way he communicated. Key points were framed as questions. The way my mind functioned, I tended to address most questions by anticipating the question that would follow. It saved time. Our dialogues went something like this:

"People have very strong opinions about you around here, were you aware of that?"

"Yes. That's been true all my life."

"Do you think its something you want to do something about?"

"Not particularly, but, I'm guessing you think I need to or we wouldn't be having this conversation."

It was serve and volley, back and forth. Sometimes he'd hit a backhand, sometimes I'd come to the net. The games never lasted long, but, they were usually enlightening and always fun. Clearly there was something he wanted me to do that he thought I would object to, and I was eager to find out what it was. I remember how he led into it.

"You know I've worked with executives like you before. You're younger than your colleagues, you think faster than a lot of the people around you and you don't have patience for people you don't respect. You also have a lot of talents to contribute. Unfortunately, these feelings that people have about you are getting in the way. Do you have any idea where this is coming from?"

"Yes and no," I said. "When we first came back I was like a bull in a china shop. I admit that. We had a lot to do and very little time to do it. I probably could have done some things differently. But I know I don't relate to people the way I did. Circumstances have changed. So have I."

"But you realize no one is seeing that," he said.

"Apparently not."

"So you have a choice. You can address it now or you can fix it on the next job. Which would you prefer?"

"I would prefer to fix it on the next job, but, you're going to tell me why I should fix it now, aren't you?"

We were both used to this type of exchange by now, so we could each enjoy the humor in it.

"The thing I don't get," I continued, "is how so many people can have these strong opinions about me when I personally interact with so few people around here."

Once I became Chief Operating Officer I had to reorganize my division. I created a Clinical Support Division like the one I had at Gen + and put Bobby, my radiology administrator, in charge of it. The service line administrators reported to Gina, someone who had reported to me at The Fort Greene Center and who I recruited to be my Deputy shortly after we returned to Woodhull in 2001. So, my direct contacts were far fewer than they had been. They consisted of the Cabinet, on rare occasions the managers who reported to the Cabinet, and the three or four managers who now reported directly to me. As usual, Kerry had a precisely worded answer that gave me a lot to think about.

"People draw their opinions from the information they have available," he said. "So if most people don't have the opportunity to get to know who you really are, then you become what people say you are."

"That doesn't make any sense," I said.

"Maybe, but that's the way it is. You're at a level now where most of the opinions people have about you will be based on perception. That's why you have to fix it now."

He didn't know it, but, I'd already decided that I was going to go along with his recommendations, whatever they were. And it wasn't for the reasons that he and Donna probably thought. It wasn't because of concerns about my career or even because I worried about the opinions others had of me. Good or bad, I seem to have been born with that gene switched to the off position. He caught my attention when he said that these perceptions were getting in other people's way. I was hindering not helping and that was the last thing I wanted to do.

When we join an organization we join a story in progress. It is the story of how the culture in that place was created. As we thread ourselves into that storyline we become part of how that culture perpetuates itself. I've learned to be mindful of this but it's a lesson I learned the hard way. Every story, every culture is a village and every village has its cemeteries.

I traveled to Egypt many years back and as we drove through Cairo en route to our hotel in Giza, the tour guide pointed out the window to rows and rows of single-story huts. Even from the distance you could see that the structures were no bigger than a single room. There were women and children tending to the concerns of the day. Clotheslines were draped from house to house with tattered garments being dried by the stale stiff air of the Middle East at noon.

Cairo is a dense and gritty metropolis, but I'm from New York. In fact everyone on our tour was, so we'd seen urban images before. I wondered why this tour guide felt the need to point this one out. But this village wasn't like anything we'd seen before. It was a cemetery. The city had become so overcrowded that the poor had taken up residence in the mausoleums, using crypts as shelters and coffins as dining tables.

In the midst of dire circumstances, we do what we need to do. So that what was once shocking and unthinkable, distasteful even detestable, becomes first a necessary evil and then a commonplace occurrence remarkable only to the tourist passing through. You can come into a place with the best of intentions. The burnt-out street light that needs replacing, the faded facade in need of a fresh coat of paint, the fix may be obvious, but there is a story behind it all. Try to change it without knowing the story and your efforts might come back to convict you. This is where the ghosts in the cemetery come in.

A friend of mine once had a boss describe her using a cemetery analogy of his own. He said, "When you have to get from one side of a cemetery to the other, there are two kinds of people. The kind that go around the headstones and the kind that run right over them. You're the 'knock them down' kind." Perhaps that's why she and I were friends because so was I.

Like me, you can feel that you have a compelling reason for getting to the other side of the graveyard. What are a few overturned headstones in the service of a cause that will benefit the living? But ghosts talk. When you are long gone into the village, they rise from the graves you've disturbed. So that everyone who passes through after you only hears ghost stories. The living might say "she ran through the cemetery to pull someone out of a burning barn." But the ghosts say "she knocks over headstones." That's how perceptions are formed and that's why you can't fix it on the next job.

When I told Donna that I'd agreed to do what Kerry asked me to do she said, "I've got to tell you, I didn't think you'd go for it." But she didn't need to worry. I understood exactly what I was being asked to do. It was time to go back into the graveyard and pick up some headstones.

CHAPTER ELEVEN
JANUARY, 2004

ANOTHER NEW YEAR FOUND us still tugging the factory toward dry land. Cumberland proved to be an unexpected challenge for me. But it wasn't the staff this time. In fact, I found that Cumberland's staff responded quickly to my requests. All they wanted in return was equal time in the spotlight to have their accomplishments recognized, which was only fair. My particular burden was Cumberland's Community Advisory Board (or "CAB"). Like The Fort Greene Center, Cumberland was located in Fort Greene but unlike The Fort Greene Center, it was in a far more residential section, surrounded by high-rise public housing.

The residents had lived there for generations and many of them had been members of Cumberland's CAB since the facility was a hospital. As far as they were concerned Cumberland was still a hospital and they wanted their own CEO to prove it. Having the network Chief Operating Officer as their administrator did not impress them in the least, because it meant that I wasn't their administrator full time.

Cumberland also had its own Auxiliary. Just like a hospital auxiliary, their function was to raise money for Cumberland. Most of the money they raised came from vendor commissions that they had nothing to do with securing. But the little ladies of Cumberland's Auxiliary were always so sweet. Their chairwoman reminded me of my grandmother and they never gave me a moment of trouble. But those feisty little senior citizens from the CAB gave me the blues every chance they got.

Our monthly marathon meetings always started off cordially. "Dr. Best . . ." I'd received my Ph.D. the previous December and my staff started a wave of people calling me Dr. Best, even though it was something that I never asked anybody to do.

"There are just a few things we want to bring to your attention." Then the barrage would begin. There was a CAB member in the building on a daily basis conducting inspections. "We found a piece of paper on the floor by the play area and it took all day for somebody to pick it up."

Their reports always contained an impressive level of detail. And every now and then they would venture into territory where they knew they didn't belong.

"When is that staff in the pharmacy going to get a raise?"

"Now ma'am," I always tried to make a point to include a "Sir" or a "Ma'am" in my responses. I was raised right. "You know that personnel issues are beyond the purview of this Board."

Of course they knew. But they liked to make friends with the staff and the staff liked to use those relationships to slip in their requests. I'm certain that's how the vice-chairwoman and I ended up in a perpetual tango over a door.

"I would like to request that the laboratory be given a Dutch door," she said one evening. That's how it started.

"Why do they need a Dutch door?" I asked.

"It would really help them keep their area organized," she said.

I wasn't persuaded so I respectfully turned down the request and expected that to be the end of it. It wasn't. One way or another she found a way to bring that Dutch door back to the table at every meeting. And at every meeting I tried to find a different way to explain to her that it wasn't going to happen.

"Ma'am, we can't make a Dutch door fire safe," I said once. "It has a split across the middle."

She replied, "But they don't make fire in the lab do they?"

This went on for months. Sometimes she'd try to sneak it in at the end of the meeting.

"Just one more thing. The Dutch door for the laboratory still hasn't been delivered yet. Can you find out about that for me and get back to us at the next meeting?"

"I can get back to you right now," I said. "It hasn't been delivered because I'm not ordering one. Ma'am, I already told you that."

It wasn't dementia or Alzheimer's. This grey brigade was in full possession of all their faculties. They'd come teetering into the meetings, aluminum foil and Tupperware dishes firmly in hand so that they could squirrel away the leftovers from the dinners we served them. And they would use their faculties to beat me over the head every third Tuesday of the month.

Fortunately for me, the CAB always took the summer off. The break would turn out to be crucial for me. With all the progress that we'd made in other areas of the network, we still hadn't turned the corner with Nursing. Despite our success during the 2002 survey, the relationship between Donna and Nigel continued to deteriorate as the complaints about Nursing continued to mount. The department felt isolated and defensive. Nigel felt isolated and defensive. It was a no-win situation. Donna reached the end of her rope and felt she had no choice but to pull the plug.

She arranged for Nigel's transfer to the Nursing Affairs Division at Central Office. But until she could come up with a replacement, she would in essence be running our nursing department herself. While I, like most people who worked with her, thought she could do just about anything I didn't think she really wanted to do that. I think timing more than confidence was the reason why she put Nursing under Operations when I asked for it. She was candid with her concerns.

"You have more than half of the hospital already. Nursing is the biggest department we have. There comes a point when even you can become ineffective."

She had a point and I acknowledged it. I wasn't being motivated by a "God-complex." I wasn't even certain I could fix what was wrong. I wasn't a nurse. But I also knew that the department's problems weren't the result of a deficit in nursing competencies. They were having leadership problems.

I walked the floors. I had developed relationships with some of the frontline nurse managers over the years. The kinds of things that they complained about came down to not feeling supported and no one in Operations ever complained about that. As a department, Nursing had either by circumstance or by their own choosing become an island unto themselves. It wasn't working for them or for the hospital. They needed to be brought under somebody's big tent. I thought mine was as good as any.

So on July 1, 2004, Nursing became a part of Operations. And no sooner was the decision made than my beloved boss threw me a curve ball. She decided to select someone for the Acting Chief Nurse Executive who was quite familiar to the executive staff – Angela Highland. Donna gave Angela to Nigel when she removed her from the Cabinet. Nigel put her in charge of Nursing Education, a job for which she was tailor-made. He struggled in his communication with her as much as anyone, but somehow they settled into an uneasy coexistence. Most people forgot she was still around.

191

In my personal dealings with Angela, I would have no problem describing her as one of the sweetest, most caring people that you could ever meet - sometimes. Then there were other times when she could make you so frustrated that you wanted to strangle her until she lost consciousness. You didn't want to kill her. You just wanted her to be silent and still.

I thought my biggest problem was going to be trying to navigate around her difficulty in getting to a point that someone could understand. That turned out to be the least of my problems. Whatever some of my colleagues may have felt about my taking over yet another major department in the hospital, those emotions were immediately overwhelmed by their feelings about having Angela back on the Cabinet. The reaction was swift and severe. No one wanted her back. In truth, I didn't want her either. It was nothing personal, but, I thought she was going to be too much to manage and that's what I told Donna.

"So who would you prefer?" she asked.

When I mentioned the name of the person I wanted to give the job to, Donna jumped back in her high-backed chair and made the sign of the cross.

"Was that really necessary?" I asked.

I knew that the person I wanted was a mixed bag herself. She was experienced and competent, but, from a temperament standpoint, she was a loose canon. When it came to intimidation, among the nurses at least, her reputation surpassed mine times ten. She told me herself that whenever she walked into the nursing station on one of the units there was one nurse who would immediately burst into tears. And that was before any words were exchanged. She didn't even know why the nurse would start to cry but the woman wouldn't stop crying until this manager left the area.

Donna was adamant that my first choice was a brand of fanatic that would never work and that was the end of that discussion. The decision was made and I honored it. Our concession to the Cabinet was that Angela would report to me and would not, therefore, be a member of the executive leadership team. And there marked the source of contention between me and the newest member of my team.

The Chief Nursing Executive had always been a part of the Cabinet. The position was a part of the Cabinet at most (but not all) the hospitals in HHC. When Angela was appointed to the position, albeit in an Acting capacity, she logically assumed that this meant she would be back on the Cabinet herself. When she found out that she would not, she uncorked a private label brand of passive-aggressive resistance. And she was just smart enough to be extraordinarily good at it. The opening sorties in our own little Vietnam began within days of her appointment. And like the original, it got ugly fast.

First she resorted to what she knew best. She pulled out state law and implied that it required her to be on the Cabinet. When we shot that down, then it was JCAHO. When that didn't work, then she didn't know anything.

"Angela, Quality Management is waiting for your monitoring reports," I would say.

"I didn't know. Nobody told me."

"Okay. I'm telling you now. They're overdue."

"Well, I don't have a budget."

"Yes you do. Your requisitions are being processed aren't they?"

"Yes, but I don't know what it is. Nobody tells me anything."

"Angela, you know everything I know."

It was like this at every one-to-one supervisory meeting we had. I started receiving letters from the nursing union complaining that "nursing leadership is not included in decision making." Then Angela would challenge me at meetings in front of her staff, something I normally would have squashed with a mallet. But the nursing department had just joined Operations and I knew they were nervous about it. The last thing they needed to see was me clashing with their boss.

And she was quite shrewd in using her personal relationship with Donna. She would send her cryptic emails implying and sometimes saying outright that she "wasn't feeling supported" or issuing veiled threats about resigning. She had the ability to take frustrating to a whole new level.

I would go to Donna. Donna would send me back to "work it out." I tried, but, we weren't making any progress. More than anything else I was losing my patience. Trying to come up with points to Angela's endless counterpoints was consuming all my time. Fortunately, I did have a diversion.

That summer, Ira, Simon our new CFO, Brian and I went to Washington, D.C., to attend a two-day training at the Ritz-Carlton on how to build a world-class customer service culture. We returned from the conference full of excitement about how to translate what we'd learned into something we could use at the network. But it wasn't going to be easy. I still remembered that boring customer service training the entire corporation had been forced to go through in 1998 and I knew that the staff would remember it too. We were going up against a "been there, done that" mentality. They'd lived through countless brilliant ideas by executives who didn't last long enough to see the paint dry on their parking spaces.

I knew that if we just got in a room and designed some program, then tried to force it on the staff, it wouldn't matter how great an idea it was. The staff would greet it with a great big yawn. I had an idea about how to approach it, but, I knew I was going to have a tough time selling it to Ira. He loved coming up with "novel approaches" and force-feeding them to the staff. Then he would become so enraptured with his own ideas that he could exist in a complete state of denial about the fact that nobody was paying them any attention. Remember that this was the man who created that "Atlas" model. It can probably still be found stuck in the corner of nursing station bulletin boards on dusty, coffee-stained paper that nobody ever looks at.

But, there were times when Ira's short attention span worked to my advantage. He was excited about the new program in the beginning. He even came up with the name we eventually gave it, the "Platinum Experience." But as it happened, we were beginning to receive national press attention for another program we developed called "Artist Access." It allowed local artists to exchange their talents for healthcare services. Every week some media outlet was looking to do a story and they wanted someone to interview. Ira was in rapture. So when the time came to work out the details for rolling out the Platinum Experience, Ira was sufficiently distracted. We were actually able to launch the program with thought and deliberation. And to my surprise it worked.

I'm convinced that the Platinum Experience was a success because we included everyone in the process of developing it. This was one of the ways I put my research degree to work. We conducted at least ten focus groups using a cross section of staff and we asked them why they thought we didn't have a customer service culture. They were very interested in telling us what we did wrong and what we needed to change to do a better job. Their suggestions became the "new rules" that we were going to adopt as a network to govern how we treated each other and our patients. We called these new rules the "Platinum Principles."

We put up posters and made overhead announcements. We even came up with a Platinum Pledge that the staff signed and we posted it in the lobby. In the beginning, the only time the staff mentioned the Platinum Experience was when they were pointing out which Platinum Principle their supervisor was breaking. But I considered that a victory. At least they were talking about it.

With all this activity going on I had to do something about Cumberland. I had my hands full. The CAB would be reconvening in September and I would have to concede the truth of their accusations that I wasn't giving Cumberland my full attention. I wasn't. Donna and I had a talk and we decided to take a chance on a manager who had worked in Cumberland's chemical dependency program for decades. We knew the CAB would approve and he had a good rapport with the staff. He even knew how to take direction. But he was another HHC "character." He had the kind of penetrating gaze that could easily be mistaken for the prelude to a psychotic break. And sometimes his passion for the place would spill over and leave a stain.

But we couldn't come up with any other options, so Donna and I crossed our fingers and put him in the job. He didn't last thirty days. Brian, Dr. Wallace, the Chief of Woodhull's Emergency Department and Chair of our Patient Safety Committee, and I were in Boston at an *Institute for Healthcare Improvement* conference. Brian stepped out of the room to take a call. When he returned, he calmly informed me that my new administrator at Cumberland had just gotten into a fist fight with one of the patients. I stared at him in disbelief. I'd never known Brian to lie, but, I just couldn't accept what he was telling me. I stepped out of the room and called the office on my cell phone. I didn't even get the chance to ask Donna whether it was true.

"Now I have to fire him. I have to fire him!" she said. "But I can't fire him. He's too close to retirement. This job is all he has. I don't believe this!" She was beside herself.

"So it's true?" I asked.

"Yes it's true! They were rolling around on the floor like a couple of hooligans. Now I've got to find a corner to stick him in."

I appreciated her dilemma but in truth, I was only thinking about myself at that moment.

"Donna."

"What?"

"Please don't send me back to Cumberland." I don't recall ever sounding as desperate as I sounded at that moment. "I can't do another CAB meeting. I just can't do it. If that little lady asks me for a Dutch door one more time I think I'm going to kill myself."

Donna was unmoved.

"Then you'd better come up with something because I'm not going to the meetings for you!"

Meanwhile, there must have been something in the air at Cumberland. Donna decided that it was time for Jackie to do something more than plan parties for the network to earn her pension. And Jackie had wanted to be promoted to the title of Associate Director for as long as I'd known her. So Donna obliged, but, in return for the promotion, which included a raise, she had to leave her comfortable surroundings at Cumberland and move over to Woodhull.

Jackie had been reporting to Elliot. To his credit, he'd made a valiant attempt to grow a spine when it came to supervising her. But in fairness, I think even Hercules would have broken a sweat trying to corral Jackie into conventional conduct. The only department that had managerial openings was Psychiatry (insert your own joke here). She would have to report to Wayne, which wasn't much of an improvement over Elliot. But perhaps being in the same building as her boss might give her more structure, something she clearly needed.

Donna had discussed the plan with her and Jackie agreed. She was telling everybody at Cumberland, "Donna needs me to help her out. They got a mess over there. I've got to go clean it up, y'all." But when the day came for Jackie to actually vacate her office, all hell broke loose. I'd just returned to Woodhull from a visit to one of the off-site clinics. When I stopped by Donna's office to tell her I was back, the tone of the conversation between her and Mimi made it sound like there was some sort of natural disaster occurring at Cumberland.

"What's going on?" I asked. Mimi couldn't contain herself.

"Jackie won't leave her office."

"What do you mean Jackie won't leave her office?" Then Donna upped the ante.

"She just finished cursing me out over the phone," she said.

I gave Donna the look I usually gave her when I caught her embellishing. She did that sometimes when she told a story. But Mimi responded for her.

"She's telling the truth. I could hear Jackie through the phone all the way from my desk."

I took a seat on the couch. I wanted to be comfortable, because I was about to preview one of Donna's dramatic presentations. She started off calmly.

"I picked up the phone," she said. "And I said 'Hello Jackie. What's the matter?' and then she started screaming at me."

That's when I got excited. Donna took off her glasses and adjusted herself in her seat. She was going to reenact the whole thing right there before my eyes. And I had a feeling that this performance was going to earn her a Tony Award for sure.

She squeezed her face tight, put her hand up to her ear like she was talking on the phone and screamed at the top of her lungs.

"AAAAHHHHHH!!!!! HOW COULD YOU DO THIS TO ME! HOW COULD YOU DO THIS TO ME!!!!"

From that point on, Donna never said "she said" or "I said." She just acted out the entire scene switching from her part to Jackie's part and back again.

"Jackie. You need to calm down."

"I WILL NOT CALM DOWN! I WILL NOT CALM DOWN! They shittin' on me! THEY SHITTIN' ON ME!!! EEEEEEEEEWWWWWWWWWWWW!!!!!!!"

Donna's adorably round face was red and contorted. She drew her hands up like claws on either side of her ears. And when she yelled "EEEEWWWW!!!!" she made her voice ring like a rotary telephone. I was on the edge of my seat.

"Jackie. Jaaaacckkeeeee. If you don't stop screaming. I'm going to have to hang up."

"Don't you hang up on me!! DON'T YOU HANG UP ON ME!!! They're trying to pack up my stuff!! They're putting me out!!!! I JUST GOT MY NEW FURNITURE!!!!!!! AAAAAAAAHHHHHHH!!!!!!"

"Jackie, you've known about this for weeks."

It was amazing to watch how effortlessly Donna could shift back and forth between Jackie's hysteria and her own calm demeanor.

"And you!!!!! YOUUUU!!!!!!!!!!!!!!! I MADE YOU!!!!!!!!!!!! I MAAADE YOOU!!! EEEEEWWW!!!!!"

I gasped, "No she didn't!"

"Yes she did," Donna replied.

It was the only time Donna came out of character and it was just for that moment.

"You made me Jackie? Gee I thought it was my 30-year career here but . . . ."

"THAT'S RIGHT I MADE YOU!!!! ALL THEM PEOPLE I INTRODUCED YOU TO!!!!! AND THIS IS HOW YOU THANK ME!!!! EEEEEEEEEEEEWWWWWWWWWWW!!!!!!!!!!!!!"

"Jackie. I can see we're not going to be able to have a conversation right now. Go put some water on your face and get yourself together and then you can call me back."

Donna mimicked hanging up the phone and then she went right back to signing some letters on her desk as if nothing had happened. I was exhausted just from watching her. As performances go, it was brilliant. So much so that I demanded three encores, which she dutifully provided.

"You have got to be kidding me," I said.

She shook her head.

"Nope. I called one of the doctors over there and asked them to go check on her. They called me back and said Jackie was crying and screaming so bad that they had to throw water in her face and threaten to sedate her just to get her to calm down."

"Over an office?" I asked.

"Over an office."

It wasn't too long before Dana knocked on the door. From the look on her face I knew she had somehow been involved in the mêlée. Donna started laughing immediately.

"Ms. Wilson," Dana said. "I have never seen anything like it in my twenty years here."

"What happened Dana?" I asked.

"I went over there to move her and she was in the office with her staff. She tried to slam the door in my face." Dana seemed incensed all over again just at the thought of it. "But I knocked it back open before they could lock it," she continued. Dana was a big girl, the perfect one for the job. "She said, 'I'm in a meeting. You have to leave.'"

"What did you do?" I asked. It was more drama and I have to admit, I loved it.

"I didn't even respond to that," Dana said dismissively. "I told her staff to get out and then I closed the door. I said, Jackie we can do this any way you want to do it, but, one way or another, you're leaving this office today." The more I heard the more amazed I was.

Then Dana turned to me. "Is she on drugs?" she asked.

"No. Jackie doesn't have a drug problem. Jackie has a Jackie problem."

She eventually got herself together and vacated her office. Like so many people before her, she also discovered what a truly gracious boss we had. She called Donna a few days later to apologize and Donna accepted the apology without giving it another thought. Ironically, for all her objections, the move turned out to be the best thing that ever happened to Jackie. The new position suited her nicely.

Having Jackie surgically removed from Cumberland still didn't resolve my administrator dilemma. It took some time, but, I finally came up with the perfect solution – Cora. She'd worked at Cumberland before so the staff knew her. The CAB would love her and she had really been functioning as the de facto Director of Ambulatory Care ever since I made her a redesign coach for our internal teams. I knew that promoting her to Associate Executive Director for Ambulatory Care would disrupt the service line model. But I also knew that she and Gina could work it out.

The year 2004 turned out to be the year that I had to take a closer look at my staff and myself. When I found myself still battling with Angela two more months into her appointment, I decided that we'd reached the breaking point. Donna and I would have to have a talk about it.

"Can I come in?" I said.

"Sure. What's up?"

I was careful not to approach Donna the way I did after I blew up at Brian. I'd had my fill of parent-teacher conferences.

"Where do I start?"

"Uh oh," she said. "I know that look."

She was expressing only half-hearted concern.

"I'm reaching the end of my patience with Angela," I said.

"The two of you will work it out."

"I don't think so," I said.

"Try."

"I've been trying."

"Well go back and try again."

"Donna, I'm serious."

"If this is the hardest thing you have to deal with, you don't have any problems."

Why did she say that? I was doing so well up to that point. I don't know if it was what she said or how she said it. There was a chortle in her voice and I was not in a laughing mood. Self-restraint threw up its hands in defeat, slipped down through my vertebrae and tiptoed out the back door. I responded before I could catch myself.

"That's not the point!" I snapped. "This isn't about being the hardest thing I have to deal with. She's taking up all my time with her nonsense. You didn't want to deal with her. That's why she's reporting to me. Why should I have to put up with it?"

I was truly fortunate that by that point in our relationship, we were more like mother and daughter than boss and employee. Donna stopped smiling and sat back in her chair. I probably should have been scared, but, I was too full of fire to have good sense.

"I see," she said.

"I'm sorry. I don't mean to be insubordinate, but, I've been working around Angela's neurotic behavior for two months now. I guess I'm not able to find the humor in this as easily as you are."

"I get it. What's the problem now?"

"It's the same problems we've had from day one. She's acting out because she doesn't report to you like Nigel did."

"That's not going to happen so she might as well get over it."

"That sounds good, but, it isn't happening. Every chance she gets she comes up with some way to insinuate that she can't do her job because she's not on the Cabinet. She's challenging me in front of others and the rest of the senior staff wants to hang her from the nearest flag pole. It's just too much."

"You can't handle that?"

"You know I can handle it and it would have been handled, but, her friendship with you isn't helping matters."

Donna didn't like that accusation.

"What's that supposed to mean? She's not getting any special treatment from me. And I never told you to give her any."

"Okay. But she still has access to you."

"So what?"

"So I think you're enabling her."

I'm not sure where I pulled that comment from, but, I wasn't backing down from it.

"Oh really?" Donna said with a raised eyebrow. "In what way?"

"You've shown me the emails with all of the whining"

"I don't pay any attention to that."

"But does she know that?"

"So what do you want me to do, Candis? You want me to stop speaking to her? Is that it?"

"No. But . . ."

"And by the way Missy," Donna added. "*You're* the one who asked for Nursing."

"I asked for Nursing. I didn't ask for Angela," I quickly replied.

The banter between us was fast and furious and it was showing no signs of letting up.

"We both know why she has this job," she said. "There was no one else to do it."

"Well . . . you know my feelings about that. I still think we should have gone with . . ."

"Forget it! I told you. She's crazy!"

"THEY'RE BOTH CRAZY! What's the difference? I could have handled that brand of crazy better than the one I've got right now!"

My arms were flailing in every direction. I think this may have been the only time in our entire working relationship that Donna and I actually had something that could be classified as a fight. Fortunately for both of us, it didn't last too much longer.

"Where are we going with this?" she asked. "We can't change Nursing Directors again. People will start thinking *we're* the crazy ones! That department is on the verge of collapse as it is. One more change and we'll never be able to fix it."

She had a point. I had no choice but to concede it.

"Well, at least stop coddling her?" I said.

"I don't know what that means," she replied coolly.

Donna was not the passive-aggressive type. She was more of the aggressive-aggressive type. But with the way she folded her arms and looked at me over her glasses, that comment came as close as she could get.

"It means that the next time she calls you or emails you that she's having second thoughts, please don't talk her into staying," I said with a composure that now matched hers.

And then we traded places. I was calm and she was agitated.

"That's not what happened!" she said.

"Okay fine. But can we just agree?" I said. "The next time she threatens to quit, let her! I'll take my chances with Looney Tunes cast member Number Two."

"Fine," she said.

And with that I left her office. That was a Friday.

The following Monday I went to Angela's office for our regular supervisory meeting. She welcomed me in with a warm smile. Then we began to talk. I made a suggestion, she agreed immediately. I could feel myself peering at her slightly askance. Then she asked me for advice about how to handle something. I turned all the way to the side as I stumbled to find an answer. My mind was preoccupied with the thought, "Who are you and what have you done with my Nursing Director?"

After we finished our meeting I backed out of Angela's office and sprinted to Donna's.

"Did you have a conversation that I should know about?" I asked.

"Why?" she replied.

"Because I just had the most pleasant one-to-one with Angela that we've had since we started working together. She never once said she didn't have any information. She agreed to everything I asked her. I didn't recognize her."

Donna took her glasses off and started to laugh.

"Not fifteen minutes after you left my office on Friday, I got an email from her."

"What did it say?"

"It was another one of those 'I just don't know whether I belong here. I'm not feeling supported' emails. She picked the perfect time to send it. I went up one side of her and down the other and I ended it with something like 'if this isn't working for you, feel free to leave at any time.'"

I couldn't even imagine how Angela took that.

"Did she respond?" I asked.

"Sure, with four words. 'No problem. I'm fine.'"

And with that closing salvo, the war was over. We turned a corner and Angela and I were finally able to concentrate on Nursing – together. I would say it was a growth experience for all involved. But I had one more member of my team that I still had to deal with. I think Donna and I were having lunch in her office that day.

"So how's your group doing?" she asked innocently.

I should have been suspicious. Donna never acted innocent.

"Fine," I said.

"Are you sure?"

"I was. Do you know something that I don't?"

"You don't think your staff is having a hard time with the fact that they don't report to you directly anymore?"

This was one of the moments in my career that demonstrated how thick I was when it came to interpersonal matters.

"What are you talking about?" I asked.

"The Dolls miss you. So does the rest of your group. Can't you tell? Miles just isn't quite the same," she said. The only response I could come up with was "Huh?"

When I left Gen+ the person Luis decided to replace me with was someone I thought was totally inadequate to the job. When Donna told me about it, I knew from the quality of her laughter that she agreed with me. "Before you say anything," she said, "let me just add that there is no one else available within the network to take over your spot and Luis will not let you leave until they find a replacement." These new facts changed my perspective considerably.

"You know, now that I think about it," I said. "She can do this job. She can definitely do this job."

Now Donna was laughing at me. "I thought that's what you'd say," she said.

"No, I'm serious. That team is so strong they don't really need supervision. There's no way she can mess that up."

When will I learn never to make those kinds of statements? Within one year of my departure, Carlos quit, Juan took a job with Sasha of all people, and Mr. Miles, the gentleman of all gentlemen, got into such a nasty scrap with my replacement that before I knew it, he was on his way to Woodhull. I was thrilled to have him back on my team. But when I reorganized the division he had to report to Bobby, the former radiology administrator who was now in charge of all the Ancillary services at the network, including Food Service. Once I became COO, I was particularly careful to select the two most agreeable members of my staff to supervise the others. I couldn't understand why Donna thought the staff was unhappy.

"It's not their supervisors, Candis. They just miss you. They miss interacting with you directly."

I tried, but, I just couldn't understand what she was talking about. She finally gave up on that topic and shifted the focus. "Well, you need to speak with Gina. She's struggling."

"Struggling?" I said.

I was stuck on stupid that day.

"Yes. I think she's overwhelmed. From what I hear, when you send her to meetings to represent you, she doesn't make decisions. She says she has to check with you first."

"That can't be right," I said. "I don't expect her to check with me before she makes a decision. In fact, nobody on my staff has to do that."

"Just talk to her," Donna said. "Maybe she's not getting support from the Dolls."

That concerned me. The very thought that they weren't supporting each other was incomprehensible to me. I went to Gina first and asked her if she was having any trouble. She said no. So I asked her if she would mind if I talked to the service line administrators alone. She said she wouldn't. I was really upset with them by the time the meeting took place. I let them know in no uncertain terms, how bitterly disappointed I would be in them if it turned out that they were not being supportive to Gina. They listened, but, they were quiet - too quiet.

"Is there something I should know?" I asked. They all exchanged glances. Then Chrissy chose to break the silence.

"I'll speak up," she said. "It's not that we don't support Gina. We do."

Right away I saw the room come to life. Everyone was nodding.

"It's just that it's not the same as when we reported to you," she continued.

Not this again, I thought. What was everyone talking about?

"Please don't tell me you miss me," I said. "My office is in the same place it's always been."

"We do miss you," Chrissy responded. "But that's not what I'm talking about. When we reported to you, if we got stuck and we went to see you, we left your office with clear direction about how we should proceed."

Now Marie jumped in, "Yeah but when we talk to Gina she just says, 'I'll talk to Candis. I have to get back to you.' Everything is 'I have to get back to you.' That can take weeks. We're not used to that."

Then Jasmine jumped in, "And her secretary is no A.J. ... ."

A.J. was my secretary. She had a low-key demeanor, but, she was the best secretary I'd ever had. She kept things running so smoothly I tried to make her take vacation when I took vacation just so that I wouldn't have to be without her.

"When we gave things to A.J. for your signature she would either call us right away or most of the time she would go ahead and take our paperwork wherever it needed to go. But this one? Things just sit on her desk. We follow-up to ask her what's going on and she's too overwhelmed to respond. She's only got half the responsibilities A.J. had!"

It was the biggest slice of humble pie I'd eaten in years.

"Okay. I'll have a talk with Gina," I said.

Before I left, Vanessa, the Emergency Department administrator said, "But we would like to come by and see you now and again. Sometimes we just need some of that essence of K. Candis Best." She made everyone laugh so hard that for a moment I forgot to feel bad about how difficult the transition must have been for them. But laughter or no laughter, I did feel bad and I was about to feel worse. I was about to know firsthand how Donna must have felt. For the first time in my career, I had to have an uncomfortable conversation with someone I cared a lot about.

We met that afternoon.

"Gina, are you sure you're not feeling overwhelmed in this position?" I asked. I didn't know how else to start the conversation.

"Yes. I'm sure," she said.

"Then I have to ask you something. I'm hearing that you won't make a decision until you check with me first. Is that true?"

"Well . . . ," she said. My heart sank. The way she was straining to find an answer gave me the very answer I dreaded most.

"Most of the time," she continued, "I feel like I know what the right decision is. But I just want to check with you to make sure it's okay."

I sat back in my chair too stunned to speak. I couldn't believe that this had been going on and I didn't know about it.

"Gina, I don't send you to meetings on my behalf just for you to bring back information," I said. "I could send A.J. to do that. You're an executive now. I expect you to make a decision. Are you afraid of making a mistake?" She didn't respond to the question one way or another.

"I need you to make decisions," I said. "Even if you make the wrong one, it's better than not making one at all. We can always fix it on the back end."

"I know. It's just . . . ," she said.

"It's just what?" I asked.

I really needed to know how we'd had such a serious miscue. Then I was struck by a horrific thought. "Oh God," I said. "Please don't tell me after all these years you're scared of me too!" She started to laugh.

"Of course not," she said. "That's not it."

That was a relief. Then she said, "I just don't want to disappoint you."

It was a touching sentiment. Gina was a hard worker. There was never anything that I'd ever asked her to do that she didn't throw herself into wholeheartedly. This was a big promotion for her. I wanted to see her succeed. It was also the first time that we'd ever had this kind of conversation. She'd always excelled at everything

I'd given her in the past. I didn't want this to crush her spirit.

"You won't disappoint me," I said. "Go ahead and take a risk. If you fall, I'll catch you. That's what I'm here for. I thought you knew that."

"I do," she said.

That was as close to the planet Touchy-Feely as I could get. It was time to get back to Vulcan. "So do you want this job or not?" I asked.

"I do! I do!" she said.

"Alright, then you've got to act like it. Speak up at the meetings I send you to. Don't let people push you around. And by the way, you're going to have to do something about your secretary."

I never liked to get involved in those kinds of decisions, but when she picked her secretary I knew the person wouldn't be able to handle the increased responsibilities once I promoted Gina. And I'd told her so.

"No. I'm going to take care of that right away," she said. "I'll give her something else to do."

She seemed to be regaining the color in her face. But I had one more piece of advice for her.

"And no more coming in here with your hair still wet and flip-flops on. If you want people to take you seriously, you have to look the part." I couldn't believe those words were actually coming out of my mouth. I was channeling my old boss, Charles Montgomery.

"Okay," she said smiling. "Do you want me to start wearing stockings in the summertime too?"

"Let's not get carried away with ourselves," I replied.

I would turn down an appointment to the Supreme Court if it meant that I had to wear pantyhose in the summertime. That was something I always felt strongly about. Somehow I'd been able to stay true to those convictions throughout my professional career. As my profile became more elevated, that conviction turned into a royal decree for all the female members of my staff.

"Are we straight?" I asked.

"Um hmm," she said.

"Alright, get to work," I said with a wink. After that conversation, I felt confident that things with my staff were back on track. And just in time, because I still had to complete my assignment from Kerry.

It was relatively simple. It required me to go to the Cabinet and the Chiefs of Service, share with them what the consultants had learned about the way I was being perceived by others and offer each of them an opportunity to share their feelings on how they were "experiencing" me.

Kerry and I discussed the mechanics of how to set the meetings up. It would start with a group announcement at a Cabinet meeting and a meeting of the Chiefs of all the clinical departments. Then A.J. would call each member individually to ask if they wanted to participate. It was up to them to accept or decline and I specifically told her to schedule the meetings so that I would come to them. The conversations were more illuminating than I had anticipated. My first session was with Wayne, our Psychiatry administrator. It was clear from the outset that he'd spent a considerable amount of time preparing for our meeting.

"I never really had a problem with you," he said. "You've always been nice enough to me. But you are a little distant."

"Distant?" I asked.

"Yeah, I mean we've worked together for how many years? And I don't really know anything about you. In fact, I remember going to one of the HHC Christmas parties. I ran into someone who worked with you at Generations + and I remember him saying, 'she doesn't give up any information.' You're not an easy person to get to know."

I couldn't disagree with him. But that's what this exercise was about so I tried to be accommodating.

"What kind of information are you looking for?" I asked.

"I don't know if you own your own house or you rent?" he asked. "Do you have a boyfriend? Do you two live together?"

What the hell does that have to do with anything? But as that thought crossed my mind, I remembered one of Kerry's admonitions about these exercises. He said, "This isn't about what you think, it's about what they think. Don't judge, just listen. If you find that you're doing most of the talking, you're doing something wrong." So I listened.

Wayne continued to share his thoughts. "You're always the last one to come to a meeting and you don't sit with everyone else. Your body language says you're not one of us." My mischievous mind thought, "I'm not. I'm a Vulcan. Continue." I needed levity during these exercises. Fortunately, I learned how to amuse myself at an early age. That said, I wasn't missing his point. I really hadn't been aware of how much of my actions were being watched by others. And I certainly wasn't aware of how they were being interpreted. I was already seeing the value of agreeing to do this. Then Wayne said something interesting.

"Some of this I think you can do something about. But some of these opinions have nothing to do with your behavior," he said. Intrigued by that comment, I fine-tuned my antennae. "Like I was talking to one member of the Cabinet," he continued. "And they were going on and on about you. 'Now she's got a Ph.D. How many fucking degrees is she going to get'? and I thought, what's that got to do with anything? And they were focusing on stuff like where the interview was going to be held."

I interrupted him.

"I said I was coming to you. Why would that be a problem?"

"I don't remember what you said," he replied. "It didn't really matter to me either way. But they seemed to think you said that we had to come to you. And this person said, 'she's the one that's fucked up, why do we have to come to her?' "

Wayne continued with his critique, but, I was lost in thought for a moment. Despite his feeble attempt at preserving the anonymity of his confidante, I knew exactly who he was talking about. There were only two people on the Cabinet who were wired that way and he was only friends with one of them: Gretchen.

When A.J. gave me the list of the people who'd agreed to participate, she told me that Gretchen wouldn't say yes or no. She wanted to talk to me on the phone first. I knew it wasn't going to be a simple matter with her. We had developed our own history over the years and none of it was pleasant.

Shortly after she took over the Quality Management department, Donna gave Gretchen the nickname "Chicken Little" because according to Gretchen, the sky was always falling. Even the few friends she had among the leadership team complained about that aspect of her personality. They just didn't tell her to her face. Putting her in charge of a department whose primary function was to identify what was wrong was like putting a drug addict in charge of the pharmacy.

That said, I think I could have managed the criticism for awhile if that was the extent of it. But she whined and there was no Spock in me when it came to whining. I had very strong emotions about it. I didn't like it, I couldn't stomach it, and I didn't permit it among my staff. Since Gretchen didn't report to me, I couldn't banish the practice when it came to her. All I could do was medicate myself with eye-rolling.

But among the people who found her caustic to work with, the most common complaint was that she was condescending. I was amazed by how much hostility could be contained in such a small frame. On top of that, she smoked. Between the bitterness and the nicotine I couldn't figure out how her body maintained its molecular cohesion. I still think one day someone's going to go into her office and find that she's disintegrated into a smoldering heap of lava pebbles.

Gretchen and I ran into difficulty early. The person I was at the time we started working together in 2001, took a full-throttle approach to any slight real or imagined. Where most people would just shrug off her comments or dictatorial emails, I pounced. We became adversaries quickly and I take as much of the blame for that as anyone.

Given our respective positions in the organization, I was the one who had the power. So the obligation rested with me to look past her shortcomings, whatever I thought they were. Unfortunately, I had a difficult time with that task and it permeated my every interaction with her. If my staff had a problem with any other member of the leadership team, I would usually tell them to try to work it out. But if it involved Gretchen, I jumped in with both feet, guns blazing, especially if they complained to me that she had belittled them in some way.

And on the few occasions that she fired a bullet of condescension directly at me, I responded with Hiroshima. That would usually send her running to Donna to complain and I would receive an email or a phone call of mild reprimand. "Candis, did you really have to slap her that hard?" Donna would say to me.

I was still fixated on Wayne's comments and I couldn't figure out why I would have said that the meetings would be in my office when I had specifically made arrangements to go to each of them. Perhaps it was a Freudian slip. Whatever it was, it brought to light the only concern I had about this assignment and I raised it with Kerry right away. I could stand criticism. I could even stand harsh criticism. What I couldn't stand was insincerity. I knew that going through this exercise with Gretchen and Maura was going to be a waste of time because they weren't going to be sincere. They were going to use it as an opportunity to play games. As we say in my neighborhood, I quit kindergarten because of recess. I don't play games when it comes to business. But apparently the games had already begun.

I asked Kerry if I could leave some people out of the exercise and I told him why. But before he could respond I anticipated what his answer would be and I gave it back to him. ". . . but you're going to tell me that that's precisely why I need to leave them on the list, right?" His response was blended with laughter.

"You're something else, Ms. Best. That's why I love talking to you."

I spent ten minutes on the phone with Gretchen and I could hear her twirling her hair. "I think I need to understand what you want to accomplish with this. Perhaps you could give me a list of questions you want to go over." I had to breathe deep to keep my composure. "This isn't my meeting, Gretchen. It's yours. It's your opportunity to tell me what if anything about our interactions is causing you to experience me as a hindrance. And what you think I should do to fix it. I won't be doing the talking, you will."

Kerry and I had gone over this language carefully. But knowing what Gretchen said to Wayne made it difficult for me to neutralize my disdain. I thought that if her comments to Wayne reflected the way she really felt, why bother to meet? Nonetheless, I treated this like any other commitment. I'd made it and I was sticking to it, all of it. She finally decided that she did want to meet so I went up to her office, prepared to swallow hard and bite my tongue. The meeting started simply enough and she pulled no punches.

"I don't know what anyone else has told you, but, it's no secret that we don't really work well together." This was her moment. My job was to facilitate it.

"Okay. Why do you think that is?" I asked.

"It's difficult to communicate with you. I think you can be hateful and mean-spirited."

What could I say to that? I'd been called a lot of things over the course of my life and I knew most of the ugliest labels. But to the best of my knowledge those were two words I'd never heard used to describe me. Interestedly enough they were two words that I had heard used to describe *her*. However, this was still her meeting so I remained silent.

"I'll show you what I mean," she continued.

She got up, walked over to one of the file drawers in her desk and pulled out a piece of paper. It was a copy of one of our more spirited email exchanges. It was clear that she viewed my words as "hateful" and "mean-spirited," but, not her own. But that's not what surprised me. What surprised me was that the email was three years old! Despite Kerry's thoughtful and timely advice about reserving judgment and limiting my responses, I just couldn't help myself.

"You've been holding on to this for three years?"

But that was why I needed to have that meeting with her. I know that now, but, unfortunately at the time I still didn't get the lesson. So I squandered the opportunity. Instead of biting my tongue like I was supposed to, I confronted her about what she'd said to Wayne. When she squirmed around a response, trying to neither confirm nor deny what I already knew she said, she lost any remaining shred of credibility in my eyes. That meant all bets were off. Any possibility of mutual growth and cooperation floated right out the window. Before long we both had swords drawn. Instead of gathering valuable insight into how I could meet her halfway, the meeting spiraled out of control and we resorted back to hurling sludge at each other across the conference table.

When you have two people carrying such dense debris on the mantles of their person, it's difficult if not impossible for anything good to pass between them. For as long as we worked together, nothing ever did. Every person that comes into your life is teaching you something. I suspect that the lessons we keep repeating are the ones that come from the people we don't get along with. We have a tendency not to listen to the teachers we don't like. It took a long time for me to figure out the lesson that Gretchen came into my life to teach me. Emotions will always overwhelm good judgment if you let them take the lead.

My meeting with Maura was far more benign. She too reached back into the past, bringing up how hurt she was that I didn't come to her first about my idea to redesign the inpatient service. This time I just listened and kept my opinions to myself. The meeting ended up being little more than thirty minutes of exchanging oxygen for carbon dioxide.

Later as I was preparing to write this book, I had occasion to look back over my notes from those meetings. There were comments from both Gretchen and Maura that I appreciated very differently being able to read them with the benefits of time and distance. One said she didn't feel like she was being listened to and the other didn't feel that she could speak to me. If that's how they felt about the Chief Operating Officer, then I was indeed getting in their way, something for which I deserved a failing grade. But at the time I blew right past it.

My meeting with Ira was surprisingly brief. He said, "Now that I think about it, things have gotten better between us. And it must have been something you did because I don't remember doing anything differently." He was the only one to acknowledge that I'd made an effort and I appreciated it.

When I met with Lorenzo it didn't take long for me to figure out that he was trying to recast the meeting into a therapy session. I found that comical to say the least.

"You've changed, Candis" he said. "You've changed. You were more fun when you were here the last time."

I knew what he meant because he'd said that before. Lorenzo had some peculiar habits. At social functions he would often appear to have started the party without the rest of us. As it pertained to me, in lieu of a simple greeting he would grab me out of a crowd and slobber on my cheeks or squeeze my love handles. I would have to wiggle out of his reach and run away to hide behind the nearest potted plant. I found it all harmless back in 1999. But when I came back to Woodhull, I was a woman on a mission. I didn't have any patience for that sort of behavior. His was just another tombstone that I knocked over without giving it a second thought. Apparently he did.

"When you come into a room, it's as if all the air is sucked out of it. Everybody stiffens up a little," he said. "Doesn't it bother you that you have that effect on people?"

"Not at all."

That probably was not the response that Kerry would have coached me to give, but, Rome wasn't built in a day.

There were other observations from other people. I learned that some of my colleagues resented my relationship with Donna. They thought I enjoyed privileges others didn't have. Obviously, she and I had become close over the years. But if anyone thought that she said yes to everything I asked of her, they grossly overestimated the extent of her fondness for me. I was also described as abrupt, aloof, unapproachable and intimidating. After the third or fourth time I heard those descriptions I couldn't find it funny anymore. I had to be getting in people's way if they shook with fear every time I walked into the room.

There were few things besides Brussels sprouts and lima beans that I wanted to avoid more than getting warm and fuzzy with the people I worked with. The description of the man who was a great humanitarian but just didn't like people, probably applied to me at that point. But I was learning that trying to lead people without getting close to them was like trying to swim without getting wet. Kerry came into my life at the perfect time to help me figure out how to strike a balance between what others needed from me and what I could live with giving.

But there was one other recurring theme that I had to address and it had to do with my staff. I didn't realize that in the process of getting their work done, my staff was actually fueling some of the ghost stories being told about me. During one of our divisional meetings I told them about the feedback sessions I was conducting with the Cabinet and the Chiefs. I always kept them informed about everything that was going on. Our meetings were free-flowing so they felt comfortable sharing their opinions. To my surprise they were outraged.

"This is garbage," Marie said. "You're the one keeping things moving around here and they're criticizing you? When do we get to tell them what we think about them?" There were more comments of that general tenor. It was sweet.

"Thanks for defending me," I said. "But it really isn't necessary. I volunteered to do this. But there's something I need to ask you. One of the things that came out during the consultant's interviews was that you all use my name like a sledgehammer. Is that true?"

The silence was deafening. No one asked me what I meant. They knew exactly what I meant. "So it is true," I said. After a few more moments of awkward silence, someone finally owned up. As usual, Chrissy was the first to speak.

"I guess it's true," she said. "But that's the only way you can get people to respond sometimes."

Once one started, the rest chimed in.

"We try to work with the other departments, but, sometimes you have to go back to them over and over again to get them to do their part. Who has time for that?"

Apparently saying something like "Fine, then I'm going to tell Ms. Best" worked wonders for getting calls returned. And copying me on emails was feared like a 9mm semiautomatic pistol to the forehead. As the confessions continued to spill forth, I didn't know whether to laugh or cry. Now I understood how the legend of the "Terror Queen" continued to grow despite my efforts to craft a softer, gentler image. If you see someone jump at the mention of a name often enough, you'll start jumping too. It's like the bell and Pavlov's dog. My own mother had the opportunity to witness it first-hand.

She'd stopped off at one of the delicatessens across the street from the hospital and she was standing in line to pay for her food. She noticed that the young man in front of her was wearing a Woodhull I.D. card so she struck up a conversation.

"You work at Woodhull?" she asked him.

"Yes, ma'am."

"Oh, so does my daughter."

"Really?" he said turning toward her, "What's her name?"

When she replied "Candis Best" the man shouted "Ms. Best?!" He grabbed his food and ran out the door without even taking his change. I'd bet my tax refund that he wouldn't have known who I was if we passed each other in the hallway. But that didn't matter. Ghosts keep the legends going and they are notoriously hard to kill.

But a sledgehammer has two sides. I addressed one side with my team. But the other side needed to be addressed by the Cabinet. My staff made an excellent point during our unscheduled rap session. They used my name because they believed that they couldn't get what they needed any other way. And they were right. I didn't expect them to check with me before they made decisions, but, many of my colleagues had not similarly empowered their staff. It made the task of working collaboratively at the department director level a frustrating experience for everyone.

My essence was far from the only cause of dysfunction at the network. In fact, Kerry's exercise seemed to lift a lot of it. But once the spotlight shifted from me, we were left with the same problems we'd confronted from the beginning. With all the progress we'd made, people still weren't working comfortably together across divisions. The network staff didn't function as a team because the senior leadership didn't function as a team. It didn't take long for that to surface with the consultants.

Donna shared information at our Cabinet meetings and we had superficial conversations, but, there was little-to-no honest dialogue going on at those meetings. The dialogue happened when the factions broke off after the meeting was over. The department directors took their cues from us and their staff took their cues from them. All the special consultancy projects in the world weren't going to change anything until we addressed that.

I've always been taken with the notion that God speaks to us in a whisper. It is a statement often quoted that I no longer believe. God doesn't speak in a whisper. It only appears that way because we're not listening. The turning points - those life-changing moments, whether they happen inside or outside of a religious context, tend to fit your frequency. Those of us who require a thunderbolt to the forehead will eventually receive one if repeated flashes of lightening don't do the trick. We will attract them like magnets.

I can remember my grandmother dragging me to church when I used to spend summer vacations with her in Baltimore. Every Sunday someone would get "filled with the spirit." First came the crying, then the twitching, followed by an anointed version of jumping jacks. The man or woman would jump straight up and down, eyes closed with their arms sweeping in and out in a lateral motion like a swimmer's breast stroke. In short order, two ushers dressed in white from the tips of their cotton gloves to the soles of their nurse's tennis shoes, would appear at the side of the newly converted. One would take one arm, one would take the other and they would be off to the pulpit.

Every Sunday I would watch this transpire (sometimes involving the same person I'd seen get the spirit a few weeks earlier). Even at an early age, I remember thinking that if that was what I had to do to get "saved," I'd just have to drown. No thunderbolts for me, thank you, a simple tap on the shoulder will do. And that's just what I received. There comes a moment in our lives, and for some of us there will be several such moments, when time slows just a bit. The muscles in our stomach contract just enough to let us know that the ground beneath our feet is starting to shift. These are the beacons.

Our lives are not linear. We are continuously circling the crossroads that mark the turning points in our lives. If you miss the road sign, the next beacon might be in lights. If you miss the lights, the next beacon may be accompanied by a horn. But if you keep missing the beacons, that crossroad will be the place where you total your car. Whatever the signs are for you, you have to slow down or you'll miss them.

Every day above ground is an opportunity and I believe that every opportunity is an opportunity for greatness. But individual greatness is never an exit off the interstate. It's at the end of the side road that has no street sign. The beacons are the only way to find it. There comes a time in every life when you must turn off the main road and turn off you will.

In September of 2003, I was recruited for a job in Baltimore to be president of a 200-bed hospital. It was a great opportunity. I went back and forth through several rounds of interviews until it was down to me and one other person. But I was torn. I was engrossed in two relationships I didn't want to leave, one with a person and the other with my church. When I didn't get the job I was actually relieved because in the process, I'd awakened to the feeling that something important was about to happen in my life and whatever it was, it would be happening in New York. It was a tap on the shoulder.

If you have ever had a foot or a leg fall asleep, the process of waking that body part up is unforgettable. First you feel nothing and then you feel everything. From the end of 2003 forward, it was as if I was waking up from the inside out. I felt and noticed everything that was happening and everyone that was passing in and out of my life. Even though I didn't get the job in Baltimore, the CEO of that hospital system, and I struck up a friendship that continues to this day. On more than one occasion, he has been the source of valuable advice to me.

Then Kerry came into my life. I have no doubt that had our interaction happened a year earlier it would have gone very differently and we would both have been disappointed. It seemed like everywhere I turned I saw beacons. Even though most of the time I had no idea what they meant, I saw them, or I felt them and I knew they meant something. At first, it was extremely unsettling to have these little strobe lights going off at different times through different people and not know why. But eventually, I learned to trust that the meanings would reveal themselves soon enough.

CHAPTER TWELVE
DECEMBER, 2004

BY THE TIME WE approached the end of 2004, the gentle tapping on my shoulder had turned into a full body massage. I could not shake these feelings and they were getting stronger. The only words I could find to describe it was that I felt like I was being "called" for something. When I mentioned the feelings I was having, during a family dinner one evening, I remember my sister giving me a puzzled look. "So you're going to Divinity School now?" she asked.

I saw the equally bewildered looks on my parents' faces and it all came together in my mind in a way that forced me to laugh. In the African-American community, the term "being called" is usually reserved for the ministry. So when I used that expression to describe my feelings to my family, I should have anticipated the ideas it might cause to spring to their minds.

After my most recent graduation, despite my assertions to the contrary, they were convinced that I had some pathological obsession with going to school. Add that to my growing involvement at church and I could see how they might arrive at the wrong conclusion. I quickly set about to clear up that bit of confusion. I'm no big fan of celibacy and the way I can curse? "No," I said. "I'm not going to Divinity School. I don't know what I'm being 'called' for, but, I know it isn't the ministry."

Right around this time, the Chief of the Department of Medicine was preparing to leave us. He'd come to America from the Dominican Republic to become a physician and had spent his entire career at Woodhull. He was a nice man, good-looking and popular within the community. But he ran the largest clinical service at the hospital and the improvements we'd made were catching up with him. He was like most of the people who'd spent their entire careers at Woodhull. He didn't know how to make widgets unless the factory was under water. When his service began to dry out, he responded like a fish.

Professionally, Woodhull was all he'd ever known. Being witness to him preparing to leave was as difficult to watch as it was for him to do. My feedback exercises coincided with his departure so I went up to his office to visit with him. Our session was far more relaxed than the others had been. Given the circumstances, it wasn't surprising when the conversation soon shifted from me to him.

"How are you holding up?" I asked.

"Pretty well. It's time," he said. "But you know, I'm going to miss this place."

He talked about his family and told me amusing stories about his days as a resident at the hospital. We laughed together, but, his laugh was labored. Then he turned to me and took my hand. He looked deep into my eyes and said, "Candis, I want to tell you something."

The shift in his voice and his body language captured my attention. He said, "Whatever you do, don't trust Ira Gold." This wasn't the first time someone had said something like that to me, so that wasn't what surprised me. It was the way he said it. There was no mistaking how strongly he felt about what he was telling me.

We all knew that he didn't really want to leave. But as much as I liked him, it was time for a change in the Medicine service. His department came dangerously close to losing its residency program on more than one occasion because he didn't know how to accept help. The negotiations regarding his retirement involved many people, not just Ira. He obviously thought his leaving was part of some plot that Ira engineered. I didn't want him to leave filled with that kind of bitterness, especially when I didn't think the reasons behind it were accurate.

"Don't focus on Ira," I said. "This isn't about him." But he wouldn't let it go.

"I'm telling you. He can't be trusted. Watch your back."

At that moment, I was more concerned about the person I was with than I was about myself. "I live my life focused on putting my best foot forward," I said. "I try not to cause harm to anyone else and I sleep well at night because of it. My back will take care of itself."

My response clearly surprised him. He sat back in his chair and just stared at me for a moment without saying another word. It was as if he had learned something new about me, something that he wished he had more time to explore. "You've changed," he said with a gentle smile. I smiled back and wished him well. The depth of how much I was changing was still to be tested.

December of 2004 also marked Angela's six-month anniversary as the Acting Chief Nursing Executive. Acting appointments are only supposed to last for six months at HHC. She wanted to know if she was going to get the job and I couldn't blame her. I would have wanted a decision if I were in her position. I had a dilemma and I was not going to wrestle with it alone. I went to have another talk with Donna.

"Angela's been "Acting" for six months," I said. "She wants to know what we're going to do."

Donna looked up at me with genuine surprise. "Has it been six months already?"

I knew how she felt. That was my response when Angela brought it to my attention. I'd hoped that Donna would make the decision for me, but, she had a surprise for me. She punted.

"So what do you want to do?" she asked with an unfamiliar air of apprehension. Judging by the look on her face, she was not going to weigh in on this decision at all. And for once I really wanted her to.

I thought about it for a moment and then I said, "Give her the job."

"Really?" Donna replied through an expression of utter shock.

I could see why she would be stunned. But what were my options? Sure, Angela still had a lot of problems directing her department. She didn't have many strong Associate Directors and the bench beneath them was even weaker. She had a lot of ideas about how to fix that, but, I wasn't convinced that the solutions she was proposing were going to yield the results she thought they were. But to her credit, morale within the department was starting to inch up.

More than that, she was present and she was truly making an effort. There is an old saying in hospital administration, "As nursing goes, so goes the hospital." For six months she'd been holding that nursing department together with spit and chewing gum. It wasn't pretty, but, it was holding. Running the nursing department at Woodhull was a difficult job. There wasn't really anybody around that I could be certain would do it any better. The only alternative was to string her along for a few more months while I looked for somebody else, and my conscience wouldn't let me do that. Whatever her shortcomings, she'd earned that job. We'd just have to figure it out together.

Chapter Thirteen
Spring, 2005

THE BEGINNING OF 2005 marked its own period of upheaval for HHC. There were always those who believed that the motivation behind all of Dr. Chang's grand ideas owed as much to his desire to build a platform for him to get a better job, as it did to his love for HHC. If those rumors were true, his plans took a long time to yield fruit. But when they did the fruit was juicy. In February of 2005, Dr. Chang announced that he was leaving HHC to accept a position with a large system in California; a position that had to be paying at least three times what he was making at HHC. The race was on to find a successor.

The whirlwind that accompanies the selection of a president for HHC is only slightly less hysterical than trying to predict whether the winner of the Kentucky Derby will win the Triple Crown. It's a brand of speculation that only gets wilder and more absurd the longer it goes on. The mayor had lived through that once when he picked Dr. Chang. It was clear that he wanted to pick his replacement in a hurry.

One of the circulating rumors that quickly appeared to be accurate was that whoever the new president was going to be, he or she was going to be Hispanic. Billionaire or no billionaire, even Mayor Mike knew how the rules of engagement worked in Gotham. We already had an African-American as Chairperson of HHC's Board of Directors, so a matching set was out of the question. Chocolate would have to sit this one out and vanilla had fallen out of fashion more than a decade ago. They weren't even discussing a Caucasian candidate. But apparently the mayor also wanted someone who was familiar with HHC. That narrowed the field considerably.

The person who got the job joined the Corporation a year before I did. Gilberto Galan worked for a few years at the Queens Network managing ambulatory care and managed care. Then he became HHC's General Counsel, which is where I first came in contact with him. Woodhull came under scrutiny by the state Attorney General's office after a local community group accused the hospital of having inadequate translation services.

We were already developing a comprehensive program when the story broke. So when the Attorney General's office launched an investigation, we agreed to a stipulation that was basically the policy we had already written coupled with an agreement to submit annual compliance reports for two years. The program was going to be supervised by Gina, so I worked with the General Counsel and his staff on the negotiations. In the process, Gilberto and I established a rapport.

When the Sr. Vice-President of the Queens Network retired at the end of 2004, Dr. Chang appointed Gilberto to replace him. This was a surprise to everyone, primarily because Gilberto didn't have any experience running one hospital much less a network that had two. So you can imagine the shock-trauma that occurred when just three short months after that appointment, he was named the Acting President of HHC.

It hardly seemed like three years had passed but once again we found ourselves back in Joint Commission preparation mode. This was the first year that JCAHO was piloting the unannounced survey process and we volunteered for it. But after a shockingly bad mock survey, Donna pulled us out of the pilot. That meant our survey would be occurring sometime in November and the countdown had begun. It was the week before the Memorial Day holiday. Donna and I were sitting in her office chatting about one thing or another as we frequently did, when Mimi interrupted us to tell Donna that she was holding a call from the president. I asked Donna if she wanted me to leave, but, she gestured no as she answered the phone.

"Hi Gil, what's up . . . no, not really . . . sure, when can we expect you? . . . Alright, Hospital Police will be waiting for you at the entrance to escort you to my office. I'll see you in 20 minutes." Then she hung up.

She looked over her glasses at me and I looked over my glasses at her. We were having another one of our telepathic conversations and we were both thinking the same thing: "Uh oh."

When the president decides that he needs to see you immediately that's news. But if it's important enough for him to come to you, your life is about to change. Donna broke the silence.

"What do you think *that's* about?" she said.

"You know what *that's* about."

"What?"

"It can only be one thing," I said. "You're going to Bellevue."

The Sr. Vice-President of Bellevue's network had been under investigation for months. Everybody knew it. And Bellevue had also been struggling to maintain its "flagship" status, so it wasn't going to be a job that just anybody could walk into. Donna had been HHC's relief pitcher for years. When they were going into the late innings, down on runs, she was the first one they called up from the bull pen. But as usual, she tried to act like the matter was up for negotiation. She immediately raised the curtain on another one of her one-woman shows.

She banged on the desk. She marched back and forth. "I'm not going! He can just turn that car right around if that's what he's coming here for because I'm not doing it! I'm sick of being shipped around! Well, I guess this is it. This is the year I'm retiring because I'm not going!" I sat back in my chair, crossed my legs, ate some candy from her desk and watched the show. I'd seen this one before. It was a revival of her performance when Dr. Ferdinand asked her to come to Woodhull. But I always enjoyed her monologues.

I waited for her to finish and then I said, "Yeah, right. Listen, your ass is going to Bellevue. I know it and you know it. The only question I need answered right now is what's going to happen to me?"

Mimi stuck her head in and announced, "He's on his way up." I sprinted out of Donna's office, went into my own and closed the door behind me. The tingles and the taps were on overdrive and I had a feeling that I was about to find out why. After about twenty minutes, Mimi called me on the intercom. "You can come back in." I entered Donna's office cautiously. She didn't have to tell me to close the door.

"So?"

"You were right," she said.

"What happened?"

Bellevue's CEO had a meeting with the president earlier that morning. He'd spent the previous day answering questions. They had him in a corner and there was no getting out. Allegedly (for legal reasons I must use the word "allegedly"), there were copies of checks with his name on it, and whatever he was mixed up in involved a hospital vendor. He *allegedly* tried to explain away the transactions as loans. But, however he explained it, by the end of his meeting with the president he was out of a job.

233

Donna was perplexed. "Why would he admit to a loan? You can't take a loan from a vendor. He had to know he was going to lose his job." I knew why. "They had copies of checks right? Then he had to say something. Admitting to a loan only gets him fired. Admitting to a kick-back means he's going to jail."

I felt bad for the guy. The Sr. Vice-Presidents were a mixed bag of personalities. And while nobody was going to mistake Bellevue's chief for Einstein, especially after this stunt, he was a really nice guy. I liked him personally. I couldn't for the life of me figure out why he would let himself get mixed up in something like this. Nonetheless, I was sorry to see him go out like that.

According to Donna, Gilberto was beside himself. We both knew why. His appointment wasn't permanent yet. Six weeks after he became president, Jacobi Hospital was the source of a scandal involving hundreds of abnormal pap smears where the results had never been communicated to the patients. It was a huge story in all the local papers and quite an embarrassment. Gilberto took the rather Draconian step of firing John Fortunado, the Sr. Vice-President of the North Bronx Network. Holding the leader accountable is one thing. But most people thought that under the circumstances, firing the CEO was a bit extreme. Now he had no choice but to fire another one. The Corporation only had seven Network Sr. Vice-Presidents and now, including the vacancy created when Gilberto was named president, they were down by three in less than three months.

Under the circumstances, Donna didn't put up much of a fight, although she refused to commit to going permanently. The most immediate concern was that Bellevue was also going through a JCAHO survey that year. It was scheduled for August, less than three months away. Their mock surveys had been worse than ours so she had her work cut out for her. "So when are you leaving?" I asked. "You know I'm going on vacation next week. I told him it's a trip out of the country. I can't cancel it. He doesn't want me to go to Bellevue for one day and then leave so they're going to wait until I get back to make the announcement."

"What about North Brooklyn?" I asked. It felt like my stomach had congealed into the kind of gelatin mold that has bits of fruit in it.

"You're it kid," she said with a smile. "He didn't even hesitate when I asked him. His exact words were, 'Candis can take over here. That's the one thing I'm not worried about.' "

"But take over how?" I pressed.

The president had several options in a situation like this. I could take over in the capacity I was in as Chief Operating Officer. Or he could appoint me Acting Executive Director but *not* Sr. Vice-President. That would mean that I would still have to report to a corporate officer and there was no telling who that might be. Donna felt certain that I was getting the whole "kit and caboodle." But, until there was a formal announcement, there was no way to be sure. All we could do now was sit and wait. I was sworn to secrecy about what I'd just learned, so I was forced to do my waiting in silence. I returned to my office.

The next two weeks were curiously unsettling for me. Confidence is one of the things I took extra helpings of when God was passing out portions. I knew I could handle the mechanics of the job. But I wasn't so mad with hubris to not understand that the mechanics were only *part* of the job. I loved being Chief Operating Officer. In fact, I thought it was better than being CEO. You had almost all the power of a CEO, but the buck stopped with someone else. So much of holding the top spot required the talents of a diplomat. I knew that wasn't high on the list of my strengths.

But that wasn't my biggest concern. It was obvious to everyone that Donna had been grooming me to replace her when she retired. But despite what I'm sure most people thought, I wasn't salivating for her job. That's because as wonderful and talented as my staff was, I didn't have a "me." I had staff members who were smarter than me. I had staff members who worked harder than I did. I certainly had staff members who were more personable than people believed me to be at the moment, and as a group they were awesome. In fact I can say without hesitation that they were a more cohesive team than the senior cabinet, and as a result far more effective at what they did. But there was something above and beyond that in the relationship that Donna and I had developed over the years.

There is no more vulnerable position than being on top. Trust is everything. I'd been Commander Riker to Donna's Captain Picard through 9/11, the 2003 blackout, and more than one bout of unfathomable choices by the staff, where the only thing that kept us from setting depth charges in the basement was a round of apple martinis. I would have walked into the bowels of Hell for Donna without blinking an eyelash and she knew it. I had my share of shortcomings, but, anytime someone else tried to impale me with an arrow because of them, she stepped in front of it.

The cumulative effect of all that history meant that in a crunch, in moments where there was no time for thought or conversation, she knew she could leap without looking. No matter what else was going on with me, I'd have hold of her lifeline. Having that kind of relationship with your second-in-command gives you a peace of mind that is a little less reassuring when you have to piece it together with three or four people.

But none of that mattered now. It was going to be what it was going to be. All I could do was ride it out. The decision about Bellevue's new CEO may have had to wait, but announcing the departure of the current one couldn't. Gilberto sent the Corporation's Chief

Operating Officer, Vincent DiNapoli, over to run Bellevue until Donna returned from her vacation. But since everyone knew he wasn't staying, that did nothing to stop the rampant speculation about who Bellevue's new Sr. V.P. was going to be. I was fielding calls nonstop from people trying to get me to confirm that Donna was getting the job. Unfortunately for the gossip mongers, not talking is something I can do without effort.

When Donna finally returned from vacation, she and the president agreed that she would come to Woodhull first, to inform our senior staff of the changes. Then the two of them would go to Bellevue together later in the day. It was being presented as a temporary reassignment. She was still maintaining that she didn't want to start over with a new network yet again. I remember one of our last conversations before she left.

Even on its worst day, Bellevue was and would always be the flagship of the Corporation. It's the hospital designated to treat the President of the United States if he's injured while he's in New York City. It's affiliated with one of the most prestigious medical schools in the country and running that hospital is the job that everyone wanted. I told her what I thought.

"Donna, what you've done here is nothing short of a miracle, but it's a miracle that will be forgotten as soon as we walk out the door. As much as I hate to admit it, it doesn't matter what we do. Woodhull will never be Bellevue in the eyes of the rest of the world. Retire when you want to retire, but, when you go, go out on top. After the career you've had, HHC owes you that job. Don't let him give it to somebody else."

I didn't know exactly how the state of affairs would ultimately play out, but, I was certain of two things. First, Donna wasn't coming back to Woodhull. And second, that was the last conversation we were ever going to have with her as my boss. I'd been in the Corporation seven years at that point and I'd spent almost six of them reporting to her. We had come to the point every mentor and protégé must reach. I'd reached this moment before. So I knew that when it arrives, you have to pause to mark the moment.

I didn't attend the staff meeting where she made the announcement. I knew how the range of emotions would run. Some people would be surprised, some people wouldn't. Some would meet my appointment as the new sheriff in town with ambivalence if not satisfaction; for others there would be tearing of clothes and gnashing of teeth. I'd already gone through my goodbye ritual with her. It was their turn. I didn't want to intrude.

Donna gave each of them an opportunity to speak with her privately before she left. I waited until I thought the last of the tribe had gone and then I went into Mimi's office. It served as a sort of anteroom to Donna's office. Her door was open so I could see Lorenzo and Ira standing in front of Donna's desk. They couldn't see me and I couldn't hear what they were saying; but there was definitely some clothes tearing and teeth gnashing going on. My suspicion about the tenor of their conversation was confirmed when they turned around, saw me and froze, and then scurried past me without looking me in the eye.

It was only at that moment that the magnitude of what I was facing really hit me. I was accustomed to working with a team of my choosing. Being able to select people whose styles meshed with mine had been one of the keys to my success. Now I would have to lead a team with more than one member who I wouldn't turn my back on in a dark alley. My mental ramblings must have been etched on my face when I went into her office because Donna took one look at me and burst into a belly laugh.

"What's funny?" I asked.

"You," she said. "All of you. Everyone's acting like the world's coming to end."

"Everyone?!" I shouted.

It was worse than I thought. But she was quick to reassure me.

"No no! Not everyone, just the usual suspects. You know who they are. Gretchen and Maura are ready to fall out and die. The only other people that asked to see me were "Mutt and Jeff". I think Wayne's actually happy about it. He's got a better shot with you than he had with me."

"I could see how excited Ira and Lorenzo were," I said.

She relayed the gist of their conversation.

"I asked them, 'What do you think she's going to do? Run around chopping heads off? Candis isn't insane. Everything with her is about what makes sense. She's not going to do anything to get in the way of things moving forward. And I'll tell you something else. Gilberto likes Candis. He thinks very highly of her. So if you think you're going to stir up trouble for her with him all you're going to do is make yourself look foolish. You need to relax.'"

"From the looks on their faces," I said. "It doesn't look like your little pep talk worked."

"They asked me why I couldn't supervise you from Bellevue," she said.

When I heard that, I went from concerned to pissed off.

"What did you say?" I asked.

"I told them that you don't need supervision anymore. Not that I had much luck trying to supervise you anyway," she said with a wink. I needed a laugh.

"Besides, I'm going to have my hands full," she continued. "I won't have time to be thinking about what's happening over here."

I guess I still didn't look reassured, so she stopped gathering her belongings and put her hand on my shoulder.

"And I don't have to. You'll be fine. Don't give these knuckleheads another thought. You're ready for this. You know what to do. Just do it."

Looking back, I guess that was the day when the purpose of those feelings I'd been having began to flower. Ready or not, it was show time, or so I thought. At the time I was convinced that moving into the top spot was the mysterious calling that I was being prepared for. I had no idea how wrong I was.

CHAPTER FOURTEEN
JUNE, 2005

ONE OF GILBERTO'S INSTRUCTIONS was that he
didn't want any major changes made during this interim
period. I remained in my office and Donna left her office
exactly as it was. Mimi went with her to Bellevue, but,
that was fine. A.J. was more than capable of stepping up.
But there were some changes I had to make. I had to
have some of my own people around me. So I put
Bobby, Gina and Cora on the Executive Cabinet along
with Angela – there was no way to avoid that. My first
test came immediately.

Just before Gilberto's big visit, Donna told me
and Brian that she wanted us to take an inpatient unit
out of service and she wanted it to happen by June 1st. I
did what I always did. She gave me an assignment and a
deadline and I went to work. The rumors had just begun
about the governor convening a hospital-closing
commission. So everyone was sensitive about their
occupancy rates. We'd been working on our rates for
over a year, but, we could not consistently stay above
80%. Taking a unit out of service made sense. But by the
time the effects of the decision started to be felt, I was
the boss and everyone was complaining.

It was taking longer for patients to move from
the emergency room up to beds on the inpatient units
after they were admitted. This was a statistic that we
were winning awards for just months earlier. Dr.
Wallace, our ER Chief, was livid and you didn't want to
make him angry. He was a lean and mean 6'6 with wire-

241

rimmed glasses. The more excited he got, the thicker his Jamaican accent became. But he was easily the most widely respected Chief we had.

When Donna wanted to check the pulse of the medical staff and she wanted to talk to someone whose opinion she valued, she didn't call Ira or Lorenzo, she called Michael Wallace. I had good working relationships with all the Chiefs because their administrators reported to me. He certainly was one of the ones I also had a lot of respect for and I believed he felt the same way about me. I needed it to stay that way now more than ever. I should have been able to rely on Ira to help mediate this type of issue. I *should have,* but, I couldn't.

Trying to run a 400-bed hospital with Ira Gold as the Medical Director was like trying to take the SAT exam with a puppy in the room. You can't assign a task to a puppy. It does what *it* wants to do. So it runs around, getting in the middle of everything, making a mess that you're going to have to clean up later and you still have to finish the exam in the time allotted. This was the source of all the early conflict between Ira and me over the years we'd worked together. Relations between us had improved and I really didn't want to see things devolve back to the way they'd been in the past. But it wasn't looking good.

Since he had not been in on the initial decision when Donna made it, he decided that he was going to throw up his hands and play the piccolo for the choirs of naysayers. All anybody wanted to talk about was reopening the unit that we'd closed. I couldn't do it. The staff had already been reassigned and all the equipment had been redistributed. But I wouldn't have done it even if I could have, because we didn't need another 34-bed unit. What we needed was to be more efficient. That was something that no one could deny when confronted with the facts, not even Ira. But it was easier to complain than to come up with a solution, especially when the new captain was still getting her sea legs beneath her.

I knew I couldn't respond to the behavior the way I would have in the past. If I had been dealing with my old team I wouldn't have had to. When I said, "Do what you have to do, just fix it," that's what they did. My people didn't whine they worked. But I wasn't just dealing with *my* people anymore. I had a dilemma. Thank God for the relationship I'd developed with Kerry, the consultant.

After I finished my feedback exercises, he left the door open for me to use him as a sounding board. I'd reached the point where I knew I really needed one. I shared the details of everything that was going on. I was being regularly bashed for a decision that wasn't even mine, although it was one I agreed with wholeheartedly. The first thing he said was, "You know you can't say that this wasn't your idea. You're in charge now."

I knew that. I wasn't intending to. But I also knew that people weren't responding to the decision the way they would have if Donna had still been there. It's not that people didn't complain when she was around. They did, but, not with the vehemence that I was experiencing. And while she didn't like whining either, she clearly had a higher tolerance level for it than I did. Otherwise, some of the gold-medal winning whining champs that we had on the Cabinet would have been on the slow boat to China long ago. I attributed it to the fact that she was both a mother and a grandmother and I was neither of those things.

Once I'd laid everything out for Kerry, he agreed immediately that the leadership team's behavior was unacceptable. I appreciated the validation he gave me at that moment, because I was starting to question my own sanity. And it kept getting better because much to my surprise, he actually advised me to do the very thing that I wanted to do. "You need to confront this head on," he said. "Let them know what kind of behavior is acceptable from a leadership team and what kind is not. They don't have to like the leader's decision, but, once the decision is made, they have a responsibility to execute it. Disagreements are held in private or not at all. They can't act like they're not involved. Let them know that they have a choice. If they're not up to the challenge, they should make other plans."

I was relieved. But just because we agreed in principal, that didn't mean that I still didn't need advice. As most great minds will acknowledge, it's not what you say, it's how you say it. Thanks to my lingering reputation as "Xena the Warrior Princess," I knew I needed to convey this message in as temperate a tone as possible.

I decided to stick to the facts, but, I avoided singling anyone out. I knew who was whipping the troops into a frenzy and who wasn't, but, I kept my comments general. I relied heavily on Kerry's examples about the role of leadership and talked about what "any leader" would expect from their team instead of what I expected from them. I finished by reframing the issue and shifting the burden to me.

"I respect how much pressure this change is placing on everybody, including the change in leadership," I said. "But there's work to be done and I need everybody on board to do it. We are not reopening 10-100, so that is no longer going to be part of our dialogue. What we can discuss is what we need to do to ease congestion using the space we have available. Tell me what you need me to do for you, within that context, and you have my word that I will make it happen."

I watched the body language carefully. Cora, Gina and Bobby were looking at their new colleagues with bafflement. Their expression read, "I don't know what's wrong with these people. Let's just get to work." Gretchen and Maura were looking down at the surface of the conference table with defiant expressions. Brian was smiling, Yvonne was looking through her performance evaluations report, Simon was looking at spreadsheets, Wayne was looking confused, Elliot was looking clueless, Angela's arms were folded and Ira was doodling. But I decided that it was a start. We would move forward from there.

We continued to struggle with patient flow for another month or two. But eventually things started to improve. And just in time, because just as we were bringing one fire under control, I turned around and found myself being handed a grenade without the pin.

CHAPTER FIFTEEN
JULY, 2005

I HADN'T FORGOTTEN WHAT the consultants told Donna. The staff loved those events we used to have and they missed them. So it occurred to me that another event was precisely what we needed. And I had the perfect excuse. It had been exactly one year since we launched the "Platinum Experience," our bold, new customer service program. At a point in time when initiatives like this one were usually dying on the vine, the Platinum Experience was still alive and kicking. This was my opportunity. We were going to celebrate the program's first anniversary with a "Platinum Day." I told Yvonne what I wanted to do and she went to work. We filled the auditorium with balloons and gave out awards. It was a huge success.

While I had everyone's attention, I decided that this was a good time to unveil our network goals for the upcoming year. July 1st marked the start of a new fiscal year and in terms of our financial position, the North Brooklyn Network was starting out ranked second to last in the Corporation. The governor's proposed "rightsizing commission" was now a reality. So our performance was no longer just an internal matter. On top of that, we'd just received the results of our annual employee satisfaction survey and it showed a lot of room for improvement.

I decided to put it all out on the table. I wanted every employee from the clerk at the front desk to the surgeon in the operating room, to know just what we were up against. And then for some reason I made a bold prediction. I highlighted every one of the indicators where we were doing poorly and pledged that by this time the next year, we would be celebrating success. It was beyond bold. It was outrageous now that I think about. I stepped in front of the camera like Joe Namath predicting victory in Super Bowl III and I had absolutely no idea how we were going to pull it off.

As July came to a close, it was early enough that I was still feeling optimistic. It appeared that the Cabinet was settling down and the emergency room was getting back to normal. For a brief moment in time, life was good and I felt like the master of all I surveyed. Then I received a call from Gretchen. The Department of Health was in the building to conduct an unannounced review of our outpatient dialysis unit. This was not going to be pretty.

That unit had been a problem since before we came back in 2001. In fact, we weren't even supposed to be performing outpatient dialysis. Lois made arrangements with Kings County Hospital back in 1998 for Woodhull's kidney failure patients to go there. But no matter how many times we tried to close that unit, it would miraculously open back up. It was like a dandelion weed. And every time the unit was surveyed the report was scathing. I took a deep breath and waited for the worst. Gretchen came to my office around noon. "It's bad. It's really, really bad," she said.

I was concerned, but, I have to admit, I really didn't take her seriously at first. This was Chicken Little after all. That's what she always said. But at one o'clock when Brian and Ira came into my office looking ashen, I knew her comments were more than hyperbole this time. I gathered them all together in the conference room to give me a briefing. But no one was talking in full sentences. I was trying to piece together what they were saying, but, it wasn't until I heard someone say "pull our license" that I really got nervous.

"They're looking for things we can't produce," Gretchen said.

Then Brian said, "They're citing our reverse osmosis unit for something I can't fix. I think they're wrong."

"I don't think that argument will fly," I responded.

Gretchen turned to me and said, "The reviewers want to have an exit conference in conference room one at four o'clock. Nursing is looking for the maintenance logs, but, I don't think they exist. I don't know what to do." I could feel the agitation level rising and I knew I needed to rein it in and fast.

"Let's not panic," I said. "Go help them."

Everyone left the suite. But I didn't know what to do either. So I called Donna. All she said to me that day was, "Candis, you have to get in this." I didn't wait for the exit conference. I went to see the surveyors then and there.

They were patient with me as I asked them to explain the basis for their concerns. The more they explained the clearer it became that they were standing on stronger ground than we were. One of the first things I did was to tell Brian to stop trying to prove them wrong. I could see we weren't going to win that argument. What scared me the most was that they weren't being unreasonable. But they were unambiguous about their intentions. Unless we came up with something fast, we were looking at the kind of citation that could have shut us down, not just one unit, but, perhaps the entire hospital. I believe the term they used was "jeopardy status."

A fleeting mental image of a lobby full of reporters and Central Office personnel descending on me like the dementors in a *Harry Potter* novel was all the motivation I needed. From that point on everything was a blur. All I can remember was going into lawyer mode. For every concern the surveyors raised, I tried to negotiate a compromise that we could meet and they could live with. We came up with a little, they gave a little. We had a setback, but, they gave a concession. This went on for about an hour. But eventually I started to see daylight.

We were running out of time because one way or another, they were leaving at 5 o'clock. They were prepared to return to address the policy issues. But they weren't leaving us with our license unless we came up with a satisfactory response to their safety concerns. We finally came up with a plan that they could live with. Just as we were going over the final agreement, the unit chief for the dialysis program strolled into the room. As I was going over the agreement one last time, she overheard me and interrupted.

"Why are we doing that?" she asked.

I could feel my blood beginning to percolate, but, I couldn't make a scene in front of our guests so through clenched teeth I said, "Doctor, if you have a question you can discuss it with the Medical Director." She didn't get the hint.

In an insistent and almost accusatory tone she said, "But what is this about? Why do we need to do this?"

The surveyors looked perplexed. I looked over at Ira. I thought, "This is one of your people. Take care of this." I know my face conveyed my thoughts as effectively as the spoken word. But he responded by shrugging at me with a what-can-you-do kind of look. Then he glanced back down at his paper and that would be the extent of his contribution until the surveyors left for good.

I was obviously on my own. But we'd come too far for me to let this little garlic knot of a woman throw a monkey wrench into a plan that was being so precariously held together. Necessity dictated that the time for diplomacy had come and gone. I turned back to her and I said, "Go sit down and be quiet." That hint she got.

As the surveyors explained it to me, they were applying their review standards far more rigorously than they had in the past. Every hospital they'd inspected that year was running into some sort of trouble. I promised them a thorough plan to correct the deficiencies and assigned the project to Gina. We had a young lady who had worked as a manager in one of our clinics, but, she proved to be a little too rigid for that job. She was exactly what we needed. I had Gina reassign her and her sole responsibility was to make sure we did what we said we were going to do. The state was so pleased with our response that they accepted our final plan without amendments.

It was a bellwether moment if ever there was one. No one challenged my authority or questioned my decisions that day. No one was offering opinions. Nobody said a word. It was one day when no one wanted to be sitting in the big chair. I'd never felt so alone. I truly understood what it meant to have the buck stop with me. But singed as I may have been by the experience, I'd survived to fight another day and I was grateful.

As WE MOVED INTO late summer, I began to feel more comfortable in my new role. I decided to stop second guessing myself and go with what had gotten me to where I was – my instincts. Most of the successes I had enjoyed were the result of focusing on building strong teams. I may not have gotten to pick all the members this time around, but, I was convinced that it was still the best strategy. We had to change how the leadership worked together or we'd be dead in the water.

So I decided to kick away the crutches. I collapsed all the major goals that we needed to work on into three groups and I called them "Leadership Circles." Every member of the executive staff including both the Cabinet and the Chiefs of Service had to serve on one of the Circles. Going forward, these Circles would be in charge of directing our efforts. I wasn't expecting them to stand up and applaud the idea. And they didn't. But they didn't reject it out of hand either, so I was encouraged.

The two Circles that were responsible for technology and customer service initiatives jumped in with both feet. They held their first charter meeting and came up with their first set of objectives within a matter of weeks. Unfortunately, the group handling the network's most pivotal work, like our finances and the upcoming survey couldn't seem to get out of the gate. Ira, Gretchen and Simon were in that Circle. When Simon came to me to tell me that they couldn't decide on who would be in charge of what, laughter was my first response.

"This isn't really that hard," I said. "Why don't you begin by setting priorities for the work we need to focus on for the next six months? Who is in charge of what will take care of itself. I'll give you a head start. Don't we have a JCAHO survey coming up? How's our spreadsheet looking these days?"

He grinned sheepishly, "I get it. I get it. I'll go back to the group. We'll be ready by the next meeting." We were lucky to have Simon. He was smart and well organized albeit just as much of a bean counter as Tom had been. Simon's nose was always buried in a ledger book. But he had an eager spirit and the right attitude and for me attitude was everything.

When Donna was still our leader the Cabinet meetings typically involved her giving us an update on what was shared at the Corporate Cabinet meetings at Central Office. Then we'd go around the table and everybody reported on what they were doing. But there was no collaboration. We talked at each other not with each other. Now that I was on the Corporate Cabinet I decided to share information through email updates. The Cabinet could read what I brought back from Central Office just as easily as they could listen to me tell them. I wanted our meetings to be used for exchange. Any comments I had to share were limited to the first 10 minutes. After that, the meetings were the group's to run, but, they would run them as teams, not as individuals.

It was awkward at first. This approach meant no more grandstanding. No more killing trees to hand out folders full of information no one ever looked at and then boring everyone to sleep with how eloquently you could read what was in them. This was difficult for some of my new team and not surprisingly, most difficult for the Cabinet members in the Leadership Circle being run by Ira, Gretchen and Simon.

"How are we supposed to inform the rest of the Cabinet about the information they need from our departments if only one person gets to speak from each team?" Gretchen asked as our new format got underway.

"You decide as a team what to present," I responded.

"But what if my work doesn't fall under my team?"

"It will fall under one of the teams. You'll just have to share the information with them so that they can incorporate it into their reports."

I knew where the resistance was coming from. But I could also see a spark in the eyes of more than half the Cabinet. We were onto something and they were intrigued. We pressed onward. One of the benefits of this new way of working was that the Cabinet was forced to work more closely with the Chiefs of Service. We went from weekly Cabinet meetings and quarterly joint meetings with the Chiefs to bi-weekly Cabinet meetings and monthly joint meetings. Everyone liked that change.

Despite some early false starts, the members started to adjust to the Leadership Circle concept and it began to yield intended benefits right away. Cabinet meetings always took place around meal time, either breakfast or lunch. Donna was a stickler about serving food. It was that charm school thing. Hospitality was always important to her. In the past, some ate before the meeting started and the rest grabbed something to go after it was over. But I noticed that after we changed the format, the group stayed together after the meeting to eat and talk. This was a good sign.

I wish I could say that all was proceeding on such a rosy path. I had no illusions about having won everyone over. I suspect there was a powwow the day Donna left, to draft the charter for the "Candis-must-die" committee. And I'm pretty sure I know who those charter members were. But to credit their shrewdness, when they adjourned their secret meetings, they left the pins and T-shirts in the room – all except for one. Maura could not seem to accept that I was now her boss and it showed.

Both she and Gretchen continued to position themselves in the bi-weekly Cabinet meetings, like the left and right lieutenants of the pout brigade. They sat in their chairs with rigid expressions and their arms folded across their chests. They didn't participate in the conversations unless you count sulking as communication. But I could handle that because it wasn't that much of a deviation from what they had always done.

But, Maura was dancing on the edge of a very weak limb and for some reason she never noticed that she was out there all by herself. We were having one of the special team meetings that Gretchen set up to prepare us for the JCAHO survey. These meetings were focused around the JCAHO regulations that were posing the biggest problems for us.

Interdisciplinary care planning was killing us. It was probably one of the most important standards that JCAHO reviewed. We had to demonstrate that the doctors, the nurses, the nutritionists, the social workers and the pharmacists were talking to each other about the care they were providing to the patients up on the inpatient units. We were doing it, but, we couldn't seem to prove it consistently.

We had a fairly large group on this team. It was me, Ira, Gretchen, Wayne, Bobby, Angela, The Director of Inpatient Psychiatry, and Maura. We reviewed the results of the Quality Management audit reports and they were terrible. They'd been terrible for awhile and they weren't getting any better. I asked for solutions, but, what I heard were excuses so I said, "Forget about what we did in the past. Obviously that's not working. Get a group together and look at this again."

Everyone nodded in agreement and we were about to leave when Maura interjected, "Can I just say something?"

"Of course," I replied.

She then proceeded to talk about how difficult it was to get anything done because people didn't do what they were supposed to do and on and on. She may have been right, but, I couldn't see where she was going. As I'd said to them countless times, I needed specifics. Tell me who isn't doing what you need them to do and I'll have a conversation with them. Tell me what supplies you need that you don't have and I'll get them for you. But this wasn't that kind of speech. It was the kind that implied that the problem couldn't be fixed. That was the wrong speech for me.

When she finished I said, "I don't really understand your point, Maura. Every person sitting at this table is a part of the leadership. So if this problem can't be fixed by the people in this room, then who is supposed to fix it? The clerks?"

To which she responded, "Whatever!"

Time stood still. Everyone sitting around the conference table froze where they were. They were all facing in my direction, except for her. She'd arrived to the meeting late, so she was sitting behind me in a chair against the wall to my right. I turned around slowly to face her and in that moment there wasn't anyone else in the room but the two of us. I resolved that I would speak to her in a calm and controlled voice.

"What did you say?"

I don't know if it was the look on my face or the looks on the faces of the people now positioned behind me, but, Maura tensed up in her seat and quickly changed her tone.

"I – I just mean it's very frustrating."

I didn't respond. Instead, I turned back to the group and said, "So you're going to get together as a group and work on this some more, correct?" They all nodded in unison. I adjourned the meeting and asked Ira to meet me in my office.

Maura's sophomoric outbursts were not my biggest concern, not even when they were directed at me. This wasn't the first time I had to supervise someone who had a problem with reporting to me, so it was something I knew how to resolve. My problem was that she was being equally hostile towards Nursing in general and Angela in particular. In fact both she and Gretchen were making their feelings about Angela patently obvious.

The crisis point came from the fact that Maura had positioned herself right in the middle of the inpatient units as if she was their lord and savior. She may have had great ideas about how to run the unit meetings where the patients were discussed, but, she was ramming those ideas down everyone's throats. It was causing a backlash.

Beyond that, I knew that both of the pout lieutenants were treating Angela disrespectfully, because I'd seen it with my own eyes. When I confronted Gretchen about her part in it she said, "Angela is hateful and mean-spirited." That's when I realized that Gretchen had a tendency to project.

I'd be lying if I said that Gretchen and Maura were the only ones who had a problem with Angela. Almost everyone on the leadership team had a problem with Angela at one point or another. Putting her back on the Cabinet didn't seem to make her any less annoying to her colleagues. But Gretchen and Maura were the only two who weren't even attempting to be civil towards her. I suspected that even some of Angela's own nurses were sick of her. But the one thing that nurses will do is close ranks. They can complain about each other all day long, but, the minute an outsider does it they start sounding the war drums.

Whatever Gretchen's shortcomings were, she did have a good relationship with her own staff. That meant that a battle between her and Angela became a battle between Quality Management and Nursing. Maura's staff operated more out of fear than love. So if she had it out for Angela, her staff simply wasn't willing to risk extending an olive branch for fear of having Maura's wrath turned on them. I was sitting on the makings of a full-scale jihad and the survey was less than three months away.

When Ira walked into my office I didn't mince words.

"This business with Maura can't continue like this," I said.

He jumped right on the bandwagon.

"I know. I don't know why she's acting like this. I'll talk to her."

"I know you like her," I said. "Have a conversation with her. She's headed for a bad break."

No one will ever believe it, but, I was pulling for Maura as hard as anyone. I had no desire to make any major changes with my own position being so uncertain. But if I'm going to crash and burn, I'll light the pilot light myself. I was not about to sit around and watch other people play with matches at an oil refinery. I did my best to stack the deck in Maura's favor. In addition to asking Ira to intervene, I gave two of my plants on the Cabinet an assignment. Gina and Bobby were the only two people on the Cabinet who got along with both Angela and Maura.

I begged them. "Help me with this please. I need you two to be the UN peacekeepers here. Maybe if you can keep them focused on the plan, they won't focus on each other." Eager as little chipmunks, they jumped right on it.

"No problem," they said. I told the interdisciplinary care planning team that they had two weeks to come up with a new plan. I gave them three. Week after week I saw little to no movement. Then one of my peacekeepers came to me expressing visible frustration.

"I'm finished," Gina said. "I can't do it anymore."

"What happened?" I asked. "We were sitting in the conference room after the meeting. I thought the three of us could talk. Then Maura made a really nasty comment about Angela, but, she said it in Spanish so that Angela wouldn't understand what she was saying." I'd never seen Gina look the way she did at that moment.

"I can't stand when people do that," she said through gritted teeth, her plump little face contorted by abhorrence. "I was so disgusted I told her, 'Maura, I have to go' and I got up and left. I'm sorry, Candis. But with that one, I wash my hands like Pontius Pilate." Gina actually slapped her hands together twice and walked out of my office.

"Terrific," I thought. "Now what do I do?"

I decided to call her peacekeeping partner into my office to see if he'd had better luck. But when I asked him how things were going he collapsed his upper body like an accordion. Bobby was one of the members of my staff who I would describe as the most positive person I've ever met in my life. Yet somehow he managed not to be annoying with it. We've all met people who are always so cheery that they can actually get on your nerves after awhile. But Bobby didn't get on your nerves because you could tell that he was one of those rare individuals who saw the good in every person or circumstance, before he saw anything else.

One day a group of us decided to go out for lunch. Bobby was driving and he was trying to parallel park on one of those narrow side streets in Williamsburg. He was halfway into the space when in typical New York driver fashion, a woman pulled up beside him so close that he couldn't complete the turn. Everyone in the car was cussin' and fussin' about how inconsiderate she was, but not Bobby.

In a calm and optimistic voice he said, "No, no she'll do the right thing." She'll do the right thing? Was he for real? We all just stared at him. And there he was sitting there smiling, patiently waiting for her to do the right thing. And that's exactly what she did. She backed right out of his way. I think that was the day I started calling him Mr. Pollyanna. From that moment on I was convinced. Bobby wasn't born he was plucked from a sunflower.

Having worked together as long as we had, I knew what his body language meant. It meant that someone had done or said something that wasn't nice and the very thought of having to repeat it was causing him physical pain. I could wait for him to tell me on his own, but, that could take forever. The only way to get it out of him now was the Heimlich maneuver. "Spit it out, Bobby. What's going on?" I said.

He started with a heavy sigh, "Oh God. . . we've been trying to set up this meeting since you asked us three weeks ago. We went to Angela and she agreed. Then we went to Maura and she agreed. But when I told Maura that I had to confirm the time with Angela, she said, 'No! Let's just the three of us meet. I don't want to meet with her!' "

He looked at me with a pained expression and said, "I don't know what else to do."

"That's okay," I said. "Unfortunately, I do."

At the next team meeting I walked into the conference room still hoping for a last-minute miracle. I would have settled for a sliver of progress even though it was now September. The entire team was already seated at the table and it was unusually quiet. I took a seat.

"Okay, where are we?" I asked.

When no-one said anything I knew it was going to be a short meeting.

"Have we made *any* progress?" I added.

"Not really," Gretchen responded dryly.

"Okay. Thank you," I said. I pushed back from the table and left the room. I'm sure they were stunned. I went back to my office, sat in my chair and took a deep breath. Then I called Donna.

"I need to do something drastic and I want to run it by you first because if you think I'm overacting I know you'll tell me."

"Okay," she said.

"I'm reassigning the case management department."

She paused for a second.

"Okay. What happened?" she said.

I told her everything that had been going on since she left. Other than the call I made to her during our dialysis crisis, I'd made a deliberate decision not to call her about what was going on. For one thing, our problems were heating up during the period when she was days away from Bellevue's survey. So I knew she didn't have time to be focusing on Woodhull's problems. Beyond that, I needed to figure out how to do this job on my own.

It turned out that she already knew about a lot of it. Ira spoke to her after my conversation with him. He told her that Maura and I "weren't working well together" and her response to him was vintage Donna. "They don't have to work well together," she said.

"Candis is her boss now! Maura's the one who has to get her act together and she'd better do it quick because unlike me, Candis will fire her." "You know I never thought about it that way" Ira replied. "You're right. I'll talk to her."

Donna knew that Maura didn't belong on the Cabinet. Our work with the consultants exposed the areas where we still had weaknesses and Maura popped to the surface like a cork in a tub full of water. Donna and I had talked about it on more than one occasion. But in the years that I reported to her at Woodhull, she removed two people from the Cabinet. Both times they responded by having total meltdowns in her office. It rattled her in a way that I saw happen very few times.

She knew that if she had taken the action I was about to take, Maura would have had a complete nervous breakdown. Donna had decided that she was not going through that again. Most of the people who worked with her over the years probably thought she was made of stone. I can attest that she is not. Her exact words to me on the subject were, "let the next person deal with her." Unfortunately, the next person turned out to be me.

"What's she going to be left with?" Donna asked me.

"She'll still have social work, pastoral care and the daycare center," I said.

"She can't stay on the Cabinet if that's all she's got."

"I know. But we both know she's not really adding anything to the Cabinet."

Donna didn't hesitate after that. "You have to get through Joint Commission. Do what you have to do." Before I informed Maura of my decision, I called Ira down to my office so I could tell him what I'd decided. He let out something like a sigh, but, he didn't offer a single objection. All he said was, "I tried to talk to her." "I'm sure you did," I replied.

Our problems with the way the different departments worked together on the units threatened to derail the survey. Unlike prior reviews, the bulk of this survey was going to take place on the units. We couldn't eat up time with elaborate presentations like we'd done in the past. The surveyors were going to sit up in those nursing stations and talk to the staff. They didn't want to talk to supervisors. They wanted to talk to the people who did the work. This wasn't a problem we couldn't solve. It was a problem that required the people in charge to work together to fix it and that wasn't happening. I think Maura was relying on the fact that since Angela was so unpopular with so many people, she could run roughshod over her and nobody would care. She probably wasn't the only one. Her mistake was getting out front.

Before Ira left my office, he asked if there was anything he could do. "It's too late for her," I said. "If you want to help somebody, go help her partner in Quality Management." It was time for me to state the issue in unambiguous terms. "I'm not blind to Angela's faults. I know she frustrates people. I know she can be difficult to work with at times and she's frequently difficult to comprehend. I'm trying to learn how to speak the language she speaks just like the rest of you. But I'm not going to allow those two to continue to blatantly disrespect her the way they've been because despite what they may think, I wouldn't allow anybody to do that to them."

He wasn't doodling now. "You know, Ira, it's really sad that the only thing the Cabinet seems to agree on is how much Angela gets on all of your nerves. But you are all missing the big picture here. We can get through this survey without a Director of Case Management. We can even get through this survey without a Director of Quality Management if we have to. But we <u>cannot</u> get through the survey without a Director of Nursing." I could actually see a light bulb go on inside Ira's busy little brain.

"There is not going to be a change in nursing leadership three months before a survey," I said. "It can't happen. It won't happen. So we had all better learn to boogie with the date we brought to the dance because Angela is it! Do yourself a favor." I sent him to my peacekeepers. "I don't know how they did it, but, somehow Gina and Bobby have found a way to work with her. And I've noticed something. Since they started trying to work with her, she's started trying to work with them. I know you people think its okay to be rude and dismissive to Angela because she acts unreasonable sometimes. But did you ever stop to think that maybe if you stopped being so rude, she'd stop being so unreasonable?"

Ira leaned forward in the chair and said, "Okay, okay, okay. I got it! I got it! I'll go have some conversations."

"You do that," I said. "And pass this along. If you need to come in here every day to ask me to run interference with Nursing for you, then come. I will do it. But we have to work together." That still left me with a very unpleasant conversation to have. I called Maura into my office. There would be no easy way to say what had to be said.

"Maura, I had really hoped to avoid this, but, unfortunately I need to make a change. I'm taking case management from you . . . ." I paused for a second to brace for the explosion, but, nothing happened so I continued. "This means you're no longer on the Cabinet . . . ." Still nothing. I couldn't believe it. I was talking to the Grand Duchess of Histrionics-Ville and so far not so much as a peep. I was past the worst part, wrapping up with, "Case Management will move over to Bobby so I expect you to transition . . ." when all of a sudden, she let out a shriek.

"WHAT?!!!" she screamed.

I was so caught off guard that everything I was thinking flew right out of my head. I thought, does she think in slow motion? I should have gotten that reaction two minutes ago. I had to rewind the conversation all the way back to the beginning and start all over. I expected her to be upset. Anyone would be. And I was prepared for her to challenge the reasons behind my decision. But she didn't quite do that, at least not immediately. Instead she tried to challenge my authority to make the decision at all.

"You can't do this!"

"Yes I can," I said. "I'm not firing you. I'm just removing one department."

"Why?!!"

"Because it's a department that requires its leader to work collaboratively with other departments and you're not doing that."

"That's not true!" she shouted. "I work wonderfully with other departments. Name one department I don't work well with!"

"Nursing," I said.

"NOBODY GETS ALONG WITH ANGELA!!!"

She screamed it with such guttural force that I could swear I heard her chest rattle.

"That's not true," I said. I tried to keep things civil.

"Yes it is!"

"No it isn't. There are people who have figured out how to work with her."

"No there aren't!"

This wasn't getting us anywhere.

"Why am I being removed from the Cabinet?" Now we were getting to the heart of the matter.

The Case Management department gave Maura a level of access and authority that would not otherwise have been available to someone who only managed the other departments under her purview. So I knew giving that up would be difficult for her under any circumstances. But what she craved more than anything else was the attention that being a part of senior leadership afforded her. Maura would have sold a nonvital organ to stay in the executive suite.

When Gretchen became the Director of Quality Management, she moved up to the 10th floor. That left Brian, Maura and me in the executive suite. Each of us had a secretary who sat out in the common area outside our offices along with a receptionist. In addition to their work for us, they shared responsibility for the overall functioning of the suite – answering the phones, keeping the pantry and supply cabinet stocked, and so forth. For that aspect of their job, they reported to Mimi, Donna's assistant, with whom I had a great relationship. She was petite and cute and had this piercing laugh that could be heard through sheetrock.

But as cute as Mimi was, she was hell on the secretaries. One by one, they dropped like flies. The first to go was Brian's secretary. The woman had been with him for 17 years. Once Mimi was in charge, I think she lasted 17 weeks. Next up was Lilly. Lilly began working for me as a temp shortly after I arrived in 2001, but, her attitude suggested she thought that I should be working for her. When Maura received approval to hire a secretary of her own, Lilly leaped at the opportunity to leave me and go work for her. I use the word "leap" intentionally.

If Maura sneezed, Lilly would literally leap out of her seat to bring her a tissue. I must have heard "Yes, Ms. Flores, Yes, Ms. Flores," fifty times a day if I heard it once. I watched this with amazement and thought, "Gee. Lilly never leaped like that when she worked for me." When I asked for something she never even got out of her chair. I used to have to come to her. And forget about a "Yes, Ms. Best." If I called Lilly's name, all I got back was "yeah."

But for some reason Lilly worshipped the ground Maura walked on. And when Lilly landed in Mimi's crosshairs, what did all that hero-worship get her? I was in Mimi's office the day she told Maura that Lilly had to go. I thought to myself, this is going to be good. Princess isn't giving up her scullery maid. I leaned back against the wall and waited for the fireworks. Imagine my surprise when they never came. Maura didn't hesitate in her reply. She simply rubbed her hands back and forth like she was brushing cookie crumbs off of her palms and said, "She gotta go, she gotta go."

You could have bought me for two cents. I was so stunned that all I could do was look at Maura and shake my head. If Maura's behind had had a spot of dust on it, Lilly would have wiped it off with her genuine, imitation ponytail. And this was her reward. I seriously doubted that Maura's reaction had anything to do with Lilly's work, because I never once heard Maura complain about Lilly. That's when I figured it out.

Maura simply wasn't going to take the chance that fighting for Lilly would mean that she would have to leave the suite. To add insult to injury, she didn't even have the decency to tell her secretary to her face. She waited until Lilly went out on maternity leave and then had the human resources department tell her that she was reassigned when she got back. But the cherry on top of the banana split was still to come. Less than a year later, when we each had to put names on the layoff list, Maura had the nerve to put Lilly on it.

Somebody losing their job is never a laughing matter. I mean that sincerely. But when Lilly came through the suite to say goodbye, I have to admit that my mind went to mischief. I looked at her and I thought, you see – one lousy leap for me and you'd still have a job. I would have fought for you. If someone's not doing their work I don't care who it is, I'll let them go if they can't get their act together. But there's no way I would have ever put someone who had worked as close to me as a personal secretary does, on a layoff list. There's a little thing called loyalty.

And I'm speaking from experience because I faced the same choices Maura did. I eventually got my call into the office just like everybody else in the executive suite.

"It's not working out with A.J.," Mimi told me one day. "She's going to have to go."

I didn't hesitate either.

"Okay. Where are we going?"

I wasn't saying it for the shock value. I really meant it. Mimi's eyes widened like latex balloons.

"We?" she said.

"Mimi, you can make me leave the suite. But you can't make me give up my secretary."

"Don't get mad!"

I don't know why she said that. I never raised my voice or my eyebrows once throughout our brief conversation.

"I'm not mad," I said. "I'm just not doing it."

I guess Mimi couldn't think of a way to explain to Donna why her Chief Operating Officer was sharing a broom closet with her secretary. So she let the matter drop and we never spoke of it again. One way or another she and A.J. worked out their differences because they were best buddies right up until the day Mimi left for Bellevue.

That incident may have epitomized the difference between Maura and me. The things that were important to her weren't important to me and vice versa.

I didn't care about that suite. I cared about two things – my work and my people and I could take care of both from anywhere. There was no way for me to be certain that Maura was incapable of loyalty to other people. But after watching her over the course of four years, I knew one thing. Her first loyalty was always going to be to herself. As long as that was true, she'd never make it on any team of mine.

And she was still screaming.
"This is personal!" she said.
"I'm sorry you feel that way because it really isn't."
"Yes it is!"
"Okay then it is."
I just wanted the screaming to stop. It didn't. Then she launched into a diatribe.
"You are going to be sorry! I have taken case management to heights that it has never been before! And I . . . and I . . . and I"
I'd heard people speak like that on television - soap operas, mini-series - but never in real life. After the fourth "I," I looked over my glasses at her and said, "You did all this by yourself, huh?" She didn't get the point. It went in one ear and out the other. Mentally, she was gone. Her arms were flailing; her eyes were rolling so far up in her head that her pupils disappeared. It was bigger than television. It was IMAX Cinema.
As she continued to convulse, I took a mental inventory of the executive leadership team that I had inherited. I had a Chief Nursing Executive down the hall spinning like a cyclone; a Medical Director scampering through the hallways causing confusion; a Director of Quality Management upstairs on the 10th floor whining in perfect pitch and adorning the furrows in her brow with war paint; a Psychiatry administrator who was only on the Cabinet because he was responsible for a service

that equaled one-third of our inpatient beds, but, whose most apparent skill was checking his tie in the mirror; a Business Affairs Director who was about as useful to me as wet toilet paper; and I was supposed to work with all of this and Norma Desmond too? That was more than half the senior staff. When I took the final tally, it amounted to more plates spinning on sticks than I had limbs to hold them. Something had to give.

I cut her off mid-rant. Our conversation had long passed the point of having a purpose. "I'm sorry Maura, but, this is my decision and it's final." She stopped abruptly, like I'd thrown water in her face. "Fine," she said.

She stormed out of my office, into her own and slammed the door. I knew what she was doing. She was crying and hyperventilating. That wasn't what I wanted. I didn't enjoy making people cry anymore than Donna did. Then I thought about it and came to the conclusion that perhaps Donna was right. Maybe it was better that it came from me.

Maura was upset at the moment, but, I knew that before long she would write the entire episode off to some personal vendetta she was convinced I had against her. As hard as she was crying, had Donna been the one to remove her, she would have had the kind of breakdown people don't recover from quickly. In that scenario there wouldn't have been anybody to blame but Maura. If hating me and branding me an ogre would keep her out of a rubber room, I was happy to let that be my gift to her.

I had no interest in embarrassing her. I gave her time to move out of the suite on her own schedule. I didn't put the change in writing. I made a brief comment about it during our next Cabinet meeting and left it at that. If anybody on the Cabinet was devastated by the news they did a good job of hiding it. To the contrary, I started to see a change in the group dynamics immediately. With one lieutenant gone, the other one didn't have anybody to feed off of at the meetings. One person pouting without an echo dissipates like a scream under water. Gretchen just faded into the background and the rest of the group seemed to liven up a little.

Finding a solution to our care-planning dilemma was now a task for Mr. Pollyanna and the Puppy. So you can understand why I wasn't overflowing with confidence. But I gave Bobby clear instructions. "Attach yourself to Ira's hip and don't let him out of your sight until you're confident that whatever you guys come up with, works." I didn't give it another thought after that.

As time passed, I stuck with my plan of coaching rather than directing the staff where I thought they needed to go. Besides, I had my own assignments to finish. I'd decided to conduct a listening tour to get to the bottom of the morale issues that had surfaced during the employee satisfaction survey. I'd pledged to spend the entire month of September meeting with all levels of staff during all three tours. By the time it was concluded, I'd heard from over 1,000 employees from all over the network, in forums large and small. It was exhausting, but, well worth the effort.

In addition to gathering valuable feedback, each meeting allowed me to create my own relationship with the staff. A real one – not one based on ghost stories. It was amusing to watch their expressions as myth was replaced with reality. The "you're younger than I thought you were" or "you're shorter than I thought . . ." that I actually heard were framed by curious expressions followed by reassuring smiles that seemed to say, "aw – she don't bite."

I inhaled what they exhaled. I'd held many of these types of forums over the course of my career. They never failed to provide me with an insight I wouldn't have gained otherwise. My intention was to gather a cross section of comments and then share the common themes with the managers who I scheduled for the final listening session on the last day of the month. About a week before that meeting, I received two anonymous letters requesting that I hold a special session with the staff in the social work department. I was still mulling over the first letter when the second one arrived. I had an idea about what prompted them.

I was told by more than one source that when I'd reassigned case management away from Maura, the social work department took the move as a sign that liberation was on the horizon for their department as well. When reality set in, I guess they decided that the time had come to escalate. I'd offered other departments the opportunity to schedule their own sessions if they felt they needed one, so I really didn't have a basis for refusing this request. I had A.J. set up the meeting to take place in the auditorium.

When I arrived there were about fifty to sixty employees present. I started off by explaining why the meeting had been scheduled, that it was the result of two anonymous requests. I never mentioned Maura by name. Her name was not mentioned in either letter and I wouldn't have brought her up even if it had been. After I'd finished my opening remarks I opened the floor for comments or questions. Initially, there was only silence. No one ever wants to be the first to speak in these forums, so I expected that.

Then a young woman raised her hand and said, "I know people have things to say but they're afraid of retaliation."

"There will be no retaliation. I'm here because I want to hear what you have to say."

"You're not who we're worried about. It's hard to speak freely when your supervisor is in the room."

I offered a compromise.

"Would you feel more comfortable if the supervisors weren't here?"

When my question was met with a wave of head nodding I asked the supervisors to step out of the room. They were invited to the Administrators meeting that Friday anyway, so there really was no need for them to be present at this session. They left and the flood gates opened almost at once.

The first comment had to do with how long some of the social workers had been working for us through temporary agencies, some for as long as seven months. So we spent a fair amount of time talking about the hiring freeze and the headcount targets, what I could do and what I couldn't do. As a part of our plan to address our budget deficit, we'd committed to trimming several hundred employees from our roster by the end of the fiscal year. I'd shared this information with the staff before, but, that didn't make the pinch any less painful for the departments that were feeling squeezed. The staff from the Psychiatry department talked about their staffing levels. I knew they were feeling strained so we talked about that as well. Then the tenor of the conversation began to shift ever so slightly.

One person mentioned how difficult it was to get work done when they were constantly being summoned to meetings. Heads nodded. The next person talked about being berated by "senior level administrators." More heads nodded. I listened. Each comment seemed to illicit an addendum. I said very little. I just let them talk. Then a young woman raised her hand.

"I want to say something in defense of Ms. Flores."

Here we go, I thought. No one had mentioned Maura by name up to that point and I didn't ask anyone to give names. In fact less than half the comments made had anything to do with supervision. But just as I feared, somehow this meeting was being recast as a personal attack on Maura, despite my best efforts. I tried my best to refocus the meeting.

"I did not call this meaning because of Maura Flores. I called it because I was asked to convene it in two separate letters written by your colleagues. Obviously, they had a variety of issues they wanted to discuss. This is not about one person." But the damage was done. I think we adjourned at 1:00 p.m.

By 4:00 p.m., A.J. was buzzing me on the intercom. Donna was on my direct line.

"What's up?" I asked. I knew what lie ahead.

"Why did I just receive a hysterical phone call from Maura?" she asked.

"I don't know. What did she say?"

"She said she was being set up."

"And you believe that?"

"No. I just want to know what happened before I call her back. I didn't take the call. I got the message secondhand from Mimi."

I recounted everything that happened during the meeting, almost verbatim. There was nothing that the staff told me that I didn't already know. No matter what they said, I had no intention of making any more changes to staff portfolios before our survey. Now that Maura was no longer on the Cabinet, I expected that she would probably follow Donna to Bellevue as soon as the survey was over, anyway. I had hoped we could all just ride it out for the time we had left. Apparently I was wrong.

"She wants to come to Bellevue right now," Donna said. "She's crying and rolling around on the floor I guess. She says she can't take it anymore."

Then I really became frustrated.

"Take what?" I asked. "I've been tiptoeing around her since she left the Cabinet as it is, trying not to hurt her feelings!"

"I know. She's going to have to grow up," Donna replied. "I'll tell her she'll just have to wait until after Joint Commission."

"Wait a minute," I said. I knew that would serve no one's interest. "You know what? If she wants to go and you can take her, let her go. Why wait if she's going to be miserable? I don't need her here throwing temper tantrums with the survey a few weeks away."

"Are you sure?" Donna asked. "Who's going to handle her departments?"

"We'll figure it out."

But it wasn't that simple.

"I can't take her at her salary," Donna said. "She makes too much money for anything I have available to give her right now."

My initial reaction was pure Vulcan. I wasn't asking Maura to leave. Why should I contribute to her salary? My first answer was no. If she left, she'd have to go at whatever salary Bellevue could pay her. First Donna petitioned for her and then Yvonne, the Human Resources Director. "Candis, this is your decision, but, it'll reflect better on you if we can say that she didn't lose any money in the transfer." Reflect better on me? I wasn't asking her to leave!

But of course that was not the way the story was going to be told. I thought it over and ultimately relented. What other people were going to think really had no bearing on my final decision. The gossip mongers were never going to know about that part of the deal and I doubted Maura was going to tell anybody about my generosity. My reputation as villain or hero wasn't going to be altered one iota by whether I kept her on our payroll.

In the end, I only agreed because I knew her financial situation. A pay cut was going to be far more devastating to her than keeping her on the payroll for a few more months could possibly mean to our bottom line. So we treated her transfer like an internal reassignment and she remained on Woodhull's payroll at her full salary through the end of the year. Simon wasn't happy about it, but, that's how the deal was struck.

Despite the hiccups, we continued our march toward November. I soon discovered that Gretchen learned faster than her buddy. I never expected her and Angela to go shoe shopping together, but, they found neutral ground. And when Gretchen had enough of Angela's antics, she came to me rather than ripping Nursing apart. It was a workable solution. I never found out if Ira and Gretchen had a conversation, but, either way I saw improvement.

Gretchen even cut down on the whining and complaining and it made a difference in the dynamics with everyone else. She was making a noticeable effort which I appreciated and I told her so. The rest of the Cabinet also seemed to be making an effort at treating Angela more humanely. As a result, I was able to downgrade her from a Category 5 hurricane to a tropical depression. The team even came up with an idea for the interdisciplinary care plan. I thought it sounded a little dicey, but, Bobby signed off on it so I let it ride.

At the beginning of July, out of seven Network Sr. Vice-Presidents, four of us were "Acting." But by September two had been made permanent, yet neither Donna nor I heard anything about our fates. It certainly appeared that the Old Boy's Club that Donna used to complain about was alive and well – the two permanent appointments were both men. I assumed that Gilberto was waiting to see how Woodhull did on its survey before a decision was made about me. To my mind that was fair. But Donna's delay didn't make any sense at all. I knew she'd already told him that she wasn't coming back to Woodhull no matter what happened. Despite her initial reticence at the reassignment, she'd made it clear that she was willing to stay at Bellevue. But he was as silent on her status as he had been on mine.

Preparing for the upcoming survey, however, kept me entirely too preoccupied to spend any time worrying about that. One of the things that did not change when Donna left was Woodhull's ability to produce head-scratching moments. Survey preparation meant bringing back the outside consultant we'd used during our last survey. But since her findings had always coincided with someone being removed from their position, her arrival had come to be greeted by the staff the way a mouse greets a cat convention. On the morning of this most recent arrival, it was greeted with a high-pitched scream from the basement.

"Can I talk to you for a minute?"

I've learned from experience that when a conversation begins with "Can I talk to you for a minute?" and the staff member who says it looks like they just knocked my toothbrush into the toilet by mistake, I'm not going to like what they're about to tell me.

"Sure Dana. What's up?"

"I wanted to make sure I had all the facts before I came to speak with you," she said.

She waited until she was all the way in my office and had adjusted herself comfortably in the seat across from my desk before she spoke again. There was no doubt about it now. I was definitely not going to like what she was about to tell me.

"Sometime on Sunday a patient eloped from one of the Med/Surg units," she said. Then she hastened to add, "Hospital Police performed a complete search of the building from top to bottom, just like our policy calls for."

The added emphasis on that last statement told me that she was describing something that the staff did right, but, that I would soon be hearing about something they did very wrong.

"Okay," I offered with caution. There had to be more.

"Well, this morning when one of the secretaries from Hospital Police opened the office, she found the patient lying on top of one of the file cabinets," she said. Considering how quickly my heart rate accelerated, my outward appearance and the timbre of my voice remained remarkably placid.

"He's dead?"

"No! No! No!" she said. "He was just sleeping. We took him to the emergency room. He's going to be fine."

Now that the worst-case scenario had been eliminated I could feel my heartbeat returning to normal. But I knew the relief wouldn't last. What she'd told me so far still didn't make sense for so many reasons. I knew once I heard the whole story I wasn't going to feel any better. First, the administrative offices for Hospital Police were located in the basement in a non-patient-care area so what was the patient doing there? Second, how did he get into an office that should have been locked? And third, he disappeared from the unit on Sunday. We were having this conversation on Tuesday, so where had he been all day Monday? From the look on Dana's face, we were about to get to the part of the story where she explained how my toothbrush landed in the toilet.

"It seems that he found his way into the interstitial space. Once he got inside he must have gotten disoriented and he couldn't find his way out," she explained.

When I heard that, my chest filled with so much emotion that all I could manage to get out of my mouth was Dana's name. And I used the same disappointed tone my mother used to use when I marred an otherwise flawless report card with a "D" for behavior because I refused to adhere to the high school dress code. Dana knew where I was headed after that.

"I know, I know," she said. She certainly did.

Woodhull was constructed with a floor of mechanicals between every occupied floor. This interstitial space was a vast, gray, dusty, dimly lit expanse that was crisscrossed with catwalks. It was deceptively dangerous because in the low lighting, most of what appeared to the naked eye to be a floor was nothing more than the acoustic ceiling tile to the floor below it. And it did *not* support a person's body weight. Dana was the one who woke me up at three in the morning two years earlier to tell me that one of our employees had wandered off the catwalk and had fallen through the ceiling two stories to his death. It was a moment that no one would ever want to relive again.

"We kept finding holes in the ceiling tiles in different offices in the basement yesterday, but, we couldn't figure out why," she went on to say. "He must have been trying to find a place to let himself down."

While I was relieved that our patient (who our creatively macabre emergency room staff had now dubbed "Spiderman") had the presence of mind to look before he leaped, I was still numb from the absurdity of it all.

"So what you're telling me," I said, "is that a patient has been lost in our ceiling like a giant gerbil for the past 24 hours?"

For some reason I felt the need to say that out loud, as if the story might not sound as ludicrous in the retelling. But it did.

"Yeah," Dana offered shamefacedly. "That's what it looks like."

"The poor thing must be hungry," I said.

"I guess so," she said. "The secretary said he ate all of the candy from her desk. Then he must have climbed back up on the file cabinet and fallen asleep."

I didn't want to laugh. We were pretty damn lucky that the worst this patient suffered was dusty pajamas and hunger pains.

"I want every door to the interstitial spaces secured and the staff in-serviced all over again on the importance of keeping them locked."

"I'm already on it," she said.

She was out of her seat and on her way to the door, so I knew the worst was over. It seemed safe to console myself with a restrained giggle as I thought, "This job just keeps getting better and better."

The next day I had to contend with the exit conference from the consultant. Donna and Gretchen loved this woman. My feelings about her on the other hand were mixed. She was highly competent and extremely knowledgeable about the JCAHO standards. But I'd begun to suspect that Gretchen was using her like a submachine gun; pointing her at her enemies and firing until the clip was empty. By the time the consultant had finished her report, my suspicions were more firmly rooted than ever.

First, this consultant was always brutally honest. But because she was also a nurse, she usually made a point to include positive as well as negative comments when it came to the nursing department. Not this time. She didn't have one good thing to say about Nursing. The nursing department managers and supervisors were crestfallen. I shared the look of surprise that also blanketed their faces. I already knew that at least one of the head nurses on the units had done extremely well during her interview. Yet the consultant never mentioned it.

But when the woman cited us for lax security because of the "patient that wandered into our mechanical space," I looked straight at Gretchen. Only the executive staff knew about Spiderman. The consultant couldn't have known about him unless

Gretchen told her. When I confronted Gretchen with my suspicions later that day, I must have caught her by surprise. She couldn't come up with a plausible denial fast enough so she admitted that she was the leak, and tried to justify her treason by saying that the consultant "had a right to know."

I decided to sit in on the impromptu nursing confab that Angela organized after the exit conference. Just as I expected, they were beating the war drums over how lop-sided the critique was. They were more convinced than ever that the quality management department was out to get them. I had to approach this powder keg carefully. If I even hinted that I shared some of their suspicions, it would only have made matters worse. But with weeks to go until the survey, I also didn't want them to feel abandoned and retreat in anger.

"I know about all the areas where you've improved even if the consultant failed to mention them," I said. "Now we have to focus on the rest of it."

That seemed to make them feel a little better. I knew I needed to start with a word of encouragement for fear of losing them forever. But I also wanted to nip the fomenting hostility towards Gretchen and her department in the bud. Besides, the consultant's criticisms weren't without merit. So I added, "If you think somebody's trying to set you up, then don't give them anything to find." We were too close to turning a corner to have it all fall apart now.

NOVEMBER ARRIVED LIKE A thief in the night. It seemed that one minute I had six weeks until the survey and the next I was staring down the barrel of a shotgun. After Woodhull's performance during the 2002 survey, the Network Sr. Vice-Presidents were convinced that the key to success was being surveyed first. Not surprisingly, Luis lobbied hard to make sure Harlem was first in line. It didn't help. The Joint Commission did away with scores, but, that did not eliminate a basis for comparison – or competition.

Now, instead of which hospital had the highest score, the new HHC benchmark was which hospital had the fewest "Requirements for Improvement" or "RFIs", the most severe kind of citation you could garner during the survey process. Tracking RFIs or even potential RFIs was a daily ritual during the survey period. The national average was 7 but no one in HHC wanted to be anywhere near that number. The current #1 on the leader board was Queens Hospital with 3. It was an impressive feat considering that they were the only HHC hospital that year to actually go through with an unannounced survey. You really had to be doing something right to do that well when you had no idea when the surveyors were coming.

I couldn't get a straight answer about the exact number of RFIs Harlem ended up with, but, they certainly weren't putting any pressure on Queens. After a brief break, our survey was scheduled to begin

November 7th. We arranged a series of morale-boosting events just as we'd done in 2002, leading up to the Friday before the survey. At the last minute I decided that I wanted to hold an interdenominational prayer service. Woodhull had a phenomenal Pastoral Care department with clergy from Christian, Jewish and Islamic faiths represented. And the department director's enthusiasm when it came to organizing activities to encourage staff was unlike anything I'd ever witnessed in my life.

They scheduled the service for Friday, November 4th, which was a special treat for me. It also happened to be my 37th birthday. When I entered the auditorium there were about 20 people assembled. As usual it was a wonderful program. Each member of the clergy offered something insightful and uplifting. And as an added surprise, one of our former employees who also happened to be a featured vocalist with the Brooklyn Tabernacle Choir joined us to sing a few selections.

When the time came for me to deliver closing remarks, I approached the podium still deep in thought. But when I turned to face the audience I was surprised to see that there were more than 100 people staring back at me. I had been so engrossed in the program, in addition to trying to find the Bible passage I wanted to share, that I hadn't noticed the steady trickle of employees who had chosen to join us that afternoon. Seemingly without effort, the Bible opened to precisely the passages I'd been looking for: Romans 8:28 "We know that all things work together for good for those who love God [and] . . . are called according to his purpose," and verse 37 " . . . in all these things we are more than conquerors . . . ." As I looked out at the smiling faces, I felt an overwhelming sense of peace and gratitude. And I shared those thoughts with everyone present.

Monday morning started at 5:00 a.m. I woke up, got ready, said a little prayer and headed to the hospital.

The first day of a Joint Commission survey feels like being a child on Christmas morning – a mischievous child. You know that you deserve as much coal as you do treats, so you're eager to find out just how accurate Santa's naughty and nice list is.

I made my way over to the conference center on the other side of the hospital around 7:30 a.m. HHC's Sr. Assistant Vice-President for Regulatory Affairs attended all of the surveys and she was already seated in the conference room when I arrived. The remainder of the Cabinet and the Chiefs of Service were beginning to assemble. One by one the surveyors began to arrive and they were seated in a separate conference room we'd arranged especially for them. When it came to orchestrating survey week, I'd learned from the master working under Donna. We had fine china and the best food, courtesy of my Mr. Miles. We'd also anticipated every need the surveyors had with respect to assembling the information they would require to get started.

The opening conference started at 8:00 a.m. We'd rehearsed all the introductions and the PowerPoint presentation down to the minute. Everything was arranged to proceed without a hitch. So of course when it was time for me to begin the slideshow, the program froze. I must have done fifty presentations in my life and that had never happened to me before. It's at moments like that when you can actually feel time playing hopscotch across your face. But we made our way through it and before I realized it, the opening conference was over and the surveyors were back in their room preparing for the day ahead.

After a few deep breaths and shared laughs at the miscues, everyone moved with dispatch to their prearranged assignments. For the first time I was faced with the highly unusual and equally uncomfortable task of having to go back to my office and wait. For as long as I'd been in healthcare I'd always held the kind of position that required me to be right in the thick of things during a survey. Those were the moments when I did my best work. But I wasn't the "go-to" girl anymore. I was the CEO and CEOs don't walk with surveyors. They don't check or double-check. The time for that was past. All I could do was trust the staff that did the work – the trustworthy and the untrustworthy alike. As a leader, these are the moments when you reap what you sow.

When I returned to my office, there was an email from Donna waiting for me. It contained a scripture from the Bible and a word of encouragement to go with it. She sent me one every day that week. Each evening after the surveyors left for the day we would speak. At the conclusion of the first day Gretchen told me that it looked like we would be receiving two RFIs so far. We still had four more days to go. At that rate we were risking the possibility of being placed on "conditional accreditation" status. If that happened, I'd be lucky to hold on to any job at HHC much less the one I was hanging onto by the tips of my fingernails.

When Donna called later that evening, I was counting the aspirins in my desk drawer to see if I had accumulated enough to euthanize myself.

"Take a deep breath," she said. "They have to see three instances before they're required to make it an RFI. Don't panic yet. Go refocus your people." So that's what I did.

Of all the places it could be, our wobbly table leg turned out to be in the department of Psychiatry; the impregnable domain of Lorenzo the Great and Wayne, the immaculately attired tie-checker. I was so annoyed with them I could barely speak, especially since the surveyors were finding problems that we'd already discussed. Our best hope was to dazzle them during their scheduled tour of the units. For once in his life, Lorenzo was humble. After our staff-only briefing, he and Wayne quickly disappeared upstairs.

Tuesday went better and Wednesday's tour of Psychiatry was flawless. It went so well in fact that when we all came together Wednesday evening after the surveyors left, Lorenzo announced in a loud voice complete with pompous affectation, "I feel vindicated!" I'll never forget the look on the face of HHC's Sr. Assistant V.P. She looked like she was thinking the same thing I was thinking – "Is he out of his mind?"

Every seasoned hospital administrator knows that no matter how well prepared you are, no matter how good your team is, on any given day someone can find something moldy in the corner of your kitchen. There are simply too many moving parts in a place that never closes. The scare that Lorenzo's service received that Monday was well justified. All he should have been feeling at that moment was lucky. Even I couldn't believe how diplomatic I was in my response. Especially considering how asinine I thought his comment was under the circumstances.

"I think it's a little premature to start celebrating," I said. "We still have two more days to go. This is the time when people start to lose focus. Go back to your staff. Keep them informed, but, let's keep it together."

Even with my cautions fresh in their minds, I knew the staff was feeling pretty good. I couldn't blame them. I spoke with Donna later that evening.

"So how's it going?" she asked.

"Donna, it's going so well I'm starting to get scared."

We were getting the benefit of every lucky break. I don't want to diminish the work the staff had done. But I'd been through surveys where staff would do the most bizarre things, like moving old furniture out into the hallway just as a surveyor was coming through.

Whether it was sabotage or thoughtlessness, I knew from experience that there was no possible way to have complete control over the actions of 2,000 people. When things go as well as they were going, you have to take the time to look up to the heavens and say, "Good looking out, God." Actually it wasn't the front line staff that scared me. It was the ones with ego-involvement.

By the time we reached Thursday afternoon, we were down from five surveyors to two – the nurse surveyor who was also the team leader and the physician surveyor. The others had concluded their responsibilities and left their reports. The administrative surveyor gave us one RFI that we were contesting because we believed he was misapplying the JCAHO standards. Judging from the demeanor of the nurse and the physician, it appeared that they were pleased with what they were seeing. So all we needed to do was manage the balance of their visit and we would be in good shape.

The final day would begin with a Leadership interview. Then the nurse surveyor had scheduled interviews in the conference room for the balance of the morning. After that, she had a little time left over to walk around the hospital before she and the physician surveyor would have to begin compiling their final report. I doubted that she was going to take advantage of that time. The physician's schedule on the other hand was completely open after the Leadership interview. But he had been so impressed with everything he'd seen that I believed he would be open to suggestions for how he should spend Friday morning. So I gave Ira a very specific assignment.

After our interview, he should talk the physician surveyor into sitting in with the nurse on her interviews. If that failed, we agreed that he would take the physician to the emergency room so that he could see all the new technology that the staff had to work with. The physician

surveyor had a background as an ER physician, so I
thought he would like that. I knew that Dr. Wallace ran a
tight ship so I didn't have to worry about any surprises.
The objective was to keep the surveyors as stationary as
possible. The less they saw, the fewer opportunities they
had to discover some new problem that they hadn't seen
before.

Around 1 p.m., I received word that the
surveyors expected to end early. They were inquiring
about whether the exit conference could be moved up
from 4 p.m. to 3 p.m. That was a very good sign. Of
course I agreed and then I reached out to Gilberto to
make sure he could make it to the hospital by 3 p.m. He
could. I asked A.J. begin calling the Chiefs and the
Cabinet to tell them to assemble in the conference room
at 2:30 p.m. I arrived in time to see Ira walking the
physician surveyor into the surveyors' conference room.
Since Dr. Wallace was already standing in the hallway, I
was confused. I approached him.

"Weren't Ira and the physician surveyor with you
all morning?" I asked. Dr. Wallace looked perplexed.

"No. I saw them for a few minutes a few hours
ago when they passed through on Ira's tour." Ira's tour?

When I inquired further, I learned that Ira spent
the day taking the physician surveyor on a top to bottom
tour of the hospital. I couldn't believe it. When he came
out of the conference room, I grabbed him. "Didn't we
have plan?" I said. But he waved me off. "Don't worry.
He loved us. It went great." I wanted to choke him, but,
there were too many witnesses. He and Lorenzo were
stretching our luck and my patience.

I started to feel better when I saw the Sr.
Assistant V.P. She was smiling. The president arrived
and the surveyors presented their findings to the two of
us in private before they were presented to the rest of
the staff. They were overflowing with compliments.
That was great, but, what I really wanted to know was

how many RFIs we ended up with. The number was three. That was a good number. I was satisfied.

We went into the main conference room and knowing the outcome already, I was able to sit back and observe the staff as they learned for the first time how well we'd done. My eyes were open and I heard everything that was being said, but, at the same time I was engaged in deep meditation – a place that the Abbott of the Zen Mountain Monastery refers to as the "still point." The staff erupted in applause with every compliment they received. It was a special moment and when it was over everyone was hugging and patting each other on the back. What I felt more than anything else was relief that the survey was over and had ended so well. Little did I know it was about to get better.

First Wayne approached me with his proof that the administrative surveyor's RFI was unjustified. I asked him to explain his reasoning and it was pretty sound. He had really stepped up and I was proud of him. I didn't know if there was anything that I could do, but, I said I would bring it to the attention of the team leader before she left.

As I was about to walk into the surveyors conference room, Gretchen stopped me. "Look at these two citations," she said. In addition to the administrator's RFI, we received one from the nurse and one from the physician. "The nurse and the physician pulled their RFIs from the same JCAHO standard. I think these two should be combined into one." It was an excellent argument. Perhaps we were being greedy, but, I thought, what the heck. Nothing beats a fail but a try.

With supporting documents in hand, I entered the surveyors' conference room. The nurse surveyor was a grandmotherly looking woman from Massachusetts, but, she had been all business during the survey process. I approached her cautiously. "Excuse me," I said. "Can I speak with you for a moment?" She turned around, smiled and said, "Sure, but first, give me a hug."

That was a first for me, but, boy did I appreciate it. I began with the Psychiatry petition. She put her glasses back on and furrowed her brow as she carefully scrutinized the information I presented to her. When she finished she paused for a moment and I thought for sure that she was going to shoot us down. But she didn't. We'd convinced her. She couldn't take the finding out of her report because it had been entered by another surveyor, and the computer system wouldn't allow her to change it. But she said she would flag it and that it would be removed once they returned to JCAHO headquarters. We were now down to 2 RFIs. Dare I ask for another concession? She was getting up to finish packing her briefcase when with a degree of timidity that was atypical for me I said, "Uh, there's just one more thing."

I made my pitch in one long run-on sentence and then I closed my eyes to brace myself in case she slapped me for my impertinence. I only opened my eyes when I heard her laugh. She was looking at the citations that she'd written and she said, "You're right. They should be collapsed." This was something she could change. She reissued the report on the spot. This time I asked for a hug. I left the room in a daze. Most of the Cabinet was standing in the hallway waiting. I was still in shock over the coup we'd just pulled off and I couldn't find the words, so I just held up one finger and I knew they knew what that meant.

The Corporation's Chief Medical Officer walked over to me and gave me a hug. "I'm so proud of you," he said. It's funny how you never outgrow hearing that kind of comment in moments like the one we were sharing. We held a reception for the staff up in the 10th floor solarium with dessert and a slide show featuring pictures from the weeks and months of preparation.

Once I'd finished greeting and thanking the bulk of the staff, I went back to my office to collapse.

This survey felt different from the one in 2002. It was clearly a relief for me personally and professionally that we'd done so well. But the level of elation was different. This time I wasn't exhausted and strangely I wasn't surprised. Woodhull was definitely a different hospital from the one I'd returned to in 2001. The improvements had been building for a while. So instead of retreating, I couldn't wait to set the next milestone. We had a Rocky Balboa kind of thing going on. As far as I was concerned, at this point the sky was the limit.

CHAPTER EIGHTEEN
NOVEMBER 17, 2005

LESS THAN A WEEK had passed since the survey
and there was already another big event to prepare for –
Woodhull's annual gala. One of Donna's lasting
signatures came from her insistence that the Woodhull
Auxiliary upgrade its annual fundraiser by moving it to a
Manhattan hotel. At 6:00 p.m. we would hold our fourth
event at the Ritz-Carlton Battery Park. In that short time,
the party had already reached legendary status, selling out
weeks in advance.

This year was particularly special because one of
the people we were honoring was Donna. I had a special
award for her that I was looking forward to presenting.
The day of the gala was almost always a half-day because
of the time it takes to get ready. But this year it happened
to fall on the same day as the monthly HHC Board of
Directors Meeting. That meant I had to go to Central
Office first. I brought my gown with me and Donna and
I decided we would sneak out of the board meeting early
and ride to the hotel together. Getting ready for my first
stint as the official "hostess" should have been the
biggest thing on my mind, but it wasn't. Instead I was
preoccupied with thoughts about a bizarre email
exchange that had taken place earlier that day.

In trying to keep my promise to the staff about
coming up with ways to show them that they were
appreciated, we received approval to create a quarterly
perfect attendance lottery – the first of its kind in HHC.
Employees who had not called in sick within the

291

previous three months would be entered into a lottery and five people would win $500. Announcement of the new lottery generated a lot of excitement. But for legal reasons we could only offer the program to HHC employees, not employees of the Woodhull, P.C., which included not only physicians, but, some of our technical staff as well.

At about 3:30 p.m. on the day before the gala, Ira sent the following email addressed jointly to me and Simon, our CFO, with the subject heading "Preventing Silos":

> The incentive pool awards for nonutilization of sick time and for being immunized against influenza are great ideas. However, it's wrong to exclude Medical Group employees from consideration.
>
> We all try hard to be inclusive and make everyone feel like equal partners of all our patient care and support teams. By excluding Woodhull Medical Group employees from consideration in this well publicized initiative it drives a wedge between our employees. The rumblings I've heard to date indicate the medical group employees feel excluded and like second class citizens.
>
> Please consider including all employees in this initiative.
>
> Thanks, Ira

Anyone reading that email by itself would probably find it innocuous. And taken in isolation it was. But I wasn't reading it in isolation and that proved to be true in more ways than one. Things seemed to settle down considerably after the changes in the Cabinet, at least for a while. But as the survey approached, I noticed that Ira was acting more and more provocatively towards me. It seemed that with every decision I made he wanted to do the opposite and he was quite vocal about it.

During the week of the survey he challenged me about everything from turning off his cell phone during the Leadership interview to my choice to have the celebration in the solarium instead of the auditorium. That was why I was so annoyed when I found out that he had taken the physician surveyor on a tour of the hospital, when I'd specifically asked him to keep the man in one location. It was adding up to more than a few isolated differences of opinion. I had already been mulling over having a conversation with him when his email arrived.

There were two things that annoyed me about the email. First, he knew how I felt about his addressing these types of emails to me and a member of the Cabinet as if we were both taking directions from him. He did it once before since I'd become his boss and I delicately reminded him then, that it was inappropriate. But far more important to me than that was that the email was another example of his "conducting the chorus of criticism" rather than acting like a leader.

The flu-shot lottery was a corporate initiative. I had absolutely no control over who was included or excluded. And we could not include non-HHC employees in our Perfect Attendance lottery for the same reasons that they were excluded from the flu-shot campaign. The Woodhull P.C. was a vendor. The New York City Conflict of Interest rules required us to maintain an arms-length relationship whenever financial transactions were involved. These were all things that Ira knew. Just like he knew about the numerous events and activities that we conducted every year to which all our employees were invited. I was starting to question whether my Medical Director was really just a "harmless puppy" after all.

I knew I had to tread carefully so I sent an email to Kerry to get his advice. I put everything I wanted to write to Ira in the email, but, by the time I pressed "send" my head was much clearer. When I received Kerry's response that I should have a meeting rather than respond in writing, it was already after I sent Ira this reply:

> I think it's time for you and I to have a talk. Please put yourself on my calendar at your earliest opportunity. Tomorrow will be hectic and I know you're away Friday so it can wait until next week.

Candis

That was at 4:16 p.m. on Wednesday, November 16th. The next day when I arrived at work, I opened the following email from the administrator for the Woodhull P.C.:

> I'd try to make it happen today for 15 minutes so you don't dwell on it till Monday. Have no fear when you know you are right.

Milo

Initially, was confused, but, I quickly deciphered what I was reading. That email wasn't intended for me. It was a reply to a copy of my email that Ira had forwarded to him and God knows who else. He had obviously been sharing our email communications with others. Now a few thoughts went through my mind, but, before I let conspiracy theories run away with me, I decided to send the entire email thread to Kerry to get his take on it. When he responded -- "This is a MAJOR problem – call if you want to discuss" -- I knew I wasn't completely out in left field.

I called A.J. into my office. "Did Ira put himself on my calendar for next week?" I asked.

"No," she said.

"Well, he's going to come down here at some point today and ask you if he can see me for a few minutes. Put him on the calendar for Monday."

She said okay and she'd barely stepped a foot outside my office when I heard Ira's heavy footsteps come into the executive suite. I needed time to think. I knew he was going to try to strong-arm her into getting in to see me that day. But I also knew that nobody strong-armed A.J.

The rest of the day went so quickly that before I knew it Donna and I were at the Ritz-Carlton getting dressed. I didn't bother to tell her about the emails. By that point it was starting to seem trivial. We went downstairs and found that the guests were already starting to gather. The theme that year was Mardi Gras so feathered masks and multi-colored beads made for a fanciful accent to the shimmering gowns and elegant tuxedos. It was shaping up to be a really special night.

The dining room was filled to capacity. My parents came as did Donna's husband, Richard, her son and daughter-in-law, her sisters and her brother-in-law. I knew them all well by that point, so it felt like a birthday party. Gilberto attended and we sat him at my table along with Donna, her husband, my parents, Ira, and the person I replaced when I went to Gen +. He was now working at a nearby hospital and had remained friends with both Donna and me.

After a late start, the program got underway. We honored the Chief of Radiology, the Chief of Pathology, and of course Donna. Her award was presented last. I knew I wanted to say something special to her. She already knew my feelings, but, I felt the need to make my sentiments public. Over the years, she'd looked out for a number of the people who were in the room that night; perhaps no one more than me. I decided to draw my tribute from Maya Angelou's poem, "Phenomenal

Woman." I customized it for Donna and had it engraved on a rosewood plaque.

Presenting her award proved to be emotional, awkward and funny all at the same time. Here we were, two women known least for displaying our emotions and we were both trying to fight back tears. But we made it through the presentation with mascara in tact and returned to our seats for dinner. I was moving from table to table greeting guests and returned to my table just as our dinner was being served. Donna leaned across the table toward me. "Where's Gilberto?" she asked. He had been sitting two seats away from me when I got up to start the program, but, now he was gone. I shrugged and looked around the room. Then I spotted him. He had left our table and was already eating at a table in the back – Lorenzo's table.

When I pointed him out to Donna, she looked as appalled as I was confused. This is a woman who went to charm school, remember. And though I hadn't, I knew exactly what she was thinking. We weren't at a barbeque. At a black-tie dinner, you eat where your host seats you. I decided to resist the temptation to read more into it than bad manners. Perhaps he was light-headed with excitement. He had his own reasons to celebrate that night. The board of directors had finally been given the go-ahead from the mayor's office to make his appointment permanent, earlier that evening.

Whatever the reasons for his odd behavior, the night was too special for me to let one person dampen it, even if that person was my boss. Once the band started playing and I'd knocked back two Cosmopolitans, my thoughts ran along the lines of "President who?" As usual, once the dancing started time seemed to fly by. We packed on to the tiny dance floor like straphangers on the uptown 6 train during evening rush hour and we kept dancing until the lights came up.

You can tell a woman's had a good time at a formal dinner when she's leaving the ballroom with her shoes in her hand. I sauntered over to a railing overlooking the stairs to the lobby and waved at the guests as they left. I felt like Queen Elizabeth waving from the balcony at Buckingham Palace, only I'm sure she would have been wearing her shoes not waving them. I had drifted off in thought for a moment to nowhere in particular when I felt someone move up beside me.

It was an executive from a facility in another network. We were both in the executive leadership training program that the Corporation had offered a few months earlier. So we'd gotten to know each other beyond the usually superficial greetings typically exchanged at HHC functions. I thought him to be smart and enthusiastic and more important, a genuinely nice and sincere person. These were traits that I was coming to realize were increasingly rare at the Corporation.

"Congratulations," he said also looking out at the revelers below us.

I thought he was talking about the party so I replied, "Thanks. You should come back next year. It's always like this."

"No, I'm talking about your appointment. I'm really pulling for you. It's your turn. You deserve it."

It was an unexpected but thoughtful comment and I thanked him for sharing it. But he wasn't finished. And I wasn't prepared for what he said next.

"But you know who you can't trust, right?"

He now had my full attention. I had my opinions about who I could trust and who I couldn't, but, this was an outsider to our network. What did he know that I didn't? Stumped, I asked who. Without hesitating he replied, "Ira Gold."

When he mentioned Ira by name every drop of alcohol still coursing through my veins evaporated in an instant. I was possessed with immediate clarity of thought. "I don't even like to shake hands with the guy," he continued. "I'm afraid I'll pull back missing fingers." This was now the second independent source of doubt about Ira that I was being presented with in less than 24 hours. "Candis, you have no idea how many times I wanted to call you, but, I didn't know what to say." He paused for a second and then he said "Just be careful."

He said volumes and the timing was so perfect that it was spooky. The list of people telling me to reevaluate my opinion of Ira was growing too large to ignore. But I couldn't get these particular comments out of my mind because they came from someone who had absolutely nothing to gain from sharing them with me, and no apparent axe to grind. I had a lot to mull over before my meeting on Monday.

The next day I received a call from Donna. I assumed that she wanted to talk more about the gala, which we did for a minute, but, then her tone shifted. "Listen," she said. "I called because David Tillman and Felipe Saldana just left my office and I told them that I would share our conversation with you." By this point Assemblyman Tillman, his wife and I had become very good friends. Felipe Saldana was a good friend of David's, but, was also well known to me because he had once served as the Chairperson of Woodhull's Community Advisory Board. David and Felipe had scheduled the meeting with Donna about something unrelated to me, but, my name came up as they were leaving. The general tenor of the comments was, "People are saying she's too tough. She needs to lighten up."

It was difficult for me to believe that the timing was coincidental. I decided that it was time to fill Donna in on what had been brewing back at Woodhull. She agreed that I couldn't afford to take an academic approach to this anymore. I needed to get to the bottom of what was going on. I called David first, because I knew we could have a candid conversation. He was in his car when I reached him on his cell phone and he knew immediately why I was calling. I was hoping that through his friendship with Felipe, he could shed some light on his frame of mine.

The first thing he said was, "I was as surprised by his comments as you are. Personally, I don't think you need to change a thing about your approach. You're doing what you need to do to run that hospital and that's exactly what I said to Felipe." I appreciated the support. But I really needed to know where these attacks were coming from. I asked him if he thought that Felipe would meet with me directly and David was sure that he would. "He supports you," he said. "He wants to see you get that job. I think he thought he was helping you by sharing what he heard. Talk to him. He'll be straight with you."

I set up a meeting with Felipe for Tuesday, November 22nd. In the meantime, it was time for my chat with Ira. By the time Monday afternoon arrived, I'd had the opportunity to get some more advice from Kerry. He suggested that I have the meeting someplace other than my office in a space that would convey neutrality. Donna's office was still empty and it had a seating area, so I decided we would speak there instead of having me peer across a desk at him.

I'd had the weekend to think about the emails, the outbursts and now the feedback from all the disinterested parties. But when Ira finally arrived and we walked into Donna's office together, what I really wanted to do more than anything else was to have a conversation, person to person. Despite our differences, I had actually considered him a friend. I certainly never thought he was someone who would actively try to do me harm. Something happens when you start to realize that you may have been wrong about a person. The circumstances start to recede like the scenery in a stage play when the lighting dims. Your focus narrows with your vision until all you can see is the object in the spotlight. Now the spotlight was on Ira and it wasn't the kind of attention he liked.

I sat down on the couch and he sat across from me in a chair. In situations like this I find no need for small talk. I began by asking him a question.

"Why do you think we're here?" He looked at me pensively.

"Because you don't like it when I send emails to you and other members of the cabinet at the same time."

"That's one reason," I said. "But I wouldn't have asked to meet with you about that. You and I are not on the same page, Ira. I think that's obvious, don't you?" He didn't answer. He didn't even look up at me. So I continued.

"I've watched you become more and more confrontational with me over these past several weeks. Challenging me in public, sending me emails about what you don't like instead of just talking to me, emails that I now know aren't going just to me. Did you think I wasn't going to respond just because I'm still "Acting" in this job?" The question elicited a look but he still gave no verbal response. "I know the president thinks that you were the reason behind our success on the survey," I continued.

At the HHC cabinet meeting following our survey, Gilberto congratulated me and Ira jointly even though Ira wasn't even at the meeting. I remember exchanging glances with Donna when he said it because the comment was unusual. Neither of us had ever remembered a president splitting the credit for a successful survey between the Executive Director and their Medical Director in this manner, not even this president. There is only one CEO. I wanted to at least set Ira straight on that point.

"If we had gone down in flames on that survey, you, Lorenzo and everyone else who was laying bets that I was going to implode, would have taken one giant step backward and let me take all the blame, right?"

He had no choice but to break his silence.

He shook his head and said, "Yeah. You're right."

"Yeah, well if I was going to take all the blame for things going wrong, then I'm taking all the credit for things going right."

But it was time to get serious.

"If you want this job, Ira, then come down front and take it from me like a man. Don't smile and put your arm around me in public and then sneak around behind my back complaining about me to the community. That's what cowards do."

He sprung to attention. "I never went to the community about you!"

He said it as if he'd seized upon some loophole he could actually answer truthfully about. But I was ready for him.

"Of course you didn't," I said. "That's not your style. You got Lorenzo to do your dirty work for you."

I was fishing. It was a bad cop bluff at best. No one had mentioned Lorenzo to me by name, not yet anyway. I was operating on instincts, but, Ira's body language told me that my instincts were accurate. He slumped in his chair, his face cherry red with embarrassment, and looked down at his shoes. If it had been a cartoon, this would have been the moment when a sign popped up from his shoulder blades with arrows made of light bulbs pointing to the crown of his head and the word, GUILTY, GUILTY, GUILTY flashing in neon above him. Never had a person given such a complete confession without ever uttering a word.

"There's only one bridge on a ship," I said. "There can only be one captain. We can't continue with me pulling the wheel one way and you trying to yank it from me. You can't possibly think that I'm going to sit still and allow that."

Having this conversation in the close space that existed between us was both awkward and liberating. There was no room for deception. The more I spoke and he didn't, the more I knew I was getting at the truth. "You have to decide whether you can live with that or not and that's a decision you need to give some thought to," I said.

There was still no verbal response, just more shoe perusal. But I wasn't finished. Up to that point it had been about business. It was about to get personal. I had nominated this man for an award at the local YMCA and when it was time for it to be presented, I insisted on making the presentation myself. I praised him for his work on behalf of children with asthma because he deserved it. But I also called him my friend and I was now realizing that he didn't deserve that.

"Do you have any idea how many times over the years that I've worked with you, someone has approached me to say that you couldn't be trusted? Some of them called you every kind of sleazy, backstabbing racist. I'm not talking about two or three people, Ira. I'm talking double-digits and I'm not even including the hearsay. I'm only talking about the people who said it to my face. And every single time I defended you. I really believed that they were wrong about you. Now I see that they were right all along." I paused to let him respond. But he didn't. I guess he couldn't. There wasn't much left to say so I decided to bring the meeting to a close.

"I don't know what the future holds for me. But if you think I'm going to sit by and let you trash my reputation without putting up a fight you are sadly mistaken. Do what you have to do. Just know that you no longer have the element of surprise." I stood up to leave, but, as I reached the door I saw he was still sitting in the spotlight, so I decided to leave him with one more thing to think about. "You know, Ira, when it's all said and done I'm not your biggest problem. I could leave tomorrow and Gilberto could give you this job the same day. That still wouldn't make you a leader." Then I leaned forward so that he could hear me clearly without my having to raise my voice much above a whisper. "You're not a leader if no one is following you and people don't follow someone they don't trust."

I went back to my office and sat down. There was a measure of satisfaction in knowing that I'd said everything I wanted to say to him. But I still felt the numbness of a busted lip. It was more than a little disconcerting to realize that I really did not know who my enemies were or what they were up to. And with all that I knew then, I still didn't know the half of it.

I had my meeting with Felipe the next day and he started by reiterating exactly what David told me over the phone. "Candis, I support you 100%. I want you to get this job," he said. "Both you and Donna have done wonders here. I remember what this place was like before you guys got here. Nobody who cares about this hospital wants to see it go back to the way it was. But you gotta soften up a little bit. You've got a great Medical Director. He goes out into the community and . . . ." I couldn't restrain myself.

"I've got to stop you here, Felipe, because I've heard this before. And I really need to clarify something. Both Ira and Lorenzo have gotten a lot of mileage out of taking credit for all the accomplishments and positive press that we've been enjoying in recent years. But I need to remind you of something. They were both here when this hospital was a shit hole. I can tell you the exact date when things started to get better: January 1, 2001, when that lady sitting over at Bellevue got here."

I could see a smile crease his face and I knew that meant he hadn't heard anything he could disagree with yet. I was on a roll and I wasn't finished. "Yes, Ira, goes out to the community to give speeches and hold health fairs and he organizes bike rides for the kids and that's great, but, there's one problem. That's not in his job description. When you try to get him to do things that a Medical Director is supposed to do like actually leading the Medical Staff, he's nowhere to be found. For all the attention he gets about his passion for asthma you would think our network would lead the Corporation on the asthma care indicators. Guess what? We don't. That's because he doesn't have the attention span to focus on those boring details. What we have at Woodhull is a Medical Director of Special Projects."

First Felipe began to chuckle. Then he began to laugh. "You know, you're right. I never thought about it that way," he said. But I didn't ask to meet with Felipe just to rehash who had been doing all the work at the hospital and who hadn't. What I needed to know was where he was getting his information.

There was too much at stake to be coy so I just asked him. "Can you tell me who came to you with this?"

Surprisingly, he didn't have a problem with revealing his sources. "Absolutely," he said. "It was Lorenzo, Lorenzo and that administrator of his. What's his name – Milo?"

That's the one, I thought.

"They cornered me at the gala. Actually, Milo had to do most of the talking. Lorenzo was pretty much incoherent. And I'd really like to know when somebody's going to do something about that!"

Well, it wouldn't be me. I had bigger fish to fry. We talked for another twenty minutes or so about a variety of things, some having nothing to do with Woodhull. Then he left pledging his full support. I added the new pieces to the puzzle. When Ira left my office the day before, I knew he wasn't going to keep our conversation to himself. I'd mentioned Lorenzo by name. And I knew Lorenzo well enough to know that being the kind of XY chromosome that he was, if I'd accused him falsely he would have been in my office in a flash banging his fist on my desk with righteous indignation. More than 24 hours had passed and I hadn't heard a word from him. I suspected that he was Ira's co-conspirator and the lapse in communication was additional evidence. After my meeting with Felipe, I had independent confirmation. The only question left for me was, "What do I do next?"

If I wanted to keep this job I would still have to work with these people. Donna offered to meet with them to broker a peace treaty and I thought maybe that would be enough. Despite the apparent brazenness of the espionage, I still considered it a minor wrinkle that we'd iron out and all have a laugh about in a year or so. Then came December 2nd.

CHAPTER NINETEEN
DECEMBER 2, 2005

I HADN'T HAD A one-to-one meeting with Gilberto since August and I mentioned that fact to him at the gala. So when his office called the next day to schedule one, I assumed that was why. I came into his office and took a seat across from him at the conference table. I had a lot of good news to report. Our financial position was rapidly improving and I had come up with the next milestone for us to reach. Woodhull was going to apply for the Malcolm Baldridge National Quality Award.

It was beyond ambitious. But the staff was enthusiastic about it and I really believed we could pull it off. I'd also been appointed to a leadership position with the *American College of Healthcare Executives*. The public sector had historically been underrepresented with this organization. I thought that having a Network Sr. Vice-President in such a high profile position with the nation's premiere organization for healthcare executives would be a great way to raise HHC's profile nationally.

Gilberto was finally ready to announce that Donna would be remaining at Bellevue as the permanent Sr. Vice-President for the South Manhattan Network. That left me hanging out on a limb as the only Sr. V.P. still functioning in an "Acting" capacity. Now that the survey was over and we'd performed so well I assumed my appointment was just a formality. After all, Woodhull's survey results were better than anyone could have predicted. We turned in the best performance of

306

any hospital in the tri-state area that year, public or private, and it ranked us among the top 1% of hospitals in the nation.

Despite the nonsense going on with Ira and Lorenzo, I was exceedingly confident about my prospects. So confident that as I sat down I said jokingly, "Do I need to be looking for a job?" I will never forget his response. "Actually, Candis" he said, "I'm not inclined to appoint you to the position."

The only word I can think of to describe how I felt at that moment was blindsided. Even with everything that was going on (and it seems silly to say that now in retrospect), I really didn't see it coming. Gilberto was still talking, but, I was dazed like a boxer who'd let his guard down and was surprised by a left hook to the jaw. I needed to shake it off and fast. When he said something about his hoping I would grow into the position, but, that I hadn't, that was enough to wake me up.

"Can we talk about this or have you made up your mind?"

"No, we can talk about it," he said. Looking back, I'm sure he wished he hadn't left that door open. I started with a request.

"Tell me what I could have possibly done that would warrant me being without a job." He actually seemed surprised by the question.

"No one said you would be without a job."

"You can't possibly think that I'm going back to my old job. It doesn't exist. I've redistributed my responsibilities to other people. And even if I hadn't, unless you can tell me how I failed as a Sr. Vice-President I have no reason to go back to being a Chief Operating Officer."

He began to stutter. "Well, that's your choice, but, no one is asking you to leave."

"I beg to differ. You had choices. You could have left me in my old title. You could have made me an

Executive Director only, but, you didn't do either of those things. You made me a Sr. Vice-President and Acting or not, that's the job I've done. Telling me I have to go back to my old job is a demotion. Now I have no problem accepting a demotion as long as you can tell me where I failed." He responded by becoming defensive and spouting incomplete sentences, so I pressed him on specifics. "What exactly is the problem?"

"There have been a lot of complaints about you," he said. "It's even gotten to the chairperson's office."

"What kind of complaints?"

To defensiveness he now added an air of righteous indignation.

"Don't ask me who complained because I'm not going to tell you."

I respectfully reminded him that I didn't ask him *who* complained, I asked him *what* the complaints were. He proceeded to tell me that he was hoping I would be more like Donna, nurturing and supportive. People found me to be aloof and they had problems with my leadership style.

I found a couple of things interesting about his comments. First, when he was describing Donna's qualities he used the exact same terminology to a word that Lorenzo had often used to describe her. It was becoming clear to me who the president's mystery sources were. Thinking back on his choice of dinner companions at the gala and the fact they my mutineers had used that evening for strategic fly-bys with Felipe as well, it occurred to me that I not only knew who Gilberto's sources were, but, when they'd spoken to him last.

He then began to talk about the agenda that he wanted to put forward and how important it was for him to have effective leadership at the networks. That provided me with another opening.

"Even if everything that is being said about me is true, show me how it's hindering me from being an effective leader. Where is the North Brooklyn Health Network failing to make progress?" I'd moved from defense to offense and I knew I was on solid ground. It was only a jab, but, it was a good one.

"There are lots of ways to be successful," he said, now clearly on the defense, "fear, intimidation." Now the nature of the attacks was beginning to take shape. But this wasn't going to be as easy as Gilberto thought. "So you think the employees in our network are operating out of fear?" I asked. "You think I've created a climate of intimidation and that's why we're performing so well?" I think he knew I was setting him up for an uppercut so he didn't respond. It didn't matter.

"Well, Gilberto, you know how much the staff at Woodhull likes to write letters."

If there was one thing that HHC employees in general, and Woodhull employees in particular, were not shy about it was writing letters when they were unhappy about something. As popular as Donna was, she generated a ton of mail during her time at Woodhull. The letters weren't always well-written, but, what they lacked in grammar and syntax they more than made up for in fervor, and when sufficiently agitated - volume. Shortly after we returned in 2001, an employee wrote a letter of complaint to Donna about my decision to transfer him to another department. He copied the president of HHC, the mayor, the governor . . . and God.

Gilberto nodded in agreement with my statement before he caught himself. His chin was exposed so I tapped it.

"Tell me something, how many letters have you gotten about me since I took over as Sr. Vice President?"

It wasn't a knock-out punch, but, it definitely caused him to backpedal. He didn't utter a word in response. He didn't have to. I knew there had only been one and that was the letter that Maura begged her staff to write on her behalf after I demoted her. This was a woman who could incite her staff to such a level of discontent that one of them actually staged a one-woman picket line outside the hospital during her lunch hour. Given the avalanche of mail written to Central Office about Maura over the years, he didn't dare bring that letter up. I kept swinging.

"Don't you think that if I had been flying through the hallways on a broom, someone would have written to you about it by now?"

He had no choice but to concede that round so we moved on. Since the leadership style argument was getting shakier by the minute, he shifted to the medical staff. I didn't have a good relationship with them according to his unnamed sources. This was a surprise to me as well. My relationship with the Chiefs of Service predated my appointment and I'd always thought we worked well together. Whenever they needed something done, I was the one they came to. Beyond that, I had to bring the conversation back to the survey.

"How could we have done as well as we did on JCAHO if I was making the medical staff miserable?" I asked. I knew I had a point whether he wanted to acknowledge or not. It is impossible to do well on that survey with a discontented medical staff. There are too many ways they can sabotage you. They had no incentive to cooperate if they were unhappy and there would have been very little I could have done to them if we did poorly. All of this they knew. It just didn't make sense.

That's when Gilberto said something that nearly knocked me out of my chair. I guess I mentioned that survey one time too many.

In a huff he said, "Well, Joint Commission was a little thing!"

Joint Commission, a little thing? At HHC? I couldn't believe he actually said that out loud.

Our survey took place during the same week of Mayor Bloomberg's reelection. During his final debate he was asked about the relevance of HHC. He gave a glowing endorsement of the work we were doing and talked about how proud he was of HHC's performance. If one of our hospitals had had a meltdown during the survey, it would have been a huge embarrassment for the mayor. And since Gilberto's appointment had not been made permanent at that point, the stakes were even higher for him. I had to take a deep breath before I could respond to that little gem. But I gathered my composure and said, "I suspect that had we not done well, it would *not* have been a little thing." From the wide-eyed silence I received in response, I took the liberty of counting that as another point in my column.

We went back and forth like that for about half an hour. He didn't present a single rational argument that he could substantiate. And since he refused to reveal where he was getting his information it limited where the conversation could go. As was my way, I decided that we had gone around in a circle long enough, so I issued him a challenge. What the hell did I have to lose at that point?

"Tell me what you need to see in order for you to be convinced that I can do this job," I said. "Name it and I'll produce it."

Without thinking he said, "Improve your relationship with the medical staff."

"Fine," I said. "I have to tell you that I'm still surprised by that accusation, but, I'll go back and take another look. And if it turns out that I'm as far off base in terms of my relationship with the physicians as you're implying, you won't have to remove me. I'll leave on my own. But I'd like you to do something for me," I continued.

"Go back and check for yourself. Don't rely on secondhand information. Come to Woodhull. In fact, tell me what day you're coming and I'll take the day off. Walk the halls. Talk to the people. If I've created some sort of toxic atmosphere, the staff will not hesitate to tell you. I'm not afraid of what they'll say. Scrutiny reveals nothing but the truth."

I also invited him to talk to Kerry. He was surprised to learn that I had already taken steps to develop my leadership approach. If he had concerns about my potential for growth, Kerry was as good and unbiased a voice to hear from as anyone. Before I left, he asked me not to make any changes and not to share our conversation with anyone. I agreed and with that I left his office. We never got to the agenda.

On the ride back across the Brooklyn Bridge, I was remarkably composed given what had transpired. And it wasn't shock. My sparring match with Gilberto had knocked all those cobwebs loose. I simply remember thinking, "Okay, God. You've got this one."

By the time I reached the office, Donna already knew about the meeting. Even though Gilberto swore me to silence, he'd called her to tell her about the conversation. She wanted to come to Woodhull the next day, which was a Saturday, to clean out her office. I decided that it might be a good idea for me to do the same, so I told her I'd meet her there and we could go to lunch afterwards.

By the time I woke up Saturday morning I was no longer feeling poised. I was angry. I felt used. Gilberto had never said a word to me about any of the "complaints" until he was ready to use them to chop off my head. And despite the "littleness" of Joint Commission, I knew why. He needed someone who could be counted on to make sure we passed that survey. Donna was already in her old office when I arrived.

"How are you doing?" she asked.

"How do you think?"

"You know I met with him right before you did and I tried to get him to tell me what he was going to talk to you about," she said. "If he had, I would have talked him out of it."

"Why?" I asked.

"To save him!"

Even as angry as I was, I had to laugh.

"Candis, you pushed that man all the way back into a corner," she said. "Those aren't my words. That's what *he* said."

"What did he think I was going to do?" I asked.

"You know I don't know! That's what I keep asking myself. They don't understand women like us at all. I think he thought you were just going to sit there, let him take that job from you and go quietly wherever he sent you."

"He couldn't have thought that," I said.

"Yes. I think he did. I knew that someone was putting second thoughts in his head over the summer."

That got my attention. We finished packing her things and decided to go to a restaurant to continue the conversation over lunch.

"He said something about having to talk to you, at a meeting I had with him back in August. That he was going to have to do something. And knowing you like I do, I got so scared for him," she said. "I told him, 'Do what? Gil, that conversation is not going to go the way you think it's going to go. Besides they've got Joint Commission in less than eight weeks. You need to let it ride.'"

"So the rumblings started back then?" I asked.

"I think they started the moment I left," Donna replied.

"He told me that someone came to him a few weeks after the appointment and said, 'You aren't seriously thinking about giving that job to Candis, are you?'"

I was floored and disgusted.

"Who do you think was getting in his head so early?" I asked.

"He wouldn't tell me," Donna said. "But I'm going to find out who is behind this if it's the last thing I do."

Of course I immediately thought about Shaina, the Corporation's Sr. Vice-President of Planning and resident blabbermouth. That sounded like something she would say and volunteering her opinions was certainly in keeping with her modus operandi. As I considered the possibility that she was once again sticking her beak into my professional business, it occurred to me that I had an earned coupon for a bitch-slap with her name on it. But fortunately for her, given my emerging state of divine repose, I opted to let it lapse.

I shared my suspicions with Donna.

"I'm way ahead of you on that one," Donna said. "She was the first person I went to, but, she swears it wasn't her."

"Then it must have been Ira."

When I said that, Donna froze with her fork half-way to her mouth. Her expression turned almost demonic.

"If I find out that he had something to do with this I will DESTROY HIM!"

She said it with such intensity that it was as if someone had mentioned E.F. Hutton. Everyone in the restaurant stopped and stared at us for a moment. It was a mother lioness kind of response. And it was certainly in keeping with her character and our relationship, but, it surprised me nonetheless. Our conversation returned to

Gilberto and I wondered out loud whether I'd come on too strong. I was still hoping to salvage the situation.

"As a matter of fact," she said, "he made a point to say that you challenged him in the most respectful way."

As we continued to talk I felt a certain numbness. Or perhaps it was more like embarrassment. I wasn't embarrassed about the possibility of not getting the job. There wasn't a decision I'd made that I would've changed and my record of achievement spoke for itself. The part that stung was that as smart as I was on paper, I had completely underestimated how hard my detractors would work to keep me from being appointed. It still amazes me to this day, how much treachery people are willing to engage in over a government job.

In hindsight, I had to be out of my mind to be so naïve. It was a completely one-sided campaign. They were fully organized and I was sleepwalking. There was only one side of the story being told about me because I was relying on my work to speak for me. That was dumb. After seven years at HHC, including the purgatory that followed my year with Lois, I should have known that strategy wasn't a strategy at all. Donna was already talking about us organizing a campaign of our own, but, I feared it might already be too late.

"You know I asked him what he would have done if you had just quit?" she said.

"He asked me about that," I said. "I told him I would never leave without notice."

"Yeah, well you're a better woman than most," she said. "He told me what you said, but, you know what? He wasn't prepared for the possibility that you weren't a professional."

"By the way," I asked. "What did Richard have to say about all this?"

For someone who never worked at HHC, Donna's husband always brought a novel perspective to our incessant melodramas.

"Oh," she said. "He looked me square in the eye and said, 'You know you're next, right?'"

I couldn't keep what I was thinking to myself another moment.

"Donna, I think Gilberto already has somebody else in mind for this job." She wasn't convinced.

"Nobody's coming to Woodhull," she said.

In fact, she was counting on that, but, I wasn't so sure she was right. Nobody wanted to come to Woodhull when *she* took the job. But four years later this was a very different hospital from the one we returned to in 2001. Now that all the heavy lifting had been done, why wouldn't there be someone out there salivating to bump me out of the top spot? But Donna remained optimistic.

"He said he hasn't made up his mind," she said. "We just have to get busy."

I scheduled one more meeting with Gilberto two weeks later to see if he'd reached a decision. He hadn't. He was still thinking, which meant that I had to continue acting as if nothing was wrong. Even worse, he said it might take him until sometime in January before he made up his mind. Beyond that he revealed nothing about whether he had gathered any new information about what kind of job I was doing. But I knew by that meeting that he hadn't tried, even when he had the opportunity.

I decided to poll some of the Chiefs about how they felt about my leadership before I went to the follow-up meeting I scheduled. I tried to honor my commitment to keep our December 2nd meeting confidential, by saying that I was just checking in with them to see if they were happy. To a person they all said they were. But I decided to be completely honest with

Dr. Wallace because he was the one Chief I knew I could trust. When I'd finished filling him in he said, "I'm surprised to hear you say that, Candis. I spoke with Gilberto yesterday at that conference I attended. He never mentioned you."

"You mean he didn't even ask you how things were going at Woodhull?" I asked.

"No," he replied.

I told Gilberto about the results of my informal poll when we met, but, after what I learned from Dr. Wallace, I didn't expect much of a response. But Gilberto did ask me a question.

"Do you still think you'll leave the Corporation if you don't get this job?"

I'd already given it plenty of thought so my answer was ready.

"Absolutely," I said. "And let me tell you why. I know how this corporation works. If the people who have given you reason to second-guess my abilities get their way, your decision will hang around my neck like a rock for as long as I work here. Only the next time a Sr. Vice-President position becomes available they won't have to reach for vague criticisms and innuendos they can't back up. All they'll have to say is, she already had the chance to be a Sr. V.P. and she failed. I'm not accepting a demotion. If you don't want to make me permanent, fine. But I <u>will</u> be leaving." That meeting was much shorter than the first.

On the same afternoon, Ira and Lorenzo asked if they could meet with me and I agreed. By now I knew most of the details of what they'd been up to. So I was curious to see what they hoped to accomplish, especially Lorenzo. This would be our first sit-down meeting since I'd out-ed him in my fire-side chat with Ira almost three weeks earlier. Would he try to massage the truth or would he go straight for the bald-faced lie? I couldn't wait to find out.

They came into my office and sat down in the two chairs in front of my desk. Ira usually enters a room with a fast pace and leaden footsteps but he was atypically subdued when he took his seat. Lorenzo, however, showed no such trepidation.

"Candis, I'm really concerned about what I'm hearing," he said. "I want you to know that I would never . . . ."

Okay I see we're going straight for the lie, I thought to myself.

I sat back in my chair and listened attentively for the next ten minutes as he attempted to convince me that he had never said a bad word about me or my leadership style. He wouldn't waiver from his story even after I told him when, where and to whom he'd been speaking.

"I'll call him myself!" he said referring to Felipe, full of bluster.

"You do that," I said. But what I was really thinking was, and say what? He was there remember? I knew who had reason to lie and who didn't. But that wasn't the point of the meeting so I tried to bring them back to it.

"I'm not concerned about what happened in the past. All I want to know is whether we can work together going forward."

They both nodded enthusiastically. Then Lorenzo volunteered to go a step farther. "We'll go talk to the president and tell him that we're happy with you and we want you to be appointed," he said. Ira nodded in agreement. I didn't know what to make of that offer. I knew I was talking to two individuals who were highly proficient at speaking with forked tongues. Beyond that, they were the last two people on the planet that I ever wanted to feel obligated to, even if that meant I wouldn't get the job.

"I'm not asking you to do anything for me," I said. "But you should know that I've spoken with the Chiefs myself. Not all of them, but, enough of them to know how they feel about my leadership. You two are supposed to be the leaders of the medical staff. If you're saying one thing and the medical staff is saying the exact opposite, who's going to look like the fool? Not me."

"No, No. We'll talk to the president and get this straight," they said almost in unison. After they left my office I made a mental note to self. One – go to the nearest church for holy water; two – sprinkle it on both guest chairs. You've just had a meeting with the devil and his henchman.

Before the month was out, the dynamic duo was back in my office to tell me that they had indeed met with the president, and told him that things were just rosy with us out at the network. "He didn't say anything though," they shared. Of course he didn't. He was probably trying to figure out why they were changing their story.

CHAPTER TWENTY
2006 – THE YEAR OF LIVING COURAGEOUSLY

BY THE TIME 2006 arrived, I was more certain than ever that I was in the midst of living out the purpose of my preparation. It's difficult to describe what it was like to keep the kind of secret I was keeping. I didn't know for sure who had been trying to convince Gilberto that I had no real connection with the staff, but, anything is easy to believe when you're isolated from reality. Except for the day he came to get the results of our JCAHO survey, he never stepped foot on the campus of the North Brooklyn Health Network while I was its Sr. Vice-President. If he had, he would have seen what I saw: Miracles.

As of January, I had been the Acting Sr. V.P. for eight months. That was long enough for anyone to begin to doubt whether I was going to keep the job. That certainly would have been reason enough for people to stop listening to me. Some of the things I wanted to try seemed a little outlandish even to me. But I had a vision for Woodhull. And I began to believe that we could make it a reality. The possibility of a bold transformation that had first enticed me to come to that hospital in 1998 was actually on the verge of coming true as far as I was concerned. I summed it up for the staff in my first general address to them. The tide was turning. Slowly but surely, Woodhull was beginning to be respected in the neighborhood.

It used to be that when you mentioned Woodhull in the community, the response was, "Woodhull??!!!" followed by a discursive of pejorative tales, replete with profanity. But now when Woodhull was mentioned, while you still might generate a similar response, invariably someone else would say, "But you know, I heard it's getting better." Considering where we'd come from, that was a ringing endorsement.

Our visits were going up and not just in the emergency room, where one could argue that the patient didn't really have a choice. We were doing more business in outpatient and ambulatory surgery – areas where the patients *did* have a choice and they were choosing us. I shared this with the staff and I told them that we weren't going back to the days when we were called "Woodkill" and "Killhall." I doubt I convinced everyone. I probably didn't convince anyone that first day, but, for some reason they were hanging in there with me long enough to see if I could actually pull it off.

People who I thought were biding their time until retirement were walking up to me in the hallways offering ideas on ways we could make the hospital run better. From the front line all the way up to the senior staff, I was witnessing a renaissance. I thought back to my first conversation with June, the CFO when I arrived at Woodhull in 1998. I thought about how she said that no matter how hard you tried to change things here they always changed back. Then I thought about our medicine clinic. When we started that first redesign project in 2002 their cycle time – the time between when the patient first entered the clinic and when they finally left – was 202 minutes! When they finished the redesign project nine months later it was 63 minutes. And the cycle time four years later in 2006? – 61 minutes.

Visitors to the hospital's lobby were no longer greeted by gum-smacking, civil servants who yelled at them through a hole in urine-colored plastic. The plexiglass was gone and so were any signs of employees who didn't want to be there. In their place we had Patient Navigators dressed in burgundy blazers and crisp white shirts. These were staff that I handpicked myself for another customer service initiative that actually worked. Now when patients couldn't find their way to their destination and even the new signage (that we finally installed) didn't help, these employees didn't just point the way, they provided personal escorts.

It was a program that proved so successful that the Corporation actually created a Patient Navigator title so that the other HHC hospitals could replicate what *we* were doing. And following Woodhull's lead was something that was happening with greater and greater frequency.

Mayor Bloomberg chose us for a public relations visit after our 2002 Joint Commission survey. Donna chose me to give him a personal tour of my labor of love – our newly renovated and redesigned ambulatory care clinics. He made special mention of how much he liked the restaurant-style beepers I'd introduced into the clinics to alert patients when the doctor was ready to see them. (I was determined to do away with the butcher shop-style method of summoning patients that had so tormented me during my first days at Woodhull.)

You have to understand that while mayors often conducted PR visits at HHC hospitals, in the past the only time a mayor ever came to Woodhull was if he was visiting a police officer being treated for a gunshot wound. Yet this mayor voluntarily came to see us – twice! And neither time was it because someone's life was in jeopardy. Even one of the local stations agreed to partner with us to broadcast one of their morning radio shows live from our auditorium. These kinds of events never happened at Woodhull before. But they were happening now.

There had indeed been a rebirth at our network. Nothing that Gilberto said or did could erase the fact that I played some part in it. But more important to me than any of that was the fact that the staff wanted this change for the better to continue. So I decided that if we were going to keep this forward momentum going, I would have to stop walking on eggshells. Okay, I was still "Acting." But the staff was "acting" like I had the job and therefore, so would I. I had another one of my middle of the night, wake me out of a sound sleep ideas and I wanted to flesh it out. I called Kerry and we agreed to meet on his next trip to New York.

In the meantime, I met with Simon and Yvonne to discuss raises and other staffing changes. Simon decided to use the opportunity to renew his petition for some staffing adjustments of his own. When Rhonda became the Director of Managed Care it meant that she would be reporting to him and things were not working out between them. He was stunned when I refused to let him fire her. I knew the reason for the astonishment. There were probably few people in the network who didn't know about Rhonda's strong feelings where I was concerned. But those were her feelings, not mine.

The network met its headcount target back in December, six months ahead of schedule. We'd now moved from the second-worst financial position in the Corporation to the second-best with more than four months to go before the end of the fiscal year. I was confident that we would meet our budget expectations by June. And while Rhonda had her peculiarities, I was sure she still had some talents that the network would benefit from. With all of those things being true, I had no intention of seeing anyone out of a job if I didn't have to fire them – not even Rhonda. Since Cora seemed to be one of the few people she got along with, I had Simon transfer Rhonda to her.

With each passing week our shift to a team-based approach was yielding more and more fruit. The Leadership Circles were busy conducting educational development fairs and career development counseling sessions. Even the unions were happy with us. My newly energized leadership team was also exploring ways to bring my dream of a truly paperless environment to life and completing the application for Woodhull to participate in the New York State version of the Baldridge Quality Award program. This was the source of my latest brainstorm and our latest dilemma.

It only took a small band of dedicated staff to drag the Widget Factory toward the shore when most of it was under water. The water itself helped to redistribute the weight. But we'd reached the point where there was more of our little factory out of the water than in. Legs were beginning to buckle. We found ourselves calling on the same twenty people every time we came up with a new project to undertake. I was convinced that we needed to continue to move toward teams and away from rigid structures. We just had to find a way to create more qualified team members.

By the time Kerry and I finally had lunch, I had given this a great deal of thought. The ideas that were swimming in my head were radical, but, I believed they could work with the leadership team's input. I shared my thoughts with him. As I began to describe my ideas for how we could give the staff more autonomy and move the hospital to a more team-based environment, the expression on his face grew into that of someone who appeared to think I was really on to something.

"What you're talking about would put Woodhull right at the cutting edge of the way hospitals are being run around the country. This is really exciting," Kerry said.

I was glad to know that he thought I was on the right track.

"I really have been listening to you," I said. "I don't want to just give this to the Cabinet and Chiefs as a directive. I know I'll need their help fleshing this out to make it work. Can you help me package this in a way they'll be receptive to?"

"Absolutely," he said. "Set up a meeting. You'll need about two to three hours of their time to brainstorm."

"I think it would help if someone other than me facilitated," I said. "Would you be able to do it?"

"I'd love to," he replied.

We talked more about how to present my ideas, how to give enough detail for them to understand what I had in mind, but, not so much as to foreclose the possibility of input from them. With everything we already had scheduled, I knew we needed to move quickly. But I was concerned about setting up the brainstorming meeting within the next week. Ira was away on a three- week bicycling trip in Southeast Asia. I didn't want it to appear as if I was trying to circumvent him.

"Don't worry about that," Kerry said. "You can make it clear that you're just gathering ideas at this point. No decisions will be made before Ira gets back. That shouldn't be a problem."

As we continued to talk, the conversation inevitably made its way around to my status. Although it took longer than I'd expected, Gilberto did eventually get around to speaking with Kerry. But it wasn't clear what Gilberto took away from that conversation.

"So have you heard anything?" Kerry asked.

"No. Not yet."

"This must be difficult for you," he said.

"It is, but, you know what I've decided? There is something special going on at Woodhull. I can't completely explain it, but, whatever it is, it's bigger than me and it's bigger than Gilberto. He'll do what he's supposed to do."

I sent around a general description of my ideas before the meeting. Kerry reviewed the handout to make sure it had just the right amount of detail. As I feared, a small group led by Lorenzo came to me with concerns that I was making plans without Ira. When I explained to them that all I was looking for at this point was feedback on the idea and that nothing concrete would be discussed until Ira returned, the group left satisfied. We held the meeting on Friday, February 3rd, in the late afternoon. Kerry ended up stuck in an airport and was unable to make our brainstorming session. But he sent another consultant from his office in his place.

As we'd agreed, I opened the meeting by reiterating the rationale behind the proposed project – a way to grow more teams and give them more autonomy. We also discussed the very limited scope of my expectations for the brainstorming session. Then I left the room so that the group could speak freely. They spent nearly two hours in spirited debate. When it was over, I returned to hear their feedback. The consultant had used a flipchart to write down the comments that emerged from their discussion. My eye went immediately to a statement about my "undermining the Medical Director." I was really disappointed. Especially when I learned that it was the Chief of the OB/GYN service who made the comment. We'd worked closely together on a number of projects since he joined us a few years earlier. I really thought he knew me better than that.

It turned out, however, that this isolated comment did not reflect the overall sentiments of the group. Everyone agreed that we'd achieved most of our most dramatic successes over the previous year as a result of team efforts. Nearly everyone agreed that we had reached a loggerhead with our current approach and we needed to consider working a new way. It appeared that while there were still lots of questions, everyone was willing to continue the discussion. That was all I was hoping for at that point. The meeting ended and our spirits were high.

The following Monday, we held our bi-weekly senior cabinet meeting. Ira was still away on his bicycle trip. Gretchen had left us to go work at Bellevue back in December. The members of the Cabinet who remained seemed to have developed a connection to each other that had never existed before. I'd noticed months ago that the Cabinet seemed to be spending more time together as a group. But this meeting was a real high point. All they wanted to talk about was the Friday brainstorming session.

"They are so far behind," Yvonne said referring to the Chiefs.

"You know I had to push back on some of those comments," Cora added. "It was just silly."

"They don't have as much experience working as a team as we do. It's just going to take some time to bring them up to speed." That last comment came from Wayne. I couldn't believe my ears.

This was the same group that barely spoke at Cabinet meetings other than to talk *at* each other about what "their" departments were working on. But now when they used the word "we" they weren't talking about their departments, they were talking about each other. They were cutting each other off and laughing and poking each other. Sometime during the previous six months, the Cabinet became a team and I hadn't noticed it until that very moment. They were so engrossed in each other that I don't think they even noticed that I wasn't participating. I couldn't. I was too choked up.

We closed the meeting with them giving themselves assignments about how they would move "our" plan forward. When I returned to my office, A.J. was right on my heels. First she told me that a meeting with the president had been scheduled for Wednesday. My heart raced initially. Then I thought, good it's time to get this over with one way or another. A.J. then handed me a folder with a memo on top.

I recognized it. It was another notice from the HHC Inspector General's office summoning an employee downtown for questioning. I was required to sign these memos as confirmation that the employee had been notified. I signed this one and put it back in the folder. A.J. was still standing there, so I handed the folder back to her instead of putting it in my outbox. That is, I tried to hand it to her, but, she wouldn't take it.

She was giving me one of those looks. Like Donna and me, A.J. and I had also developed our own means of communicating without talking. She was obviously making a point and it had something to do with that folder. We'd received quite a few of these notices in recent months, but, so much of my day was filled with signing documents that I didn't spend much time concentrating on what I was looking at. But I was concentrating now and it didn't take long for me to pick up on A.J.'s point.

The last twenty or more employees who had been called down to the Inspector General's office since September all had one thing in common. At one time or another, each of them had reported to me. *I* was being investigated. But that wasn't all. I linked what I was reading to what I remembered hearing about the identities of three other people who were called down to the Inspector General's office in recent weeks - Gretchen, Maura and Rhonda.

Satisfied that my eyes were finally open, A.J. took the folder from me, but, not before making a comment in that easy, sardonic tone that I had come to know so well. "Sure seems like somebody's trying real hard to find people to say something bad about you."

Gilberto hadn't made so much as a gesture toward me one way or another since our last meeting on December 17th. I was struggling to understand what kind of man I was dealing with. Was he really that callous or just clueless? He was making decisions that had people leaning either way. North Brooklyn wasn't the only network that needed a Sr. Vice-President. He still needed to backfill his own former position in Queens.

The Executive Directors at both of the hospitals in that network wanted the job and wanted it badly. Few people believed that he had any intention of giving the position to either one of them. But for some reason, he allowed them both to continue swinging in the wind in much the same way that he was handling the decision about my appointment. Whatever the reasons for the delay might have been, these two Executive Directors were both carrying long odds in Vegas as far as their appointment to the Sr. V.P. spot was concerned. But rather than put them out of their misery, Gilberto decided to make them switch hospitals for three months.

Confused? So was everyone else. From January to April of 2006, the Executive Director of Queens Hospital was sent to run Elmhurst Hospital and the Executive Director of Elmhurst Hospital ran Queens Hospital. But they couldn't change anything. And they couldn't bring any staff with them. And they had to consult each other on any major decisions. It hardly seemed worth the trouble of going.

After that bit of creative organizational thinking, I considered the possibility that the long period of silence regarding my status could be due to nothing more than the corporation having a president who had a difficult time making decisions. Whatever fate awaited me, I knew one thing. I wasn't ever going to be blindsided again. I prepared a full agenda for our meeting. Once again I had lots of good things to report.

There was a scene in one of the *Lethal Weapon* movies where the villain called an employee into his office. The man had apparently done something that he shouldn't have. During the brief conversation that followed, the villain never raised his voice or even appeared angry and the employee took no notice of the fact that he was standing on a plastic tarp. When the conversation was over, a hit-man emerged from a closet and put a bullet into the employee's head. A few scenes later, the same assassin was summoned back to the office. When he walked through the door he immediately began looking around at the floor beneath him. When the villain asked him what he was doing, the hit-man replied, "I'm just making sure I'm not standing on plastic."

When I entered Gilberto's office, I sat down across from him at the conference table as I'd done at our last two meetings. I slipped my agenda across the table toward him and then I started looking for signs of plastic. But when he didn't say anything, I exhaled and proceeded to go through my agenda. As I pointed out each accomplishment, he nodded and smiled. I told him that we were planning an off-site leadership retreat (a recommendation from the brainstorming session) and he didn't seem to have a problem with that.

By the time we reached the end of the agenda I was breathing easier. Things were going well at the network. He seemed satisfied. I put my agenda back into my portfolio and waited to see if there was anything else we needed to cover. He pushed his copy of the agenda aside, clasped his hands together and said, "I know I said I would give some more thought to your appointment, but, I'm back at the same place. So I won't be appointing you to the position."

This time I offered no resistance. I crossed my legs and leaned back in my chair as he leaned forward in his. I would estimate that Gilberto was somewhere around 6'0 maybe 6'1 when I first met him. But he began to get smaller and smaller with every meeting we had since his own position as president became permanent.

I watched his body language. His torso was slightly hunched forward with his hands still clasped on the table in front of him. He was facing forward, but, I noticed that he couldn't seem to look me directly in the eye. From the angle he was presenting to me, I could see that he had a small blood clot in the left corner of his eye. Once again, I remember hearing another one of my grandmother's Southern sayings rising in the back of my head. "You see, God don't like ugly."

He continued to speak. "Now I know you said that if you didn't get the position you would leave, but, we have a couple of options to offer you and you really need to think about it." The way he emphasized the "you really need to think about it" part, it appeared he thought he was doing me a favor. I said nothing. "If you go back to your old position, provided that you and the new Sr. Vice-President get along, in six months or so I wouldn't be opposed to you getting the Executive Director title."

If I get along with the new Sr. Vice-President? "So you've already selected my replacement?" I asked. Judging from the sudden paleness that washed across his face, I could see that he didn't mean to give that away. But it was too late. The cat was out of the bag.

He stammered a little. "Uh, Yes."

"I see. And when is this person starting?"

"Well, they have to give notice and wrap up some projects they're working on so probably some time in April."

"Um hmm," I said.

Slowly the pieces were falling into place. It was one of the loudest wake-up calls I'd ever received. He was watching me and I was watching him right back. But the tension didn't make me feel any pressure to speak before I was ready to. Instead I remember thinking,

"You little expletive deleted. You never intended to give me this job." It was almost funny.

It was the beginning of February and he had entirely too many details about my mystery replacement for this to have been a decision he'd reached recently. The delay had nothing to do with his needing more time to think about whether I could do the job. He just needed more time. This time I didn't wait until I got into the car to have a little conversation with God.

Now I knew for sure. That calling I'd been responding to over the previous three years wasn't preparing me to get the job of CEO at the North Brooklyn Health Network. It was preparing me *not* to get it. And this was one of the moments I was being prepared for specifically. When I reflected on it later and considered how thoroughly Gilberto had played me like a fiddle over the preceding months, I knew that it was nothing but the Lord God Almighty that kept me from leaping across that conference table and slapping finger stripes into the side of his face. And yet that thought didn't even enter my mind while I was actually sitting there. Those were thoughts that only came to me later.

The other generous offer Gilberto had to make was a job with Vince, the Corporation's Chief Operating Officer. I would have to call him to get more details, but, it would be a corporate officer title and I wouldn't have to take a cut in pay. I listened to everything Gilberto said and when I was ready to reply, I leaned in toward him and looked directly at him. I wanted him to know that I was serious.

"As for me returning to my old job," I said. "I've already told you my position on that. I don't know why you won't believe me, but, I'll say this one more time so that they'll be no need for you to ever ask me that question again. Under no circumstances am I <u>ever</u> going back to my old job. I don't have to think about it. I don't have to sleep on it. That's - <u>never</u> - <u>going</u> - <u>to</u> - <u>happen</u>."

Then I leaned back with a smile and said, "But I'll call Vince."

As far as I was concerned I knew everything I needed to know. I wasn't making an idle threat. I had already confronted the possibility that my time at HHC was coming to an end and I'd made peace with it. But I didn't want to be impetuous either. I had a great deal of respect for the Corporation's Chief Operating Officer. And as things were shaping up, reporting to him would mean that I would have a boss I respected a whole lot more than the one I had at the moment.

I was ready to leave when it appeared that Gilberto felt the need to show me that he was still the president.

"You're still going to need to work with a coach for a year or so," he quipped. And he continued to shrink.

"I'd already planned to do that on my own," I said. But what I was really thinking was, "You first."

He should have let the conversation end there. But he didn't. "I need you not to say anything to anybody about this," he said. For the first time in all that had transpired between us, I felt myself losing my temper. I had to take several deep breaths before I could respond, and still my jaw was tight. It must have shown in my expression because he inched back in his chair a little bit.

I'd spent the previous two months waking up every morning with a knot in my throat, one that I had to swallow each morning so that I could go into that office every day with a smile on my face. And I promised myself that I would sear those feelings into my memory so that I would never be the cause of someone else being made to feel that way.

Through clenched teeth I said, "I have been exceedingly patient throughout this ordeal. But those people want to know who their Executive Director is going to be and after nine months, they're starting to assume it's going to be me. I'm not going back there to look them in the face and lie to them another day."

He was certainly in no position to ask me for a favor. The veins must have been protruding from my neck. Either that or he decided that he didn't want to step back into the ring with me after our last match.

"Okay. Okay," he said hastily. "Can you wait until Monday?"

I agreed and then I left.

There are plenty of books to tell you how to read and navigate office politics. You need to know how to socialize strategically, how to use the fine arts of diplomacy and persuasion to win people over to your way of thinking. Being in the right place at the right time dramatically increases your odds of success in the workplace if through hard work, careful preparation and a dash of savvy you are able to predict where and when the right place and time are.

But what the books can't teach and don't tell you is that there is always an unknown variable in the equation. The very same actions can cause one person to see you as confident and another to see you as arrogant. You can be praised for being an affable individual who knows how to get along with everyone or vilified as a weak-willed bootlicker who won't take risks for fear of offending someone. It is the choices we make long before anyone is looking closely that mark the dimensions of the wooden boxes people will put us in later. The unknown variable is in the mind of the carpenter.

The only thing you have control over is the sincerity with which you approach the choices you make. You most certainly do not have control over how those choices will be received. As you live and learn and grow you are guaranteed to make mistakes along the way. The mistakes are part of the process. Clipping your own wings prematurely so that you can fit in might limit how far you can fly for the rest of your life.

I look back on some of the choices I made and I can see clearly how I could have lived some of those same moments differently. But would I go back and change them if I could? Almost without exception the answer is no. What part do you change? Remove the experience that teaches the lesson and how does the lesson get learned? We don't need leaders who don't make mistakes. We need leaders who learn from them. It makes them more knowledgeable and experienced and it also makes them more compassionate.

In the end, if you are positioned among people who want you to succeed, short of a felony, the mistakes you can make that will impede your progress will be few to none. But if someone wants to deny you a promotion or take your job from you, know that those individuals will interpret everything you do in a light that will justify their decision. And there will be precious little you can do to stop them. That's the paragraph on office politics that is rarely written.

When you set off to create the structure that will house your professional reputation, choose the design and materials with care and deliberation. But whatever the final shape and whatever the ultimate composition make sure you place its foundation on firmer ground than the opinions of others because opinions change - swiftly.

I decided to wait until after I spoke to Donna before I called Vince. She'd been in the Corporation long enough to know what kind of corporate titles I could ask for. I left a message for her, but, she didn't get back to me until later that evening. By that time I'd talked to my family, and I had already worked through whatever emotions I had been feeling about my meeting with Gilberto.

Donna and I had been talking for several minutes about what kind of positions they might offer me and whether I'd be able to keep the company car when she abruptly put a halt to our conversation.

"Can I call you back when I get in the house?" she asked. She'd called me from the car on her way home from Bellevue. "I . . . I don't even know where I'm driving. I just turned down the wrong street. I . . . I . . . still can't believe what you're telling me."

I'd been so focused on the advice that I needed from her that I failed to consider how she would take the news. She'd become as invested in my career at HHC as I had, maybe more so. And just like that it looked like it was over. Parents feel their child's pain in double doses. I could hear something like that in her voice.

"Sure," I said.

The next day I had a long conversation with Vince.

"Candis, I can't tell you how sorry I am that things worked out the way they did," he said. "In this short time that we've worked together, I thought you were doing a terrific job."

"Thank you," I said.

As we started talking about titles and what I might do in his shop, it became clear that this plan wasn't as well thought out as Gilberto made it appear.

"To tell you the truth," Vince said, "I have to think through what I would have you do. Whatever it is, it's going to upset my division some. It's just that when I found out that you weren't getting the job, I was afraid you might leave. So I asked Gil if I could offer you something with me. I wanted to do it if meant we could keep you. I just happen to believe the corporation would be better off with you in it."

The idea to offer me a job in Operations wasn't Gilberto's after all. Whoever's idea it was, it soon became clear that it wasn't going to work. One of Gilberto's many alternating versions of why I wasn't getting the job at Woodhull was that I was being groomed to be Vince's replacement when he retired in a few years. But Vince already had someone working in his division that people thought highly of. I knew the person. He and I had worked on several projects together over the years and we'd become friends. If anyone should be groomed for that job it was him, not me.

Of course Donna also asked me to come to Bellevue to be her Chief Operating Officer and Gilberto was quick to take credit for that offer as well. I knew she was only trying to look out for me, but, I couldn't spend my career following her around. There wasn't one person, not even Gilberto, who could establish that I hadn't been up to the job of CEO. So I wasn't going to take a step backwards, not even to work with Donna again. Besides she already had a Chief Operating Officer. If she removed him from his position just so that I could have a job, I had a sinking suspicion that it would be no different from what Gilberto had just done to me. There was no way in hell that I was ever going to be a party to doing that to somebody else.

No matter how I looked at it, every other job I was being offered meant that other lives were going to be disrupted just to accommodate the fact that the president of HHC turned out to be a crumb. Then Vince told me that no matter what job I took, Gilberto was requiring me to stay at Woodhull for two to three months to "transition" with the new Sr. Vice-President.

So in a nutshell, after being used for six months and strung along for three more in exchange for the privilege of being demoted, I would have to train my replacement. By the time the weekend arrived, my choices were clear. As far as I was concerned I really only had one. The new Sr. Vice-President was starting in April, so my last day at HHC would be March 31st.

It was remarkably easy for me to accept that I would be leaving HHC. At least it was at first. But the three days between when I knew I was leaving and when I could tell people, were the most taxing I faced. I received a steady stream of visitors who all wanted to tell me the same thing. I think there were more people telling me that they wanted the president to make my appointment permanent during those three days, than in all the months that preceded it. I had no illusions about whether there were people who didn't want me to get the job. That was obvious. But since no one in that contingent was bold enough to tell me to my face, the only conversations I was having were ones of encouragement.

The day after my meeting with Gilberto, Cora came to see me. Even though she had the day off she came in so that she could introduce her sister who was visiting from out of town, to the "young woman who she'd been talking so much about all these years." Cora was one of the stalwarts of my staff and someone who was close to retirement. But she was standing in my office giddy with excitement about the plans that came out of the brainstorming session the week before.

She'd gone out and brought some books with her own money. And she'd been talking to some of her colleagues about the teams they were going to form when she returned from vacation. She displayed all the glee of a child on Christmas Eve, but, I couldn't hear a word she was saying. I was taking it in like a silent movie without captions. All I could think was, "How am I going to tell her that none of this is going to happen?"

Once again my poker face must have failed me. She didn't ask me what was wrong, but, I saw her energy level begin to wane. Before too long she and her sister said goodbye and left my office with far less levity than when they'd entered it. She was one of the two or three of my closest staff members who I called on Sunday night to break the news, so that they wouldn't be caught by surprise at the Monday morning meeting. After I broke the news to Cora she said, "I knew something was wrong. Tell me what you want me to do."

Those three days were the ones when I wrestled with the greatest flood of emotion and feelings of regret. From the spot where I was stalled on my journey, all I could extract from the experience was that I'd had no right to whip the staff up in a frenzy of promises about my vision for the future when I didn't know for sure that I would be around to see it through. Like so many tactically oriented leaders, I still saw things in black-and-white terms. I thought about how much better it would have been for everyone if Gilberto had been up front with his intentions earlier. I would have performed my job as more of a caretaker and then this transition would have been easier for everyone.

Ira returned from vacation on the day I announced that I was leaving. I called the Cabinet and the Chiefs together at 8:30 a.m. I found it interesting that the individuals who I'd personally called the night before weren't the only faces that did not betray surprise when I announced the president's decision. It was clear to me that Ira and Lorenzo already knew. When one of the Dolls shared the news with the physicians in her service, a physician who was close to both of them responded, "I knew that weeks ago." When I heard about that comment all I could do was laugh.

We had already scheduled an off-site business planning retreat that Simon had been eager to have. As the February 17th date approached, Chrissy, who I'd recently made my Chief of Staff, told me that there were grumblings that I should cancel it since I wasn't going to be in charge anymore. I did not. We'd invited the CFO for the Corporation and the Medical Director for the corporation's health plan to present. I actually enjoyed the fact that I didn't have to expend any effort making sure the Chiefs and managers got something from the exercise. It would soon be someone else's problem. I took a walk out to the lobby during one of the breaks and on my way back I passed one of our presenters, the health plan's Medical Director, as he was leaving.

I stopped to thank him for coming. By that point the news that I was leaving had been widely disseminated throughout the Corporation. He took the time to tell me that he was sorry to see me go and that he also thought I'd done a good job while I was in charge. Then he said, "I'm surprised though. I would have made them offer me something else." When I told him that I'd been offered several positions and had turned them down, he looked at me like I'd just grown another head out of each eardrum.

I knew why he was surprised. There had been no shortage of people who tried to convince me that I had to be crazy to leave a good government job. There were only three people on the planet that knew the whole story and weren't telling me to stay, "at least until something better came along" and all four of us shared DNA.

There is something about the air down there at 125 Worth Street. Once people pass a certain number of years with HHC they start thinking that there's no living without it. But as everyone was asking, why would you leave? I kept thinking, why would I stay? The only answer to that question was money. There are some things in life that are more important than that. I wasn't independently wealthy by any means. In fact, once I made the decision to leave, I intentionally refused to itemize my bills for fear that it would cause me to reconsider the decision I already knew to be the right one for me.

There are many ways to sell your soul. People don't always do it to get ahead. I'm convinced that most do it because they believe it's the only way they can keep their head above water. I wasn't the only one to feel Gilberto's footprints on my back. I was just the only one to leave. I knew that if I stayed I would be bitter. Maybe the bitterness would subside, maybe it wouldn't. But I'd always been proud to call myself a HHC employee because of the kind of work we did. Now that I'd been up close and personal with the man who was going to be setting the vision for this organization, I had a feeling that it was no longer going to be the kind of place that made me feel anything positive.

Whatever Gilberto's reasons may have been for selecting my replacement, even poor judgment can be exercised with integrity. I imagine that the conversation would have sounded like this: "Candis, I know this isn't the news you wanted to hear, but, I'm not appointing you to the position. It has nothing to do with you. I just want my own person. But I appreciate your service and if you'll work with me during this transition, I promise I'll make it up to you."

I doubt I would have been happy about that decision, but, I could have respected the man who made it. What I know for sure is that had we had *that* conversation instead of the ones we did have, I would probably be a HHC employee right now and you wouldn't be reading this.

Emotions were becoming so raw that I was thankful to be taking a week's vacation. All of the silos that we'd spent years trying to tear down reappeared almost overnight. It was heartbreaking to watch. My sister and I drove down to Georgia to stay at my favorite vacation destination. A long drive along the coast line was exactly what I needed. We listened to Hillary Clinton's autobiography *Living History* on CD and stopped at all my favorite places to eat. But there was no rest for the weary. My cell phone rang nonstop while I was away.

First, I found out what a good friend I had in David Tillman. He immediately started putting pressure on HHC about the decision to replace me and went to work rallying as many of his fellow elected officials and members of the community as he could. Gilberto responded by accelerating the appointment of my replacement, which meant that he could no longer keep her identity a secret. Once that happened, the comparisons between me and Lourdes Peña began.

I received calls about that. I received calls from human resources because she was already requesting a copy of the Table of Organization. I received calls that her appointment was going to be delayed, then it wasn't. I didn't know how I was supposed to feel. But David would say, "Candis, we're on the side of right. Somebody needs to explain this. This isn't over yet."

My sister and I made the drive back up Interstate 95 to the New Jersey Turnpike and I can't remember a road trip with so little conversation. I was numb. But knowing that the board of directors had in fact appointed my replacement while I was away, I thought to myself, at least it's finally over. That's what I thought anyway.

We were in the car approaching the Holland Tunnel when my cell phone rang again. It was Chrissy. "I'm sorry to call you while you're still on vacation, but, you need to call Gina." "Why? What's wrong?" "She just received a letter from the Inspector General today and hers didn't look like the others. It said she should bring a lawyer. She's a wreck." Now they were harassing the people close to me? For what?

I was beyond numb at that point. My sister was able to figure out what was going on from my side of the conversation. When I finally hung up I couldn't speak. All I could do was look at her and I will never forget the look on her face. The only way to describe it is to describe what it reflected. It was the look of a person who was being prevented from doing the one thing she wanted to do more than anything else in the world at that moment – protect her baby sister.

"Don't talk to anyone else tonight," she said. "You've had enough of this. Just go to sleep and call them tomorrow. Okay?" I nodded. But as soon as she dropped me off at my house I broke my promise. I couldn't let Gina swing in the wind with indecision all night. I called her and she tried to sound calm, but, I knew she wasn't.

"I don't even know where to find a lawyer," she said. "What should I do?"

"Gina, you don't need a lawyer. You haven't done anything wrong."

It seemed as if just hearing those words from me made her feel better. "Just tell the truth. You have nothing to hide. Besides, trust me, I don't care what that letter says, you're not the one they're after."

CHAPTER TWENTY-ONE
MARCH, 2006

THE SEVEN WEEKS THAT followed my decision to leave were the salt that brought out the flavor in all the years I'd spent working for the Corporation. One of the most important lessons I learned was that periods of transition, while often unsettling, are ripe with information. And I think that's true for a very specific reason. We are never more receptive than during times of uncertainty or when we are looking for something. We could be looking for a thing or an answer or just closure. But until we reach the finish line, our eyes are wide open and our nerve endings are raw.

That's when things really got interesting because I found out that I had friends I didn't even know about. Gilberto soon found himself in the quite unexpected position of having to explain his decision over and over again. It affected him like a hot iron on the armpits of a shirt that's been worn too many times between washings.

David called me late one evening.

"Have you got a minute?" he asked.

"Sure."

"I want to share a conversation with you that I had with one of the HHC board members," he said.

I made myself comfortable because I had a feeling this conversation was going to require my full attention.

"She went to Gilberto to ask him to explain why you didn't get the job and she said he made her feel like she should be on the defensive. Can you believe it?" I could.

"So she said, 'well I was appointed to the board to represent the borough of Brooklyn. There are elected officials who are asking me what's going on.' So he asked her who she was referring to and when she mentioned my name he said, 'I've already spoken to David Tillman.'"

"I didn't know you'd spoken with Gilberto," I said.

"I haven't!"

I found David's indignation more amusing than what he was saying.

"You should know he's also trying to dredge up that garbage that happened between you and Lois back in '99."

"Of course," I said with unrestrained sarcasm. "Why not?"

Gilberto wasn't even working at Central Office when that was going on. Someone had to have fed that to him.

"Now I need your help with the next part," David continued. "He said something about you knowing for a while that you weren't getting the job."

"David, I told you about every conversation that Gilberto and I had. If he wants to count that as my 'knowing for a while' I'm sure he's talented enough to say that with a straight face."

"Um hmm," David responded. He wasn't persuaded. "Then he said that you were even working with a coach and it didn't go well."

I'd been pretty calm until I heard that.

"What?! Is that what he said?"

"Yeah. Do you know what he's talking about?"

"I'm certainly going to find out!"

The next day I put a call in to Kerry. He had shared his conversation with Gilberto with me, but, if Gilberto was telling people that my work with Kerry hadn't gone well, then Kerry definitely left something out. He wasn't available when I called and while I waited for him to get back to me, I filled Donna in on what I'd learned. She must have gotten to Kerry before I did, because by the time we spoke he already knew what I wanted to talk about.

"Candis, I don't know why he would say something like that," Kerry said. "As far as I'm concerned we haven't even begun a formal coaching relationship yet."

"I was concerned because I thought we worked well together."

"We do," he said. "I even offered to work with you formally if it would make him feel more comfortable about giving you the job. But, no, I do not believe that anything we did together didn't go well."

And the shrinking continued.

The time had come for my final report to the Quality Assurance Committee of the HHC Board of Directors. This would be my last Board Report. It was the one thing about leaving the Corporation that I was not going to miss at all. From the day I started having to attend those meetings I went through the same ritual. I would become nauseous starting the night before every meeting and I wouldn't feel better until the meeting was adjourned.

When Mayor Bloomberg appointed a new Commissioner for the NYC Department of Health, the position made him an HHC board member as well. But more important, it made him the Chair of the Quality Assurance committee. His addition to the cast of characters changed the aura of Board Report from arduous to terrifying. During his tenure he managed to strike mortal fear into the hearts of everyone who had to present before him.

When he joined the board, he immediately added fifty more indicators to the report. So right away he made no new friends. But this was a man who clearly could care less about that. What quickly made him the most feared member of the board, however, was the relentless way he pursued the case reviews.

To be perfectly candid, I always had serious doubts about whether the other members of the committee even read the reports before the day of the meeting. But there was no doubt that he read them from cover to cover. And if your plan was to bullshit your way through a response, dismiss his recommendations or argue him into conceding a point, you'd be better off donning red satin boxer shorts, hopping a flight to Pamplona and turning your ass to the bulls. You'd get the same result but with better scenery.

Most of the physicians who presented before him hated it and probably hated him because he was so unrelenting. But you had to give him credit; he always had a well-researched basis for his position. Unfortunately, Ira thought he was as smart as the Commissioner and his inability to keep his mouth closed exposed him and the rest of us to the risk of repeated impalements. Donna was a master at managing Board Report and I'd watched her carefully over the years. So when it was my turn to sit at the end of the conference table, I knew what my Number One job was – wrangle the puppy.

I came up with a plan. If it looked like Ira and the Commissioner were ramping up for a debate, a debate that Ira would most assuredly lose, I would put my hand over his hand. That meant "let it go." If he missed that signal, I would put my hand under the conference table and jab him in the thigh with a ballpoint pen. And if all else failed, I made sure I always wore high heeled shoes. I was perfectly willing to ram by heel through the top of Ira's foot until I drew blood if that's what I had to do to keep him quiet. Whatever it took, I was going to leave those meetings with my skin integrity intact. Fortunately, I never had to escalate past the first signal.

I presented at three Board Reports as the Acting Sr. V.P. I knew that everyone would be watching me closely to see how I handled myself. We made our way though the first one with very few questions, even fewer follow-ups and no outbursts. The next one went equally well. As my swan-song report came to a close, the Commissioner surprised me by giving me the opportunity to talk about our network's successes during the prior year. It was something that I thought was generous of him to do, since it appeared my leaving was going to pass without a mention at the meeting.

When it was over, one of the board members signaled that he wanted to speak to me. It was Dr. Bruno Facci. A boisterous personality with a booming voice and an irreverent attitude, Dr. Facci was every bit as Italian as the name suggests. If *The Sopranos* had added a family physician to the cast, it would have been Dr. Facci. He and the Commissioner would lock horns on occasion because Dr. Facci was the only other person at the table who couldn't be intimidated. But he had also thrown us a lifeline on more than one occasion when Ira or one of the Chiefs was sinking under the weight of one of the Commissioner's withering inquisitions.

As I approached the back of the boardroom to gather my belongings, Dr. Facci moved to intercept me with a broad smile and his arms wide open.

"Come here, young lady. Are you alright?" he asked as he gave me a hug and a kiss on the cheek.

"Yes," I said somewhat surprised by the attention.

"You got some set on you," he said. "Why'd you thumb your nose at these people?"

He still had his arm around my shoulder and the stragglers were starting to stare.

"Come on. Let's take a walk," he said.

We walked together still arm in arm out into the hallway. "

So why don't you want to stay?" he continued. "They had real plans for you."

The look of utter confusion on my face triggered a similar look on his own. It was a look that quickly morphed to anger. "Wait a minute," he said. "Gilberto told me something very specific about why you didn't get that job. If it turns out that I don't have the whole story I'm gonna be pissed."

"What were you told?" I asked.

"That you were being taken out of North Brooklyn so you could be groomed for Vince's job."

I responded with laughter before words.

"No. You don't have the whole story," I said.

"Then give it to me."

He grabbed me by the arm and whisked me into the board chairperson's office suite. It was just across from where we were standing. There were some empty offices in the back. He found one, led me in and closed the door.

"So what the hell is going on?" he asked.

I started with the meeting on December 2nd and went all the way up to the present. The more I told him the angrier he got. I was eager to hear more about what he knew and he appeared ready to tell me when there was a knock on the door. It was one of the secretaries.

"Candis, someone wants to talk to you," she said.

I stepped out into the hallway to find the Commissioner waiting to speak with me. We stepped into another vacant office.

349

"I was really sorry to hear that you're leaving the Corporation. I've been really impressed with you."

"Thank you," I said. "That means a lot to me."

"Have you found something else yet?" he asked.

"No."

"I have some openings coming up. Give me a call."

I was still thanking him as we stepped back out into the hall when in addition to Dr. Facci, I walked into a third board member who was extending her hand out to me so that she could grab mine.

"You have no idea how many people are out there fighting for you," she said. "I just wanted to let you know that."

"I'm starting to see that," I said. "Thank you."

I was standing in the chairperson's suite, surrounded by three members of HHC's Board of Directors and everyone was looking at me – the board members, the secretaries and just behind them – Gilberto. His complexion had turned the most peculiar shade of puce and as soon as he noticed that I noticed him, he turned on his heels and left. It didn't take long for me to figure out at least one of the reasons why he and the secretaries were standing around wringing their hands. They couldn't start the next Board Report because I had the quorum with me. I've always been attracted to the word surreal. But that day, at that moment, I experienced the word with all five of my senses.

"Can you wait for a minute?" Dr. Facci asked me as he followed the other board members who were being herded back to the boardroom. "I want to finish this conversation," he said.

"Okay."

I waited for as long as I could, but, I needed to get back to the hospital. I left my number with the secretaries in the office and headed back to Woodhull.

The expression of interest and support that I received from the board members that day was a precious gift to me. When I returned to Woodhull the staff had one more.

I'd just put my purse away when Chrissy came running into my office.

"Look at this! Look at this!" she shouted, pointing to the PowerPoint presentation that she had just thrown on my desk. She was so animated that I was more focused on her than on what she was trying to show me.

"What is it?" I asked.

"It's the results from the employee satisfaction surveys."

Anxiety replaced confusion. I'd asked the staff to put a rush on the results so that I could have them before I left. It was exactly one year after the previous surveys were conducted and I'd made some pretty bold predictions about improving the morale for those areas where it was the lowest. The slides for those areas were precisely where Chrissy was pointing. I guess my adrenaline levels were too high, because I couldn't focus on what she was trying show me. She finally lost patience with me.

"Look," she said "See! Every one of the groups you targeted went up - every one of them!"

And which group showed the most dramatic increase in their level of satisfaction over the year before? The medical staff. The closer I looked at the results, the more I had to smile about. In addition to the questions from the previous year, we asked the staff questions to determine whether they believed we were ready to compete for the Baldridge award. To my surprise it was the frontline staff, more so than even the managers, who gave us a resounding thumbs up. Those results meant so much to me that I literally hugged the papers they were written on once I had the office to myself.

Within a week of that final Board Report, Dr. Facci and I met for breakfast at the Brooklyn Marriott. The hotel's Archive restaurant is a popular meeting place for power breakfasts. It is impossible to go there and not run into someone you know. I found it telling that he picked it. Obviously he didn't care whether someone saw us having breakfast together.

"I just don't get it," he said. "I finally got to take a look at her resume and I just don't get it. Why her?"

It was a question more and more people were beginning to ask, thanks in large part to the fact that David Tillman had taken on my removal as his personal crusade. He managed to gather a contingent of thirteen elected officials from the federal, state and local levels who agreed to put their names to a letter that Woodhull's new city councilman had decided to send to the mayor.

He intended to ask Mayor Bloomberg to take another look at Gilberto's decision. And because they were kicking up such dust, the local press was beginning to inquire. At one point the activity gathered such momentum that Shaina called me while I was still on vacation and asked me whether they should cancel the annual Legislative Breakfast at Woodhull.

"I've made some calls," she said. "It sounds like some members of the community are planning to cause a scene about you leaving and that's really not what that breakfast is for. We think maybe we should cancel it. What do you think?"

"Do what you want," I said. "I don't really have a vote anymore."

They did. And I found it strangely ironic that there would be this much hoopla over the departure of someone who was an aloof administrator with a problematic leadership style.

Free from interruption, Bruno and I talked for about an hour. Comparing notes only brought more inconsistencies to light. I'd already figured out on my own that Ms. Peña would be receiving somewhere in the neighborhood of a 100% increase over her current salary with this appointment, something that was highly unusual for HHC. I also came to know that she was going to be paid more than I was being paid to do the very same job I'd been doing for ten months.

I was glad that we had the meeting if for no other reason than to know that I was not losing my mind. There were people - people who had no prior relationship to me - who upon learning the facts thought that what was happening at Woodhull was more than a little strange. It also didn't hurt that Bruno Facci had a wildly over-the-top sense of humor. I spent so much time laughing that morning that my food got cold.

"You know, I really didn't like the way Gilberto treated John Fortunado over that thing in the Bronx," he said. "But I knew they were going to accuse me of sticking up for the Italians, so I didn't say anything."

He was waving his toast in the air, animating every word he said with his hands. "That's why lawyers don't need to be running organizations like this," he said.

"Whoa! Whoa! Whoa!" I said. I couldn't let that go unchallenged. "Wait a minute. I'm a lawyer. Some of us know what we're doing."

"Ah, you're different," he said, waving another slice of toast, this time at me. "You have an MBA."

If that reasoning was good enough for him to let me out of the grease he was frying Gilberto in, I was willing to go along with it. "But this business with you . . ." he continued. "And the way he treated the Chief Medical Officer. I really went off about that!"

Gilberto went on a tear after his appointment to president became permanent. I wasn't the only one he'd decided to dispose of like soiled paper napkins. He chose to demote the Corporation's Chief Medical Officer, but, did it in a really demeaning way. Very few African-

Americans get to be Chief Medical Officers and HHC rarely attracts someone with one Ivy League degree much less two. When I spoke to him personally about it, he didn't even bother to hide how hurt he was about the way he was being treated. And like me, he had no idea why he was receiving the axe. He said, "All Gilberto said to me was, 'I need a different face.'"

And Gilberto never did appoint either of the Executive Directors from the Queens Network to be Sr. Vice-President. After treating them like lab mice for over a year, he reached past both of them and their Medical Director to make one of their Chiefs of Service, the new Sr. V.P.

Then at one of our HHC Cabinet meetings he introduced us all to a woman who would be taking over responsibility for marketing and public relations. But he neglected to explain the empty chair that usually contained the woman who currently had the job. The sea of confused glances that were being exchanged among us was drenching the conference table. Finally Donna dove in. "What happened to Carol?" she asked.

Carol replaced Julie, who was sent packing in 2002 shortly after Dr. Ferdinand was replaced by Dr. Chang. With a straight face, Gilberto proceeded to tell us how Carol would be "staying on to focus on public relations, which was really her strength" and how the two women would be working together. The story sounded a little suspect, but, he didn't stutter through a single word of it. So we bought it. Meanwhile, as I would later discover, Carol was already wrapped in plastic and headed for the East River.

There came a moment during breakfast when Bruno's jolliness faded. His gaze left me for a moment and I could see that he was deeply engaged in thoughts that disturbed him.

"You know, I'm starting to think that Gilberto is a liar," he said.

By that point I was of the opinion that truth was more like Silly Putty to Gilberto. It existed to be stretched, bent, manipulated and even imprinted with bizarre images so long as it took whatever shape suited his purposes at the moment. I decided not to share my opinions with Bruno. Instead I took another sip of my chamomile tea and thought, welcome to my world.

After our breakfast was over, however, I was more conflicted than ever. We had indeed created miracles at Woodhull. We couldn't have possibly put in all that hard work just to have it evaporate for no good reason. Perhaps I was letting my ego get in the way of what was best for a organization that I'd come to care so much about. I called Vince and asked if we could meet face to face. I had an offer I wanted him to take to Gilberto.

"Things aren't going well for Gil with this decision about replacing me," I said.

"I don't know that. What do you mean?" Vince replied.

"Not everyone on the Board believes he handled this the way he should have. The number of elected officials who are asking questions about it is starting to grow and I know the Corporation has had to field inquiries from the press," I said. Vince didn't agree or disagree, but, he was definitely interested in what I had to say so I continued.

"I've been treated despicably. But I'm willing to put that aside because I actually do care about what happens to Woodhull and that network. And I know that Gilberto has already gone out on a limb by naming Ms. Peña to replace me, so I want to offer a compromise."

"Okay," Vince said. "I'm listening."

Talking to Vince was like playing cards with a world-class poker player. There were no "tells."

When I moved from COO to CEO, not having a "me" meant that I still had to do both jobs. When Gilberto appointed a Sr. Vice-President who in her entire career had never held either job, he was expecting a lot. For him to put that Sr. Vice-President at Woodhull was expecting too much.

"Vince, you've been at HHC long enough to know that you can't walk into a Sr. V.P. position with absolutely no relevant experience and expect to succeed. I don't care how smart you are, there's too much about the way this place functions that is peculiar to HHC."

"Give me an example of what you mean," he said.

This was what I liked about Vince – always the pragmatist. I preferred to deal in facts as much as he did and for this part of the discussion, I only needed two words to do it – Board Report. During the last one, Ira and Lorenzo – true to their inability to keep their mouths shut – managed to light a fire under one of the board members. And it wasn't the Commissioner this time. It was a man who was generally pretty easy going. But every response they gave him only served to make him angrier.

I sat back and watched the two of them dig themselves into a deeper and deeper pit. It seemed to me to be a bit of karmic justice being exacted so why should I get in the way? But as the discussion continued to deteriorate, the scene ceased to be amusing even to me. That board member had talons on each of their throats and he was beginning to draw blood. I described the scene to Vince and then shared how I came up with a response that this board member was finally willing to accept.

"He believed what I said because I was able to give him examples of ways we'd fixed similar problems at Woodhull in the past. I only had those answers because of institutional memory. That is something she won't have."

What I also knew but didn't share was that if she intended to rely upon Ira and Lorenzo to bail her out of trouble, I would be able to see that mushroom cloud from the front steps of my house.

"If Gilberto really wants her to be a Sr. V.P. and he's serious about a transition, let's transition her in a way that gives her a chance to succeed," I said. "Let her spend the next six months to a year at Central Office with the Corporate Sr. V.P.s so she can learn about what you do. Then bring her out to the network and I'll transition with her for six months to a year."

I was trying to get to 2007 so that I could at least get Woodhull to the Baldridge competition even if I wouldn't be there to see them through it. I was absolutely convinced that by then, with the momentum we were building, the staff could win it. It wouldn't matter what happened after that. The Woodhull story would be written in an ink that no one could ever erase.

"If someone had just let me in on the master plan," I said. "I never would have made the plans I made with the staff at the network. But I've started something with them. All I want now is the opportunity to finish it."

I was willing to put my money where my mouth was. "If he's willing to do that, the Corporation won't have to find a job for me at the end of the transition. And I'm willing to put that in writing." Vince's gaze never left me. *"That's* a transition," I said. "But . . . ."

The lawyer in me was well versed in the fine art of negotiations. I knew that a single offer, especially one as radical as the one I was proposing, would be dismissed as unreasonable. So I also gave Vince an alternative. "If he's unwilling to accept that, then tell him this. I will sit wherever you want to stick me other than the North Brooklyn Health Network. All I ask is that he takes his requirement that I train my replacement off the table. Because that's not a transition, it's an attempt to use me for three more months. And after everything that's happened, he doesn't get to ask me for that."

Vince agreed to present my offers just as I'd described them to him. I left his office, but, by the time I reached the elevator I was laughing to myself. Not because I thought Gilberto was going to accept one of the offers, but because just that quickly, I realized that he wouldn't. Why would he? That would be too much like right. Vince called me back that very afternoon to tell me that Gilberto had indeed rejected both offers.

When you reach a point when you've done everything that you can do it is an important moment. But we so often miss the message. When you're looking for an answer you need to know that sometimes the help comes in the door closing. That may be the only way God can show you that you're facing in the wrong direction.

My final weeks at HHC were abounding in so many ways. For one thing, that's when information really began to flow my way. I obtained confirmation that despite his assurances to the contrary, Ira had been quite active in my undoing. *He* was the one who had gone to HHC's board chairperson to complain about me during the early days of my interim appointment. I learned that Lourdes Peña had been a candidate (and obviously the only candidate) as early as the previous August.

Her name emerged the day the announcement about my departure was made from people who didn't even work at our network. And whoever she was, Lorenzo felt so confident about his relationship with her that he was already announcing which of my ideas were going to be immediately dismantled. It was amazing how much information I received. I guess people don't feel the need to keep secrets from the dead.

The balance of March served as my farewell tour. I spent most of my days meeting with staff who wanted to say goodbye to me in person. One employee, who I only knew in passing, even requested an appointment to come to my office because he wanted to pray with me. I made more than a few close friends during those final days. The Chief of the Emergency Department turned out to be one of them. He came to visit me one day looking sullen.

"You know all the Chiefs had dinner together just a week before we found out you were leaving," he said. "Everyone was there except Ira and Lorenzo. And to a person every one of them said how happy they were with how things were going with you in charge."

Even at this late date, his comments gave me a great deal of comfort.

"I tried to get them together so that we could speak to Gilberto as a group but . . . ."

I knew why his voice was trailing off. No one was willing to go on record with their feelings. It was safer to wait until the final bell and then back whoever was left standing.

"What really gets me is that the very ones who gained the most . . . ."

Once again he couldn't bring himself to finish the sentence. Michael truly was a gentle giant. As fearsome as he could be when he was sufficiently riled up, he cared deeply about what happened at Woodhull. "I just want you to know," he continued, "I called Gilberto to let him know what I thought. After everything you've done around here, I wouldn't have been able to look myself in the mirror if I didn't say something."

When he finished sharing the details of his conversation with me I literally had to bite my lip to hold back the tears. He was speaking in such a cavalier manner that I knew he wasn't trying to impress me. That's what made the compliments so moving for me. "And I'll tell you something else," he said. "Someone came up to me recently who I couldn't have paid to say something nice about you a year ago. And he said, 'Michael, we've got to do something. Candis has got to stay.'"

It was one of the physicians from his department who was very outspoken and well connected within the Dominican community. He was also a good friend of Maura's. Michael brought him to see me a few days later. "I wanted to tell you myself," he said. "I called everyone I know. This isn't coming from the Dominican community. People have a lot of respect for you around here."

"Believe me," I said, "I already know where this came from."

We spoke for a little while longer and before he left my office he turned to me and said, "I'm so sorry I didn't get to know you better."

"That's okay," I said. "We know each other now."

The parade of visitors continued almost daily. One of the staff members who had reported to me when I first returned to Woodhull stopped by to thank me for my support of his department. It gave us the opportunity to reminisce about the past as I did with so many of the visitors I was receiving. But he and I also talked about the rumors circulating, what was true and what was not. When he left, Chrissy came to my office and I told her about our conversation.

"Do you think I should talk to the staff about why I'm leaving?" I asked. "Give them a chance to ask me questions?"

Her response practically eclipsed the question. "Yes!" she said. "Definitely. There are so many rumors going around. People want to know why you won't stay. I think they need to hear from you directly."

I had been holding monthly leadership meetings with the management staff ever since I became Executive Director. My final one would be the perfect place to clear the air. The auditorium was full of people. I'd spoken in front of large audiences before and I rarely got nervous, but, that day was different. I began with an update. I couldn't wait to share the results of the employee satisfaction surveys with the managers. They deserved as much of the credit as I did and I told them so. Then it was time for me to tread into unfamiliar territory. It was time to get personal.

"Woodhull has come so far," I said. "Farther than I think anyone could have possibly dreamed for this place. But I've gone as far as I can go with you." I don't think my mind truly connected to the reality of my leaving until I said those words. "It has been a rare honor and privilege to work with you and for the last ten months to be your Sr. Vice-President. And if there is one thing that has contributed to our successes as a network over this past year more than anything else, I think it's been our transparency. This leadership team worked very hard to make sure that everyone in this organization knew how we were doing, good or bad, and what we intended to do next. I believe it will be vital to the network's success for you to continue to do that. And I want to leave you by modeling that behavior myself."

As I prepared to open myself to a room full of people, I could feel the familiar rush of anxiety and anticipation.

"I know there have been a lot of rumors," I said. "And some of you have questions about when I'm leaving and why I'm leaving. So I'm going to open the floor to you now. You can ask me anything that you want to ask. Nothing is off limits."

As I expected, there were stunned looks underscored by total silence. I knew they would need a jumpstart so I said, "I'll start things off by repeating some of the questions that I've been asked in private and sharing my answers with you."

The first few were funny. Like, "Why didn't I move into Donna's old office?" "Was it because I was scared?" *Me* scared of all people! Then I went right to the question I knew that most people wanted answered. Why wouldn't I stay and go back to my old job? "I told you in our first meeting together that we were never going back to the days of being 'Woodkill' and 'Killhall.' We crossed a threshold that we had no reason to return to. The same goes for life. Once I've moved forward, I don't go back. That's one reason."

Some people were literally sitting on the edges of their seats. It was as if they were drinking in the words as soon as they left my lips. "But a more important reason is this," I continued. "When I took over I shared a vision with you and you embraced it wholeheartedly. For that I will forever be grateful." As hard as I tried I don't think I could have ever fully conveyed how much I meant that. "But your new Sr. Vice-President will have her own vision when she arrives. She deserves to have the same undivided attention and unqualified support that you gave me. If I stayed I would only be a distraction. So I expect you to give her your full support." And then to lighten the mood I looked over my glasses at the audience like a grammar school librarian and said "And I will know if you don't."

After that, the questions began to flow freely. Did I have any parting advice? What should they focus on now? Did I have any regrets? Then one person shouted out, "What are you going to do now?" It was the one question I wasn't prepared to answer publicly. So I had to think a minute about how to respond. I remembered a passage from Hillary Clinton's book that stayed with me after my road trip to Georgia. I couldn't think of a response that would have captured my feelings more accurately, so I simply shared the passage with them as best I could remember it.

"They say that having faith means that if you have to step off of a cliff, you are absolutely certain that you will either float safely to the ground . . . or you will learn to fly."

Just repeating those words was such a comfort to me that I couldn't help but smile as I looked out at the one hundred or more sets of eyes that were now transfixed on me. "So I guess I'll be learning to fly."

When the questions finally came to an end I thanked them all again for their support and took a seat on the stage to wait for the auditorium to empty. I should have known it would not be that simple. Our Director of Pastoral Care bounded up to the microphone with his characteristically ebullient voice and said, "I know our Sr. Vice-President isn't the touchy feely type, but, I don't think she would mind just this once and I'm sure each of us would like to say goodbye to her one last time. So if you feel like giving her a hug, go ahead. That alright with you, Dr. Best?" Then he looked at me. Under the circumstances I didn't have much choice but to agree, although, in truth there wasn't much fight left in me anyway.

I went out into the main hallway that led to the auditorium from the rest of the building and a receiving line began to form almost immediately. The hallway was wide enough for people to go around the line and leave without waiting if they wanted to. So I was truly touched and amazed at how many people chose to wait in line. Much to my surprise I actually enjoyed having the opportunity to greet the staff and reminisce with some of the ones I'd known for my entire HHC career. We'd given the managers several of those leadership fable management books by Patrick Lencioni, so a few of them asked me to sign their books. As I shook hands with each person I took a glimpse at the people behind them. Inching their way towards me were Lorenzo, Milo and Ira in a row.

It took a lot of nerve for them to stand in that line, but, fortunately for them I'd had sufficient home training not to embarrass them. First up was Lorenzo. As he approached I looked carefully at his expression. I think it was the only time that I'd ever seen this one on his face. He actually looked like he had a conscience. He shook my hand quickly, tossed me a feeble grin and then hurried off toward the elevator. Next was Milo. Milo fashioned himself a smooth operator. He extended his hand. I shook it, but while guiding him graciously from my left to my right, I could feel him trying to press in towards me. I thought, "I know this scoundrel isn't trying to hug me."

Oh but he was. It just so happened that I'd just read an article that described how to stiffen your arm to keep someone from hugging you if you didn't want them to. It turned out that I was a quick study. So was he. I stiffened my arm and when he felt the resistance he scurried off behind his boss. That left Ira. He extended his hand, I shook it and just like Milo I could feel him trying to press forward to hug me. He also met the stiff arm, but, to my surprise, either he didn't get the message or he was trying to ignore it. The harder I pushed, the harder he pushed. With my arm as rigid as I was keeping it, we looked like two loggers sawing wood.

Our little miter dance was annoying me more and more with each pass of the blade. I'd already forgiven all three of them for their dirty deeds. My faith made that a requirement. But I knew how Ira's mind worked. He wasn't trying to hug me because he was sorry for what he'd done. He was looking for cover.

The rumors about who knew what, when they knew it and who played a part in my removal were reaching a crescendo. His name was mixing right up to the top. Ira couldn't stand the thought that someone might think he wasn't everybody's All-American. If he could be seen hugging me in front of all the people who were standing in that hallway, he could then feign innocence with more conviction. I didn't think my faith required me to be complicit in that little scheme and if it did, I decided that I would just have to say an extra rosary.

We were still sawing wood as I continued to guide him from my left to my right. By now there was no way he could have been unaware that I did not want to be hugged by him. So at this point we were testing which one of us had the greater upper body strength. Unfortunately for him, it was me.

We'd reached the point where the back and forth was becoming visibly awkward. So I decided to put an end to it by giving him what I thought was an extra little push. Only between the additional effort and my attempt to direct his path, I must have generated some sort of centrifugal force. He slid with astonishing velocity. He must have traveled at least six feet down the hallway on the soles of his snakeskin boots. In fact, he came dangerously close to landing on his butt. Fortunately, he was able to keep his footing and he ran off to catch up with his pals.

For months after that, I couldn't think of Ira without thinking about that episode of the *Twilight Zone* where the monks had the devil locked in the hermitage and the stranger wouldn't believe them. How many times over the years had someone come to me with one version or another of, "The devil's in the medical director's office! Don't let him out! Don't let him out!" Every time I responded like the stranger. "Ira's not the devil. What's the matter with you people?" And just like that stranger, I lived to regret it.

If there had been any lingering doubts about whether I could have returned to my old job and made it work, they were put to rest during those last few weeks. From what I observed, it was clear that my successor would be relying on the members of Woodhull's leadership that I had reason to trust the least. The soil was no longer hospitable to the dream I was trying to plant.

Once the events unfolded that led Donna to Bellevue and me to take her place, we both thought it was divine intervention that it happened after Gilberto took over. Dr. Chang would never have appointed me even on an "Acting" basis. In all likelihood, he would have given the job to his good friend, Ira. Now that the curtain had fallen on the final act, however, I was still convinced that it was divine intervention, but for an entirely different reason. In the end, Gilberto did what he was supposed to do just as I'd predicted. By being the person that he turned out to be, he ensured that I did what I supposed to do.

When you find yourself in an environment that is no longer conducive to your growth, it's time to leave. That is a leadership lesson. But the lesson that is steeped in spiritual growth teaches you how to know when that time has come. The relationships that are most effective at spurring growth are usually the abrasive ones. It takes rough edges to smooth rough edges. But no one really likes the way that feels. That's why sometimes you need something to hold you in place until you've had a good scrubbing. But stay in that place even a moment too long and the wounds will leave scars that don't fade.

It's a critical lesson. One that is too specific to the individual to think you can figure it out based upon something you can learn in a seminar. I don't know how people make it through life without faith or how the ones who profess to have it can believe that it doesn't belong in your briefcase. My faith proved to be my most reliable source of wisdom, especially in my professional life. When you find that wisdom, it provides you with a compass that is calibrated to you and you alone. Standing in the very same spot, my compass may tell me to leave when your compass is telling you that your growth journey requires you to stay.

One of my favorite shows is *CSI*. There is one episode where Grissom, the brilliant but socially challenged supervisor, talks to one of the members of his team about how he envisions his eventual departure. He said, "When I leave they'll be no cake in the break room. I'll just be gone." That was how I wanted to leave. Vulcans have no use for fanfare. When the job is done, you move on. Period.

I spent the last week of March in Chicago attending the *American College of Healthcare Executives'* annual conference. The day before I left, I called Chrissy into my office and I gave her a single instruction. No goodbye party. This "Grissom" didn't want any cake either and I knew how much the staff that was closest to me liked to throw me surprise parties. "You know they're really going to want to do this," she said. But I was firm. "This is what I really want and I mean it. No parties."

Even that late in March, there were still people working to try to get Gilberto to reverse his decision. I was getting motion sickness from wondering whether I was meant to stay or go. On March 29th I finally received the answer I was looking for. I'd just hung up from the last of a flurry of phone calls about what people were saying and what they wanted to do about my leaving. I stretched out on the bed in my hotel room. Perhaps it was because we were entering the Lenten season, but, I felt as if I could hear Christ's last words from the cross. "It is finished."

Whatever it was, it was accompanied by a serenity that felt like a cleansing breath. The rollercoaster was finally slowing down and pulling into the station. I was glad to be getting off. But finally knowing for certain that the door I was supposed to go through was the one marked exit, didn't alleviate the uncertainty all at once. I was still left with one unanswered question. "Why didn't I get this message seven weeks ago?" That answer was still to come.

CHAPTER TWENTY-TWO
MARCH 31, 2006

IN THE 1940'S, A set of sacred texts were discovered in the deserts outside Egypt in a place called Nag Hammadi. They were subsequently authenticated as reflecting gospels attributed to some of Christ's disciples. What is most interesting about these "Gnostic gospels" is that they had been buried for well over a thousand years. And even after their discovery it took another 25 – 30 years before the rest of the world realized the significance of what had been discovered.

I pause here to share this because it symbolizes an important aspect of the life lessons I learned en route to leadership. Part of what makes the experiences we encounter during our journey through life so frustrating, is that the lessons contained in them are not always apparent. Even for those willing to accept that there is a lesson in every experience, it can be exasperating to search for meaning in a tragedy, a loss or a disappointment and not be able to find it right away. I call these the *Nag Hammadi* moments.

This journey brings with it all kinds of milestones. When we think of milestones, especially in a spiritual sense, most people are looking for epiphanies, those memorable moments when God speaks from a burning bush. And the journey does have those moments on occasion. But *Nag Hammadi* moments serve a very different purpose. They are more than guideposts to tell us that we're on the right path. A *Nag Hammadi* moment is a person, or a thing or a situation you encounter, the significance of which you <u>cannot</u> see until after the moment has passed. Those lessons are contained in the result of our cumulative experiences.

I am a native New Yorker and I was in New York on 9/11. In the weeks and months that followed, I heard countless stories of people who were headed to work at the World Trade Center, but, because of some change in their routine, they were late and their lives were spared. Imagine the man on a train who had some stranger spill coffee on his suit forcing him to go home and change his clothes. At the time he might have been obsessed by anger because of the inconvenience, or he might have dwelt on how far this detour set him back on his schedule. Then once he heard about what happened, he would be consumed by the events of the moment like everyone else. Only later after he had time to do the math, could he appreciate that had he not gone back home to change, he would have been sitting at his desk on the 92nd floor when the first plane hit his building.

The lesson from his *Nag Hammadi* moment is that the person you're cursing might just be your blessing. These moments are indispensable parts of the journey. We simply cannot gain all of our most important lessons in life through epiphanies or immediate answers to our prayers. Some lessons must have time to marinate.

When March 31st arrived, I attended a breakfast for David's father, Congressman Tillman, so that I could thank him personally for his family's support. After that I went to the hospital to turn in the company car, my keys and my I.D. card. I'd cleaned out my office weeks before so I expected the entire process to take an hour, tops. Fortunately for me, my sister was the principal of the elementary school across the street, so I planned to walk over to her office once I left and hitch a ride home from her.

On the way back to the hospital, I was able to reflect as much on what I'd accomplished as what I would be forced to leave undone. For one thing, I would be leaving without ever knowing why the Inspector General had chosen to waste four months and untold resources investigating me. They finally called me in for an interview a few days before I left for Chicago. I spent less than an hour answering their questions, questions that covered so much terrain that it was clear they were on a fishing expedition.

"Has anyone on your staff ever given you a Coach bag?"

"No."

"Are you sure?"

"I'm sure I would know. No, they haven't."

"Did your staff collect money to send you on a spa weekend?"

"Yes."

"Did you go?"

"No."

"What happened to the money?"

"I spent it on a staff outing. I believe it was a karaoke night at a restaurant in the Village."

If they were looking for an indictable crime they weren't going to find one. At one point in the interview they seemed to be focusing on my relationship with a local charity where I'd once served on the board of directors. It was clear from the slant of the questions that they were trying to infer that I pressured staff into making donations. I didn't. And judging from the sheer numbers of people they'd called downtown by the time they called me, they were having difficulty finding people who would say that I did.

By the time I had my interview I knew that the specter of being under investigation had leaked out from within the walls of Worth Street, and made it all the way to my front door. I happen to be a member of the same church as my local councilwoman. When she whispered, "I heard you're under investigation. It's getting ugly over there, isn't it?" in my ear one morning, the Inspector General's little KGB exercise stopped being funny. For all I know they still have an open file on me. It would not surprise me in the least if they were tracking down former nursery-school classmates to investigate allegations that I'd misappropriated the sand in the sandbox.

When I finally entered the executive suite for the last time it was calm and quiet just like I liked it. I sat down at my desk and my eye caught the edges of a note tucked in the corner of my desk drawer. It was something that Bobby, my Mr. Pollyanna, had written to me about a year before. I left it out of the boxes I'd packed with the intention of reading it again along with some of the other notes I'd collected over the years. Since I had a few minutes to myself, I decided to read it now. He wrote,

I want to tell you something. When I left the job I worked at before I came here, I left for three reasons. I wasn't growing, I wasn't working with people I enjoyed spending time with and I wasn't working for a boss I could admire. I've found all of those things working for you.

I felt the strangest sensation come over me. It was tingly and peculiar and I didn't know what it was. Then I heard a voice from somewhere within me say, "Candis. CANDIS! Get yourself together, woman. Vulcans don't cry!" I was relieved to hear a knock at my door. It was Yvonne, bringing me my exit papers. It took about twenty minutes for me to finish the paperwork. After I said goodbye to her I went into Chrissy's office to see if there was any other unfinished business I needed to attend to before I left. She wasn't there, but, as I turned to leave I noticed several captions on her email inbox that read "FAREWELL RECEPTION." I was livid. When she walked into the office she couldn't miss the expression on my face.

"What?" she said timidly.

"I asked you to do one thing for me."

It took her a minute to figure out what I was talking about, but, once she did she said, "I tried! I tried! I told them what you said but . . . ."

"What's so hard?"

I was so annoyed. I had my final moments all planned out. Having to schmooze was not part of the equation. I knew who the likely suspects were and they weren't that difficult to corral. Especially if they thought I was going to be upset.

"It wasn't Bobby and Gina," she said. "It was Brian." Brian?

The day I found out I wasn't going to be appointed, Brian stopped into my office to see me. I'd watched him evolve from someone who was liked, but, not necessarily respected to someone who consistently delivered; he seemed to grow three inches in height because of it. He and I both grew as a result of the support we received from Donna. But in the process, I have to admit that some of my growing came at his expense. Of all the tombstones that I knocked over in the graveyard, I would have to say his had the most tread patterns from my tennis shoes.

But he came into my office that day to tell me that he and his staff intended to write a letter to Gilberto about all the good things they thought I'd done while in charge and asking him to make my appointment permanent. I was speechless for a number of reasons. First, because by then I already knew it was too late. Second, I was trying to come up with a reason to dissuade him without breaking my promise not to announce Gilberto's decision before our agreed-upon date. But most of all I was speechless because I couldn't believe that what he was saying was coming from him. He must have been able to read the unease on my face.

"You and I have had our differences in the past," he said. "And I'd be lying if I said I wasn't worried when I found out you were taking over. But anyone who says you haven't been fair or that you haven't done a terrific job would be lying. You've made a believer out of me. You've earned this job."

There was probably nobody in the building who I'd given more of a reason to want me out than the man who was telling me this. But he had been willing to give me a chance to prove that I could be a better person and in doing so he became a better person than me. And he was one of the people who continued to treat me like the Sr. Vice-President of the North Brooklyn Health Network until the moment I walked out the door for the last time.

Chrissy said, "Brian came into my office and practically pounded on my desk. He said, 'I've worked for this corporation for more than 20 years and I've watched one Executive Director after another leave like criminals. I'm not letting her leave that way.'"

I listened to what she said and it took all of the wind out of my sails. I sat down behind her desk like a school girl who'd just been reprimanded by the principal. All I could say after that was, "Okay. I'll act surprised."

They held the party in Donna's old office – the one I'd never moved into and never would. I may have only planned to be at the hospital for an hour or two on my last day, but, it was late afternoon before it was all over. I lost count of how many people came through. Donna came back. Even my sister came from across the street. The staff gave me a memory book with pictures from all the different events we'd held over the years. The book contained personal notes by individuals and departments from all over the network. And I continued to be rendered mute by some of the people who stopped by or sent emails if they couldn't.

I knew the Woodhull staff. Some just came for the food. But so many more made a point to find me so that they could tell me some story about something I said or did that they appreciated. But the people I remember most are the people I didn't remember at all. Even with so many employees, after seven years I remembered lots of names and if I didn't remember names I usually remembered faces.

But there were people coming up to me who I didn't recognize at all and yet they had very specific and touching memories that I received like presents wrapped in a box with a beautiful satin bow. I still can't find words to describe how humbling the experience was. At one point I was listening to a testimonial from one such nameless and faceless angel. I was standing in front of Chrissy's office at the time. When the woman finally gave me a hug and left I turned around and Chrissy said, "See how many people you've touched." A party was something that I was absolutely certain I didn't want. But it was exactly what I needed.

By the time the day was over, there were so many gifts and flowers in my office that I couldn't carry them all. So Chrissy volunteered to bring them to me later. When my sister left to go back to work I asked her to take my purse because there had been so much traffic in the office that I didn't want to lose track of it. The last staff members to come visit me were our interpreters. This was one of my special programs and I'd personally interviewed each of them before they were hired. When they came up to say goodbye, they handed me a single red rose. So it worked out that this was all that I had to carry with me when I walked out of the door for the last time.

I tried to say goodbye to A.J., Bobby and Gina but one by one they each turned away from me and shook their heads when I approached. Always the outspoken one, Chrissy was the one to verbalize what they apparently couldn't. "Don't say goodbye to me," she said. "Just go." So in the end I was able to leave the way I wanted to leave, like it was any other Friday and I would be back again on Monday. I said goodnight to no one in particular and waved over my shoulder as I let the door close behind me for the last time.

I took the shortcut through the back of the building and was so thankful that I'd had the presence of mind to keep my sunglasses with me. It was the end of March, but, when I stepped outside I stepped into the most gorgeous spring day we'd had so far. The sun was perched high in a sky unblemished by clouds and the temperature was absolutely ideal. I was fighting with all my might to keep hold of my emotions and the sunglasses did a commendable job of masking the few that leaked through.

But it wasn't until I'd literally stepped my right foot off the campus for the last time that all of the pieces of my *Nag Hammadi* moment finally fell into place. I finally knew the answer to the question I'd put to God in Chicago. Every prayer had been answered with the answer I needed at the moment. If I'd heard "it's time to go" even a moment earlier I would have stopped paying attention. I would have missed all of the awful and awfully wonderful moments I had with the people I'd been working with as my days at HHC drew to a close. I would have stopped the process of my growth with the lessons I was comfortable with. I needed every second of the experiences I had until the very last one because every one of them had a meaning and a lesson tailored especially for me.

When I moved back to New York after graduating from law school, I decided to take a job at a local department store while I sorted out my next steps. The final step in the interview process was a drug test which for obvious reasons, had to be taken on the spot. There was only one problem. I didn't have to go. I went to the bathroom with my little plastic cup in hand and the very best of intentions. I tried every trick I knew. I drank water, I let the faucet run so that the sound of the stream would tease my bladder, but nothing worked. After about ten minutes I managed to eke out a pitiful contribution that was dolefully insufficient. After ten more minutes, I realized I had nothing more to give. Not wanting the store to send a search party to look for me, I decided to make up the difference with tap water.

When I got home I told my father about my day, including my standoff with a specimen cup and the ingenuous solution I'd come up with to end it. He laughed. "You realize that's not going to work," he said. "Don't you think they can tell the difference between urine and water?" His question totally dismantled the logic behind my brilliant idea, but, I didn't want to be wrong. That's another trait I inherited from both my parents. Not to be outdone I said, "If you drink enough water it comes out of you clear anyway. What's the difference?" I've never forgotten his response. "I don't care what it looks like. Nothing goes through the body without coming out changed."

Forgive me if a metaphor about bodily functions is too crude for your tastes, but, in this there is for me, an inescapable congruence with the relationship of individuals to the body politic. And this is true for leaders and layman alike. We simply cannot pass through each other's lives, no matter how sterile or anonymous we try to keep the interactions, without coming out changed on the other side. Changed by the words, changed by the deeds, changed by the memories, we are changed by the choices that we make and the choices made by those who probably aren't even thinking about us when they make them.

When we pass through each others lives we are making journal entries. These entries are made in ink, not pencil. That means you can't erase mistakes. And you don't get to clarify misinterpretations. All you can do is write your entries with deliberation and care. Be mindful in the use of colloquialisms and always use good penmanship.

Even if you know that someone took something you wrote in their journal the wrong way, there will be limits to your ability to fix it. When people feel strongly about you, they memorize your handwriting. So when they see it again the perception of what they're reading changes. Often they don't even realize it. And if the feelings are strong enough, they'll never read another word that you write. Not a lesson you need to teach or a moment you want to share, not even if what you're writing is an apology.

All these thoughts came cascading down to me as if they were being carried on the rays of the sun itself. As I exited the hospital campus for the last time and as the left foot met the right, I heard that inner wisdom summarize these lessons for me. It was speaking to me in my own voice and this is what I heard:

All this time I thought I'd come to this place so that I could change Woodhull. I was wrong. I came to this place so that Woodhull could change me.

Epilogue

It's often been said that life is a journey. Perhaps it isn't one long journey as much as it is a series of small journeys that are connected at the crossroads in our lives. And it's at these crossroads that we meet ourselves again and again, always a little different, hopefully a little wiser. I decided to write this book because of the lessons I learned on one such journey.

Simply put, it was at a crossroad where I learned to have profound respect for what it means to be a leader. I learned a great deal from my strengths and weaknesses as a leader, and the strengths and weaknesses of the people who were in leadership positions over and around me. But more than anything else, in the course of my journey I found my own definition of the meaning of "inspired leadership." Managers give their people something to do; leaders give their people something to believe in. When looked at from this perspective it's easy to see how you can have a leader in the mailroom and a manager in the White House.

The quest for inspired leadership is not a fad. It is more than a goal or a competency – it is a requirement. I wrote this book because I came to understand on a personal level that the source of a leader's inspiration will tell you everything you need to know about the direction that leader will take their organization. The nation's business schools seem to cover just about every angle of how to develop managerial and leadership skills except for that one.

The fact that this book came together as presented is due in large measure to conversations I had with my pastor while the events were unfolding. He would see me in the hallway and ask how things were going with the job. When my appointment was delayed he asked why. When he found out I was leaving HHC he asked what he could do. But it was during one of those conversations that he asked me the question that ultimately challenged me to write this book as opposed to something more conventional. He asked, "So what's your testimony?"

He actually asked me that question more than once. He had to, because I didn't have an answer the first time. I was so caught up in the experiences themselves that I hadn't stopped to consider that there were lessons contained in them or that those lessons might benefit someone else.

I suppose I could have done research on how leading from a core of your spirituality can make you a more dynamic and inspirational leader. But I didn't find my way as a leader (and grow as a person in the process) so much from what I read as from what I lived. The path we walk in life will shape the person we become long before some of us will be called to lead. All the information we need about an individual's capacity not just to lead, but, to lead as a visionary is available to anyone who would care to look at the book of that person's life. From the journey of life is written the journal of leadership – good, bad, indifferent or inspired.

We all want to bathe in the gossamer pool of visionary leadership. We quickly recognize the residue of organizations in which it is lacking. And there are innumerable books, studies and courses on its requisite characteristics. Yet, we as a nation (and a planet) continue to suffer from a cavernous deficit of inspirational leadership. So why is it so difficult to find if we already know what it looks like?

I am now convinced that the inspired leader must possess two characteristics before all others: wisdom and compassion. All the other traits required of a great leader flow from these two. Few would argue against the belief that wise men and women make the best leaders, but, how do you define wisdom and where does it come from? To be sure, credentials alone do not guarantee it. Wisdom is hollow without knowledge, but, requires more than mere intellect. It evolves with maturity, but, can be lacking in those with years of experience. Websters' dictionary defines it as "insightful understanding of what is true, right and enduring." Perhaps it is the element of "insightfulness" that makes wisdom so elusive. Insight demands that the individual be capable of reflection.

The wise person is constantly absorbing from his or her surroundings and incorporating what they learn into experiences that will form the basis for how they see the world. It is an accumulation of the elements of intellect gained over time. But what separates the wise from the merely smart is the character to apply what they know in ways that are just.

These are nuances the absence of which, are easily camouflaged by credentials deftly displayed in a curriculum vitae, a winning smile and a charismatic persona. Truly inspirational leaders are minted in kindergarten, before the first sensuous kiss of ego formation. That is when "character" is formed.

I used to believe that adults past the age of 28 don't change. While I'm now certain that most won't, I also believe anyone can if they want to. But you can't teach an adult to care about people before things unless they want to change their priorities. You can't pull the multi-hued imagery of a dynamic vision from an individual whose printer only has black ink. We have to do more than merely *want* inspired leadership. We each have a responsibility to shape it through careful and continuous monitoring of the impact leaders have on the organizations they lead.

There have been many times when I believed that this journey would be infinitely easier if we could do it without dealing with other people. But I will share with you something I once heard a talented young minister say in a sermon. "Your best you isn't in you, it's in all the other people whose lives you touch." We can't be our best in isolation. Everything that we know about what it takes to build an innovative organization reminds us of the pivotal role that interpersonal relationships play in the process. And you cannot lead from a distance. The available literature on exceptional leadership tells us that inspirational leaders create environments where their employees feel that:

- they are cared about;
- they are trusted;
- their talents and skills will be developed;
- they are appreciated;
- they can see the connection between what they do and the leader's vision for the organization;
- they are making a contribution to something important; and
- work is fun

Looking at leadership through this lens forces us to reevaluate everything we've ever learned about how to lead (and how to be led!). The people aren't one thing, they're everything. And the connection isn't flowing in only one direction. Perhaps we already know how we are influencing each other as individuals. The mistake leaders often make is thinking that our mutual interdependence stops when we pull into a reserved parking space.

I took a two-week trip to West Africa in 2000 with a small group of friends. We visited Elmina Castle in Ghana and Goree Island in Senegal. And, of course, we did a lot of shopping. As our trip was winding down, my roommate and I were sitting in the tour bus while we waited for our traveling companions to finish their last bit of shopping. It was a busy thoroughfare away from the tourist traps. Because our group was small, our guide was able to take us to the places where the locals went to shop. As we sat silently gazing out the window at the foot traffic, my roommate said, "They're so elegant."

I had to smile. I'd been thinking the exact same thing. As we discussed our reflections, we came to the conclusion that the African custom of carrying goods on the tops of their heads had caused these area residents to develop erect postures. It isn't something that we'd noticed when interacting with them a few at a time. But watching the scores of villagers move back and forth, presented us with a moving portrait of grace.

It didn't take us very long to isolate the particulars supporting our observations only because we took the time to figure it out. I reflect on that moment now because of how quickly our minds arrived at a conclusion based on those observations. Our first thoughts weren't, "look how years of carrying baskets on the tops of their heads has made their posture straight." We simply went straight to the conclusion: they're so elegant.

So much of the conditioning that we have received over the years of our individual human experiences will be read by others and reduced to short and succinct statements of fact. And we are frequently no more aware of the conclusions that others are drawing than those villagers were aware of what was being said about them from the confines of a small tourist bus. Those of us who move into leadership positions have a unique opportunity because we are creating atmospheres. What we put into that air will condition those we lead, including many who we may never meet directly.

The leader who is creating an atmosphere where people feel cared about and trusted; where their talents and skills are being developed as well as appreciated; where they can see the connection between what they do and the leader's vision; where they are making a contribution to something important, but, are also having fun -- that leader is breathing the same air. In return, she is cared about and trusted, his talents and skills are being developed, she is appreciated. That is how inspired leadership evolves. It is very much a two-way exchange. In the process something remarkable happens. When outsiders enter, they are struck by being in the midst of something awesome. Even if you can't find the words to describe it, you know it when you see it. It is the inimitable experience of being in the presence of people walking upright.

That is why we must have leaders operating from compasses attuned to a force far more profound than anything you learn en route to an MBA. What I am referring to is something more than ethics training can provide. We simply can't rely upon leaders to be guided by subjectively crafted notions of ethics and morality. There is an uncomfortable truth we must face in this regard.

Our social order has been hobbled by how unreliable the concept of "right" and "wrong" has become. We live in a global society that has learned how to convince itself of the "rightness" of just about anything. Once cast in the halo of moral correctness, individuals have felt justified to engage in the most contemptible behavior, up to and including murder. But perhaps this very limitation carves the alcove in the boardroom where faith can find its place.

There is indeed a plan at work. It's not some master plan written in a book somewhere that has already predetermined who you will marry, how many children you will have, and what kind of job you will hold. It is a plan based on the principle that the God-Universe is oriented toward what is positive, helpful and good. It is also a plan that acknowledges your power to create. When you choose to be the creator of positive, helpful and good things, that plan conspires with you to bring into your life the objects and circumstances you would not otherwise control, precisely when and how you need them to be to accomplish your goal. In other words, focus on creating something positive and see how the world unfolds before you.

There is an ancient Egyptian proverb, which says that karma brings into your life the people, things and situations that you need in order to grow.[2] The process of leading does not start *after* growth has stopped because we don't stop growing until we stop living. Leading is itself a process of growth. We are in a constant state of creation with our thoughts and our deeds. The question is: "what kind of Creator are you?" In many West African religions, it is believed that man receives his destiny before he is born. The Akan call this the *nkrabea*. But in one version of the story the Akan believe that instead of simply being given a destiny, man in his pre-earthly form tells God what he (or she) intends to do while on earth and then receives God's approval.[3] What I like about this version is that it reflects the view that we have a choice in our destiny. But it also allows for the possibility that a higher order is at work, one that is both capable and willing to compensate for our mistakes.

Not everyone is going to be Lee Iaccoca. As the saying goes, "everything ain't for everybody." But, everybody is meant to live out their full potential. Doing so accomplishes several things, all of them positive. First,

---

[2] Egyptian Yoga: The Philosophy of Enlightenment,Vol.I Ashby, M. (Cruzian Mystic Books, 2001)
[3] West African Traditional Religion, Opoku, K. A. (FEP International Private Limited, 1978)

it fuels your joy. Joy is one of the most positive and productive emotions you can feel. Yes, productive! You are never in a more effective state of mind for creating something positive than when you are joyful. Studies tell us that those organizations that are consistently voted among the best places to work are almost never the places that pay the highest salaries. They are the places where people most enjoy working.

Second, you will simply be better at the activity or activities that align with your potential. That probably sounds obvious and it is, yet it's surprising how many people are engaged in activities that they are not good at. The fact that we have the ability to choose to do what we want doesn't mean that there isn't something we were meant to do. No one chooses mediocrity over greatness. They choose mediocrity because they haven't found their greatness yet.

If you are a parent, you are a leader. If others look to you for advice, you are a leader. When you step out of your front door you have the opportunity to lead just by the example you can set by being who you are. After all, we never know who is watching. These are the legacies that each of us leaves behind. In one way or another, eventually, we are all called to lead on some level. So we each bear responsibility for cultivating the enduring source of wisdom that all great leaders require.

Believing in a plan more encompassing than our individual desires actually frees us to find our greatness, whatever it may be. It means that there is a calling for each of us to respond to. If your calling is leadership, then this plan means one more thing. It guarantees that as karma brings into your life the people, things and situations that you need in order to grow, it will also bring into your life the people, things and situations that will qualify you to lead.

Challenge yourself to take a fresh look at the path you're walking right now. What great opportunities are your current circumstances preparing you for? You may not have the answer at the moment. But know that even the greatest of journeys, like every journey, begins with small steps and seemingly insignificant choices (not unlike the one that led you to be reading these words right now). Where your path takes you next involves choices only you can make, but, ones with far-reaching implications. Whatever that journey is for you, whatever legacies you leave in the process, may your journey be a blessed one.

Made in the USA
Lexington, KY
10 July 2011